The Tyndale New Testament Commentaries

General Editor: PROFESSOR R. V. G. TASKER, M.A., D.D.

THE EPISTLES OF JOHN

DEDICATED

TO

ANOTHER 'ELECT LADY AND HER CHILDREN,
WHOM I LOVE IN THE TRUTH',
THE CONGREGATION OF
ALL SOULS CHURCH, LANGHAM PLACE

THE EPISTLES OF

JOHN

AN INTRODUCTION AND COMMENTARY

by

J. R. W. STOTT, M.A.
Rector, All Souls Church, London, W.I

Wm. B. Eerdmans Publishing Company
Grand Rapids, Michigan

First printing, February 1960
Tenth printing, September 1980

Library of Congress Catalog Card Number, 64-8801

ISBN 0-8028-1418-2

PHOTOLITHOPRINTED BY EERDMANS PRINTING COMPANY
GRAND RAPIDS, MICHIGAN, UNITED STATES OF AMERICA

GENERAL PREFACE

ALL who are interested in the teaching and study of the New Testament today cannot fail to be concerned with the lack of commentaries which avoid the extremes of being unduly technical or unhelpfully brief. It is the hope of the editor and publishers that this present series will do something towards the supply of this deficiency. Their aim is to place in the hands of students and serious readers of the New Testament, at a moderate cost, commentaries by a number of scholars who, while they are free to make their own individual contributions, are united in a common desire to promote a truly biblical theology.

The commentaries are primarily exegetical and only secondarily homiletic, though it is hoped that both student and preacher will find them informative and suggestive. Critical questions are fully considered in introductory sections, and also, at the author's discretion, in additional notes.

The commentaries are based on the Authorized (King James) Version, partly because this is the version which most Bible readers possess, and partly because it is easier for commentators, working on this foundation, to show why, on textual and linguistic grounds, the later versions are so often to be preferred. No one translation is regarded as infallible, and no single Greek manuscript or group of manuscripts is regarded as always right! Greek words are transliterated to help those unfamiliar with the language, and to save those who do know Greek the trouble of discovering what word is being discussed.

There are many signs today of a renewed interest in what the Bible has to say and of a more general desire to understand its meaning as fully and clearly as possible. It is the hope of all those concerned with this series that God will graciously use what they have written to further this end.

R. V. G. TASKER.

5

CONTENTS

CHIEF ABBREVIATIONS

Alexander *The Epistles of John* by Neil Alexander in the *Torch Bible Commentaries* series (S.C.M. Press, 1962).

Alford Commentary on the Epistles of John by Henry Alford in his Greek Testament (Rivingtons & Deighton & Bell, 3rd edition, 1866).

AV English Authorized Version, 1611.

Barclay *The Letters of John and Jude* by William Barclay (The Saint Andrew Press, 1958).

Blaiklock *Faith is the Victory* (Devotional Studies in the First Epistle of John) by E. M. Blaiklock (The Paternoster Press, 1959).

Brooke Commentary on the Johannine Epistles by A. E. Brooke in *The International Critical Commentary* (T. & T. Clark, 1912).

Calvin Commentary on the First Epistle of John by John Calvin, translated by T. H. L. Parker, in the *Calvin's Commentaries* series (Oliver & Boyd, 1961).

Candlish *The First Epistle of John Expounded in a Series of Lectures* by Robert S. Candlish (A. & C. Black, 1877).

Dodd Commentary on the Johannine Epistles by C. H. Dodd in *The Moffatt New Testament Commentary* (Hodder & Stoughton, 1946).

Ebrard Commentary on St. John's Epistles by John H. A. Ebrard (T. & T. Clark, 1860).

Eusebius *Ecclesiastical History* by Eusebius of Caesarea, *circa* 260–340, translated with introduction and notes by H. J. Lawler and J. E. L. Oulton (S.P.C.K., 1927–28; two vols.).

Findlay *Fellowship in the Life Eternal* (An Exposition of the Epistles of St. John) by George G. Findlay (Hodder & Stoughton, 1909).

CHIEF ABBREVIATIONS

Grimm-
Thayer
C. L. W. Grimm's *Greek-English Lexicon of the New Testament*, translated, revised and enlarged by J. H. Thayer (T. & T. Clark, 4th edition, 1901).

Law
The Tests of Life (A Study of the First Epistle of St. John) by Robert Law (T. and T. Clark, 1909).

Lewis
The Johannine Epistles by Greville P. Lewis in the *Epworth Preacher's Commentaries* (Epworth Press, 1961).

Liddell and
Scott
A Greek-English Lexicon compiled by H. G. Liddell and R. Scott (1843), revised and augmented throughout by H. S. Jones and R. McKenzie (1925) (Oxford University Press, 10th edition, 1940).

mg.
margin.

NEB
New English Bible: New Testament, 1961.

Plummer
Commentary on the Epistles of St. John in the *Cambridge Greek Testament for Schools and Colleges* by Alfred Plummer (Cambridge University Press, 1894).

RSV
American Revised Standard Version, 1946–52.

RV
English Revised Version, 1881–85.

Smith
Commentary on the Epistles of John by David Smith in *The Expositor's Greek Testament* (Hodder & Stoughton, 1910).

Westcott
Commentary on the Epistles of St. John by B. F. Westcott (Macmillan, 1883).

AUTHOR'S PREFACE

IF it be said (as it quite reasonably may) that one who is in no sense a New Testament scholar should not presume to write a commentary on New Testament Epistles, I would reply in respectful self-defence that I have written as a pastor and not as a theologian. Nor is this entirely a disadvantage, since insight into the New Testament literature demands some acquaintance, not only with Greek usage, but also with a local church situation such as lies behind the Johannine Epistles. Certainly John writes as a pastor to his people in language which every modern pastor will understand. He loves them. He is deeply concerned to protect them from the enticements of the world and the errors of false teachers, and to see them established in faith, love and holiness. So he appeals to what they are and what they know. He warns them, exhorts them, argues with them, instructs them. All this will find an echo in the experience of every pastor who has been entrusted by the Chief Shepherd with the care of a flock. I am hopeful that the readers of this commentary, though not neglecting academic questions raised by the Epistles, will not forget the practical purposes for which they were written.

A fuller consideration of some of the chief exegetical problems of the First Epistle has been reserved for the Additional Notes. Even so the commentary is longer than it should have been, and I am grateful to the publishers for their indulgent acceptance of it as it now stands. My indebtedness to other commentators will be apparent in the exposition of the text, although I have tried to resist the temptation to be a merely slavish copyist of abler and better men.

I pray that we may be given grace to do more than study these Epistles, namely submit to them in mind and life. The Church needs their message. To borrow John's own phraseology, we must abide in it, and let it abide in us (2 Jn. 9; 1 Jn. ii. 24).

J. R. W. S.

INTRODUCTION

THE natural place in which to look for information about the authorship of any ancient epistle is in the epistle itself. It was customary in antiquity for a correspondent to begin his letter by announcing his identity. This was Paul's invariable rule and the same holds good of the Epistles of Peter, James and Jude. The author of 2 and 3 John styles himself 'the Elder' without disclosing his name. Only the Epistle to the Hebrews and the First Epistle of John begin without any announcement of the author's name or title, and indeed without any introductory greeting. The anonymity of 1 John is not to be explained by the suggestion that the author is writing a theological treatise, or even a general or 'catholic' Epistle, as Origen first called it. Although it has a considerable theological content, it contains a genuinely personal message addressed to a particular congregation, or group of them, in a particular situation (cf. ii. 19). The 'I—you—we' form of address is maintained throughout; the recipients of the letter are the author's beloved 'little children', whose spiritual history and present circumstances he knows. Moreover, 'the writing is . . . instinct from first to last with intense personal feeling' (Westcott). It is a truly pastoral Epistle, sent by a pastor to his flock or a part of it, as are also (and even more clearly) the two shorter Epistles.

Who, then, was the author of these Epistles? Since they are anonymous there is no *a priori* need to ascribe them to the apostle John or to any other John. Nevertheless, the external evidence is strongly in favour of this ascription, particularly in the case of the First Epistle.

a. External evidence for the First Epistle

All three Epistles are found in the oldest Greek MSS. The First

Epistle is also included in the most ancient versions of the Church of the East and the West, namely the Syriac and Latin, whereas the Second and Third Epistles are not in the Old Syriac.

Commentators have found possible allusions to the Epistles of John in a number of early patristic writings. Thus, Clement of Rome twice described God's elect people as being 'perfected in love', and there is a similar expression in the *Didache*. The *Epistle to Diognetus* includes such phrases as 'from the beginning', 'God loved men' and 'sent his only begotten Son', so that we love 'him who thus first loved' us. But none of these is more than an echo of Johannine language, derived as well from the Gospel or current Johannine theology as from the First Epistle. There is no formal or exact quotation, nor any mention of John or the Epistles by name.

The earliest definite reference to these Epistles in the Fathers comes from Polycarp of Smyrna (d. *c.* AD 155), who in the seventh chapter of his letter to the Philippians, written perhaps thirty or forty years before his martyrdom, asserts that whoever does not confess that Jesus Christ has come in the flesh is antichrist. He goes on to urge a return to the message handed down from the beginning. Here are quotations from 1 John iv. 2, 3 (with a possible reminiscence of 1 John ii. 22 and 2 John 7) and 1 John ii. 24. Polycarp does not, however, attribute his quotations to John.

The first to refer specifically to a Johannine Epistle was Papias of Hierapolis in the middle of the second century, who, according to Eusebius (iii. 39. 17), 'used testimonies drawn from the former Epistle of John'.

It is not until we reach Irenaeus of Lyons (*c.* 130–200) that at least the First and Second Epistles are clearly attributed to the John who was both the 'disciple of the Lord' and the author of the Fourth Gospel. In his *Adversus Haereses* (iii. 16. 18) he quotes fully from 1 John ii. 18–22, iv. 1–3, v. 1, and 2 John 7, 8.

Clement of Alexandria, who survived Irenaeus by a few years, evidently knew more than one Johannine Epistle, since he uses the expression 'the greater Epistle', which he ascribes to 'the apostle John'. His quotations are even more numerous than those of Irenaeus. In chapters 2–5 of *Stromateis* he quotes i. 6, 7, ii. 4, 18, 19, iii. 3, 18, 19, iv. 16, 18, and v. 3, 16, 17, while in *Quis Dives Salvetur?* chapters 37 and 38, he quotes iii. 15 and again iv. 18.

Tertullian, his Latin contemporary (d. *c.* 220), made considerable use of the First Epistle, quoting it about fifty times (especially i. 1, 3, ii. 22, iv. 1, 2, v. 1) in his polemical writings against Marcion, Praxeas and the Gnostics. Origen of Alexandria, a little later (d. *c.* 255), also relied much on the First Epistle, ascribing it to John, although like Tertullian he does not quote from the two shorter letters.

The Muratorian Canon, which was probably compiled in Rome between AD 170 and 215, perhaps by Hippolytus, contains two relevant passages, though of somewhat uncertain meaning. In one the author describes how he believed John had come to write his Gospel, and immediately adds a reference to 'his Epistles' in which he claimed to write 'what we have seen with our eyes, heard with our ears and touched with our hands' (quoting 1 Jn. i. 1, 4). In the other, 'two' Epistles of John are mentioned (it is not clear which are meant); they are then described by the phrase *in catholica habentur*, which has been understood by scholars as meaning that they were recognized either 'in the Catholic Church' or 'among the Catholic Epistles'.

Cyprian, Bishop of Carthage in the middle of the third century, quoted from i. 8 and ii. 3, 4, 6, 15–17, and it is interesting to note that the passages he used are concerned rather with ethical conduct than with theological controversy.

When we reach Eusebius (*c.* AD 325), we find that he numbers the First Epistle among the *homologoumena* or 'acknowledged books', while he puts the Second and Third Epistles among the *antilegomena* or 'disputed books' (iii. 25. 2, 3).

b. External evidence for the Second and Third Epistles

The external evidence for the Second and Third Epistles is not so clear or strong as that for the First. The first definite quotation occurs in Irenaeus (*Adversus Haereses* iii. 16. 3, 8) who mentions two Epistles, ascribing them to 'John the disciple of the Lord', and quotes 2 John 7, 8, 10 and 11. Clement of Alexandria implies by his reference to John's 'greater Epistle' (*Stromateis* ii. 15. 66) that he also wrote one or more lesser Epistles, and elsewhere according to Eusebius he mentions 'the second Epistle of John' which he said was written to a certain lady who signifies 'the holy church'. It is in Origen that we come across the first explicit mention of any doubt about the authorship of these two Epistles. He knew of both, but no quotation of either has survived from his pen, and according to Eusebius he knew that they were not universally acknowledged as 'genuine' (vi. 25. 10).

Eusebius himself, as has already been mentioned, placed the Second and Third Epistles among the *antilegomena* (iii. 25. 3), although 'well known and acknowledged by most'. He adds the interesting explanation of the uncertainty surrounding them, namely 'whether they belong to the Evangelist, or to another of the same name'. In another place he states his own conviction that they were written by the apostle John (vi. 25. 10). The reference in the Muratorian Canon to 'two Epistles' of John might as easily be an allusion to the First and Second as to the Second and Third. Jerome said that the two shorter Epistles were ascribed to John the Presbyter, and, although throughout the Middle Ages the Epistles seem to have been accepted as the work of John the apostle, Erasmus reverted to the theory mentioned by Jerome. It is not surprising that this attestation of the Second and Third Epistles is scantier than in the case of the First, for they are both slight and contain little distinctive matter which would be suitable for quotation.

c. Common authorship of the Gospel and the First Epistle

Such evidence for the authorship of the Epistles as can be gathered from the Epistles themselves is indirect rather than direct. It is a complex problem, concerning the mutual relations between the Gospel and each of the three Epistles. If it can be shown that any or all of the Epistles were written by the author of the Fourth Gospel, then clearly arguments for the authorship of the Gospel will be equally applicable to the Epistles. More simply, if the Gospel is the apostle John's, then the Epistles will be also. This is not the place to attempt even an introduction to the complicated question of the authorship of the Fourth Gospel. The reader must be referred to competent commentaries on that Gospel for this subject. What must be done here, however, is an examination of the relation between the Gospel and the Epistles. The best way to proceed is to consider the evidence of common authorship first between Gospel and First Epistle, then between the Second and Third Epistles themselves, and finally between them and the First Epistle.

Even a superficial reading of the Gospel and the First Epistle reveals a striking similarity between the two in both subject-matter and syntax. The general subjects treated are much the same. It has often been pointed out that the author of each has the same love of opposites set in stark contrast to one another,—light and darkness, life and death, love and hate, truth and falsehood,—while people are said to belong to one or other of two categories, with no third alternative. They are children of God or children of the devil, of the world or not of the world. They have life or do not have life. They know God or do not know Him. In style one is aware of what Westcott called 'the same monotonous simplicity of construction', and the same Hebraic love of parallelism. The author uses few particles, and does not like subordinate clauses introduced by the relative pronoun. On the other hand, he has a great fondness for sentences beginning with certain emphatic formulae like 'This is . . . that . . .', 'By this . . . that . . .', 'For this . . . that' and 'Everyone who . . .'.[1]

When we compare the occurrence of precise phrases in both Gospel and First Epistle, we find that in fact the same divine purpose or scheme of salvation is set forth in almost identical terms. It might be summarized as follows, the reference in the Epistle being printed first in each parenthesis: In our natural and unredeemed state we are both 'of the devil', who has

---

[1] For a detailed examination of linguistic similarities and dissimilarities see Brooke, pp. i–xix and 235–242, and Law, pp. 341–363.

sinned and lied and murdered 'from the beginning' (iii. 8: viii. 44), and 'of the world' (ii. 16, iv. 5: viii. 23, xv. 19). We therefore 'do' sin (iii. 4: viii. 34) and 'have' it (i. 8: ix. 41), 'walk in darkness' (i. 6, ii. 11: viii. 12, xii. 35) and are spiritually 'blind' (ii. 11: xii. 40) and 'dead' (iii. 14: v. 25). But God loved us and sent His Son to be 'the Saviour of the world' (iv. 14: iv. 42) and that we might live (iv. 9, 10: iii. 16). This was His 'only begotten' (*monogenēs*, iv. 9: i. 14, 18, iii. 16, 18), who, though in or from 'the beginning' (i. 1: i. 1), yet became, or came in, 'flesh' (iv. 2: i. 14) and then 'laid down his life' for us (iii. 16: x. 11–18), in order to 'take away' sin (iii. 5: i. 29). To Him 'witness' has been borne, partly by men who have 'seen' and therefore 'testified' (i. 2, 3, iv. 14: i. 34, xix. 35), but especially by God Himself (v. 9: iii. 33, v. 32, 34, 36, 37) and by the Spirit (v. 6: xv. 26). We should 'receive' this divine witness (v. 9: iii. 11, 32, 33, v. 34), 'believe' in the One thus adequately attested (v. 10: v. 37–40) and 'confess' Him (iv. 2, 3: ix. 22). Believing in Him or His 'name' (v. 13: i. 12, etc.), we pass out of death into life (iii. 14: v. 24). We 'have life' (v. 11, 12: iii. 15, 36, xx. 31), for life is in the Son of God (v. 11, 12: i. 4, xiv. 6). This is to be 'born of God' (ii. 29, iii. 9, v. 4, 18: i. 13).

Those who have been born of God, God's 'children' (iii. 1, 2, 10, v. 2: i. 12, xi. 52), are variously described, in relation to God, to Christ, to the truth, to each other and to the world. They are 'of God' (iii. 10: viii. 47) and have come to 'know' God, the true God, through Jesus Christ (v. 20: xvii. 3). It may even be said that they have 'seen' God (iii. 6; cf. 3 Jn. 11: xiv. 9), although in the literal sense no man has ever seen God (iv. 12, 20: i. 18, vi. 46). Christians are not only 'of God' but 'of the truth' as well (ii. 21, iii. 19: xviii. 37). The truth is also 'in' them (i. 8, ii. 4: viii. 44) and they 'do' it (i. 6: iii. 21), for the Spirit given to them is 'the Spirit of truth' (iv. 6, v. 6: xiv. 17, xv. 26, xvi. 13). The relation of Christians to God and to the truth is through Jesus Christ, in whom and in whose love they 'abide' (ii. 6, 27, 28, iii. 6, 24, iv. 13, 15, 16: xv. 4–10) and who Himself abides in them (ii. 24, iii. 24, iv. 12–16: vi. 56, xv. 4, 5). His word abides in them too (i. 10,

ii. 14, 24: v. 38, xv. 7) and they in it (ii. 27: viii. 31). Thus they 'keep his word' (ii. 5: viii. 51–55, xiv. 23, xv. 20, xvii. 6) or 'his commandments' (ii. 3, 4, iii. 22, 24, v. 2, 3: xiv. 15, 21, xv. 10), His 'new commandment' being that they love one another (ii. 8–10, iii. 11, 23; cf. 2 Jn. 5, 6: xiii. 34). 'The world', however, will 'hate' them (iii. 13: xv. 18). They must not be surprised by this. The reason for it is that they no longer belong to the world (iv. 5, 6: xv. 19, xvii. 16), and while remaining in it must not love the things that are in it (ii. 15, 16: xvii. 15). Christ has 'overcome the world', and so also through faith in Him have they (v. 4, 5: xvi. 33). The end result of all that Christ has done for, and given to, His people is fullness of joy (i. 4: xv. 11, xvi. 24, xvii. 13).

In view of this remarkably close parallel, Alford does not seem to be expressing himself too strongly when he attributes an obstinate 'perverseness' to those who maintain a different authorship. Yet during the last hundred years or so a small but persistent minority of scholars have held that the evident similarity between Epistle and Gospel is due rather to imitation than to identity of authorship. Thus, C. H. Dodd, who argues that the three Epistles (but not the Gospel) were written by the same author, supposes that he was 'not a mere imitator' of the Evangelist but his 'disciple' or 'student', who reflected and yet modified his master's thought, much as modern Barthians accept and yet adapt the theology of Karl Barth. These scholars point mainly to three phenomena, first to words and concepts in the Epistle which do not appear in the Gospel, secondly to peculiarities in the Gospel without parallel in the Epistle, and thirdly to subtle but significant differences in doctrines which are common to both Gospel and Epistle.

Brooke analyses the fifty peculiarities of the Epistle which Holtzmann listed, and they do not amount to much in the end. The most important words of the Epistle which do not occur in the Gospel are *angelia* (message), *koinōnia* (fellowship), *hilasmos* (propitiation), *chrisma* (unction, or anointing), *antichristos*, *anomia* (lawlessness) and *sperma* (seed). But, even though these words are missing from the Gospel, it would be rash to assert that the ideas about man's sin or Christ's death or the Holy Spirit's work which are conveyed by them are absent also. To C. H. Dodd these linguistic differences are largely due to the fact that the Gospel reflects the language, thought and customs of Palestinian Judaism, whereas the Epistle is coloured by Hellenistic mysticism with its characteristic vocabulary of 'light', 'seed', 'chrism' and its abstract ideas (e.g. 'God is love'). But apart from the fact that one would naturally expect the Gospel with its Palestinian setting to be more Aramaic than Hellenistic, Neil Alexander is surely right that in the Epistle 'these Hellenistic terms often carry invisible quotation marks'. John is deliberately borrowing from the vocabulary of the false teachers he is opposing.

Peculiarities of the Gospel are fully listed in eight pages by Brooke. He gives a catalogue of 813 words which occur in the Gospel but not in the Epistle. This may seem impressive, but not when it is examined. The great majority of these words are unimportant and are used only once or twice. More notable words are cross and crucify (14 times between them), disciple (78 times), glory and glorify (39 times between them), heaven (20 times), law (13 times), Lord (52 times), seek (34 times) and sign (17 times). But of these only 'glory' and 'glorify' can be said to have any distinctive doctrinal meaning, for the *ideas* of the cross, discipleship, heaven, etc. are present in the Epistle even if the words are absent.

Turning from the words which are peculiar to either Gospel or Epistle, we must now consider those words and themes which are handled in both but with a difference, indeed, according to C. H. Dodd, 'a formidable difference'. There are seven major ones, which have been advanced as reasons for accepting a diversity of authorship.

1. In the Prologue to the Fourth Gospel the *Logos* is personal, referring to the only begotten Son, whereas in the Preface to the Epistle 'the *logos* of life' is impersonal and refers to the life-bringing gospel. This is probably true, as is accepted in the notes *ad loc.* (although it is still maintained by some that the 'Logos of life' is personal), but the similarities between Prologue and Preface far outweigh this difference and are summarized in the Additional Note on page 66.

2. The Paraclete in the Gospel is the Holy Spirit, 'the Comforter', whereas in the Epistle this title, which is found nowhere else in the New Testament, is applied to Jesus Christ the righteous, who is our Advocate in heaven not on earth. But neither concept contradicts or excludes the other. Why should it be thought impossible that both the Second and the Third Persons of the Trinity should exercise a ministry of aid and advocacy, the Spirit on earth and the Son in heaven? Besides, if Jesus called the Spirit '*another* Paraclete' (xiv. 16), who is the first?

3. In the Fourth Gospel it is Jesus Christ who is 'the true Light', 'the light of men' and 'the light of the world' (i. 9, 4 and viii. 12), whereas the message of the Epistle is that 'God is light' (i. 5). Again, both are true; they cannot be said in any way to be irreconcilable in the mind of the same author who has such a high view of the relation between Father and Son. Nor is it altogether correct to say that 'the Gospel is Christocentric, the Epistle Theocentric',[1] since in the latter the author many times uses the pronoun 'he' (*autos, ekeinos*), without specifying to whom he is referring. His allusion is normally to the Son, but he does not always consider it necessary to say so.

4. The Gospel contains the affirmation that 'God is spirit' (iv. 24), while the Epistle declares once that 'God is light' (i. 5) and twice that 'God is love' (iv. 8, 16). It is extraordinary that anybody could seriously consider these statements as being in any way inconsistent in the same author.

5. The death of Christ, it is rightly said, is presented in the Gospel as His 'uplifting' and His 'glorification'. Neither word occurs in the Epistle, where the purpose of His death is propitiatory (ii. 2, iv. 10) and brings cleansing and life (i. 7, iv. 9). But the references to the death of Christ in the Epistle are in largely polemical passages, where the author's purpose is to emphasize its benefits for men in salvation rather than its significance for Him in glorification. Moreover, teaching about the achievement of the Saviour's death cannot be said to be absent from a Gospel which declares that the wrath of

[1] Law, who himself very much modifies his own aphorism.

God abides on the unbeliever (iii. 36) and includes verses like i. 29, iii. 14–16, vi. 51, x. 11, 15, xi. 49–52, xii. 24, etc.

6. The word *parrēsia*, bold outspokenness, occurs in both Gospel and Epistle; but in the former it denotes plainness of speech to men (e.g. x. 24, xi. 14, xvi. 29 and xviii. 20), and in the latter confidence before God in prayer and on the day of judgment (ii. 28, iii. 21, iv. 17, v. 14). All that needs to be said here is that boldness should characterize the Christian in his approach to both God and men, and that there is no reason why the same author should not believe in both and write about both.

7. Lastly, the eschatological teaching is said to be different. In the Gospel, we are told, the eschatology is 'realized'. Eternal life and judgment are received now, since lifegiving and judging are the present activities of God through Christ (iii. 14–19, v. 19–27), and Jesus Christ promises to come again not in glory on the clouds of heaven but spiritually through the Holy Spirit (xiv. 15–24, etc.). In the Epistle, on the other hand, the older and more popular expectations are preserved of Christ's personal 'coming' (*parousia*, ii. 28) and visible 'appearing' (*phanerōsis*, ii. 28, iii. 2), and of a final 'day of judgment' (iv. 17). This, we are told, takes no account of the profound reinterpretation of eschatology which is given in the Fourth Gospel; it is rather the 'naïve thinking of the primitive Church' (Dodd). But this reconstruction is much too categorical, as if there were no 'popular' eschatology in the Gospel and no 'realized' eschatology in the Epistle. The truth is that the Gospel includes sayings of Jesus about His coming to take His people to Himself and about 'the last day' of resurrection and judgment (e.g. xiv. 3, v. 28, 29, vi. 39, 40, 44, 54, xi. 24–26, xii. 48), while eternal life is clearly regarded in the Epistle as a present possession, received and enjoyed in Christ now (v. 11–13). The present, personal activity of the Holy Spirit in witnessing is also taught in the Epistle; it is just not accurate to say that it contains 'no trace of the high "Johannine" doctrine which is found in the Gospel' (Dodd).

These differences of emphasis constitute no solid ground on which to base a theory of different authorship. They are sufficiently accounted for by the different purpose which the author had in writing each (which many commentators do not seem adequately to have noted) and by the interval of time which may have elapsed between the composition of each. The author's purpose in writing is known from his own definition of it. He wrote the Gospel for unbelievers in order to arouse their faith (xx. 30, 31), and the Epistle for believers in order to deepen their assurance (v. 13). His desire for the readers of the Gospel was that through faith they might receive life; for the readers of the Epistle that they might know they already had it. Consequently, the Gospel contains 'signs' to evoke faith (xx. 30, 31), and the Epistle tests by which to judge it. Further, the enemies of the truth in the Gospel are unbelieving Jews, who doubt, not the historicity of Jesus (whom they could see and hear), but whether He is the Christ, the Son of God. The enemies of the truth in the Epistle, however, are professing Christians (although John's tests show that their profession is a lie), and their problem concerns not the divinity of the Christ but His relation to the historical Jesus. Westcott summarized this distinction well in saying: 'the theme of the Epistle is "the Christ is Jesus"; the theme of the Gospel is "Jesus is the Christ". '

This double difference of purpose implies a difference of time and would seem also to establish, not that the Epistle was written to accompany the Gospel (Ebrard, Lightfoot), still less that it preceded the Gospel, but that it followed it after an interval, inasmuch as John's readers must be brought to faith through testimony and to life through faith before they could be brought to an assurance of life. Those commentators who think that the Epistle was prior to the Gospel, have argued that they detect in it embryonic ideas (about the Logos, the atonement and the last things) which only come to birth in the Gospel. But this is surely topsy-turvy. The Epistle is written to people who already know the truth and do not need anyone to teach them (ii. 20, 21, 27), provided they let that abide in them which they have heard from the beginning (ii. 24). The NEB rightly entitles the Epistle a 'Recall to Fundamentals'. John is not teaching new truths or issuing new commandments; it is the heretics who are the innovators. John's task is to recall them to what they already know and have. All this seems to presuppose on the part of the readers a knowledge of the Gospel, or at the very least of the body of doctrine contained in the Gospel. We may then agree that the Epistle is 'a comment on the Gospel, "a sermon with the Gospel for its text" ' (Plummer).

So far, then, we have suggested that the similarities of subject-matter, style and vocabulary in the Gospel and the First Epistle supply very strong evidence for identity of authorship, which is not materially weakened by the peculiarities of each or the differences of emphasis in the treatment of common themes. These are explained by the distinctive purpose behind each writing and by the lapse of time which can therefore be assumed between them. The similarity between Gospel and Epistle is considerably greater than that between the Third Gospel and the Acts, which are known to have come from the same pen; between the Pastoral Epistles to Timothy and Titus; and even, it could be argued, between the two Thessalonian Epistles written during the apostle's second missionary journey, and between the Epistles to the Ephesians and the Colossians written during his first Roman imprisonment. 'The usage suggests a writer who varies his own phrases, rather than a mere copyist' (Brooke). 'The same mind deals with the same ideas in different connections. . . . The Epistles give later growths of common and characteristic ideas. No imitator of the Gospel could have combined elements of likeness and unlikeness in such a manner. . . .' (Westcott).

d. The relation of the Second and Third Epistles to each other and to the First Epistle

It is not necessary to marshal lengthy arguments for the common authorship of 2 and 3 John; it is almost self-evident. It is true that the Third Epistle has one or two words peculiar to itself (e.g. *philoprōteuein* in verse 9 and *phluarein* in verse 10). Nevertheless, in spite of the different circumstances which evoked them and the fact that the male recipient of the Third was a person and the female recipient of the Second probably a personification, there is a striking similarity of address (from 'the elder' to one 'whom I love in the truth'), the same background situation of itinerant missionaries, the same length, pattern, style, language and conclusion. They are 'like twin sisters' (Alford). 'The similarity between them is too close to admit of any explanation except common authorship or conscious imitation' (Brooke); and the latter is hardly credible in view of the brevity and comparatively unimportant content of the letters.

If we consider the relation between the two shorter Epistles and what Clement of Alexandria called 'the greater', the divergences are seen to be insignificant. When it has been pointed out that the author of the First Epistle nowhere identifies himself, while the author of the Second and Third announces himself as 'the elder', that the tense of the verb in the expression 'Jesus Christ . . . come in the flesh' is perfect in the First Epistle (iv. 2) but present in the Second (verse 7), and that 'antichrists' are plural in the First Epistle (ii. 18), while only singular in the Second (verse 7, though he is there plainly representative of the class called 'many deceivers'), this seems to be the sum total of differences which can be discovered. In contrast to these trivial points the similarities between the greater and the two lesser Epistles are striking. There is the same emphasis on 'truth' (eleven times in the Second and Third Epistles, nine times in the First) which consists pre-eminently of the doctrine that 'Jesus Christ is come in the flesh' (2 Jn. 7: iv. 2). Loyalty to this truth is to 'have both the Father and the Son' (2 Jn. 9: ii. 23); disloyalty to it is to be a 'deceiver' and 'antichrist' (2 Jn. 7: ii. 22, 26). This doctrine is not new, but old. They must 'abide in' it (2 Jn. 9: ii. 27) and let it 'abide in' them (2 Jn. 2: ii. 14, 24). Christian ethics like Christian doctrine are not new; John is writing to them not 'a new commandment' but 'that which we had from the beginning', namely that we 'love one another' (2 Jn. 5, 6: ii. 7, iii. 11). It is in such fellowship that fullness of joy may be found (2 Jn. 12; cf. 3 Jn. 14: i. 4). Those who love and who do good give evidence that they are 'of God' (3 Jn. 11: iii. 10, iv. 4, 7); those who sin and do evil show that they have 'not seen God' (3 Jn. 11: iii. 6).

We conclude that both shorter Epistles were written by the same person and that this person was also the author of the First Epistle, who, we have already argued, had previously composed the Fourth Gospel. If this reasoning is sound, it means that whatever may be learned of the author of the Fourth Gospel from internal evidence will apply to the author of the Epistles, and vice versa; it is impossible to study the Johannine problem if any one of these four writings is isolated, not to mention also the Apocalypse. What concerns us now, however, is to enquire if any further evidence can be discovered from within the three Epistles themselves, which may throw light on their authorship. Such additional internal evidence is both the writer's apparent claim to have been an eyewitness of the historic Jesus, and the authoritative tone with which he addresses his readers, calling himself 'the elder'. If it can be shown that he wrote as a personal eyewitness and with self-conscious authority, we have gone a considerable way towards asserting that the author was an apostle, since one of the qualifications of the apostolate was to have been an eyewitness (e.g. Mk. iii. 14; Lk. xxiv. 48; Jn. xv. 27; Acts i. 21–26, xxii. 12–15, xxvi. 16; 1 Cor. ix. 1, xv. 8, 9), while the uniqueness of the apostolate was the special authority with which they were invested by Jesus Christ Himself (e.g. Mk. iii. 14, 15, vi. 7; Lk. vi. 13; Gal. i. 1).

e. The author as an eyewitness

The clearest and most definite claim of the author of the First Epistle to be an eyewitness is found in its opening words (i. 1, 3). Here John is announcing his particular emphasis. What he proclaims concerning the word of life, the gospel, he says is 'that which was from the beginning, which we have heard . . . seen . . . handled . . .'. His message is supremely concerned with the historical, audible, visible, tangible manifestation of the Eternal. He could hardly have conveyed his meaning more forcefully. He is vouching for his message from his own personal experience. It is not 'cunningly devised fables' (2 Pet. i. 16), but a historical revelation verified by the three highest of man's five senses: hearing, sight and touch.

Yes, he had even 'handled'. This claim to empirical experience he repeats, in the parenthesis of verse 2 ('we have seen it, and bear witness') and again when he resumes his theme after the parenthesis: 'that which we have seen and heard declare we unto you' (verse 3). His declaration is a testimony, and his testimony depends on the personal experience granted to his ears, eyes and hands. A similar claim seems to be made in iv. 14, 'we have seen and do testify that the Father sent the Son to be the Saviour of the world.' He is able to testify in the present because of what he has seen in the past. It is this objective testimony which the Spirit's inward and subjective witness confirms (verse 13). Perhaps a third, though indirect, allusion to the author's eyewitness experience may be found in the reference to the water and the blood in v. 6 (cf. Jn. xix. 34, 35).

Now in i. 1–3 and iv. 14 the claim to an eyewitness experience is couched in the first person plural. It is in each case 'we' who 'have seen' and 'bear witness'. The question is: whom does the author include in his 'we'? Is it merely an editorial or epistolary 'we' by which (like the royal 'we') he is in reality referring to himself alone? So Ebrard: 'St. John is speaking of *himself* and *his* announcement and writing.' His 'we' is 'full of dignity and prerogative'. That this is John's meaning at least sometimes is clear from 3 John 9, where he slips from the singular, 'I wrote unto the church' into the plural 'but Diotrephes . . . receiveth us not'. The RSV significantly maintains the singular, 'Diotrephes . . . does not acknowledge my authority'. Similarly, in verse 12 and the AV rendering, 'we also bear record; and ye know that our record is true' becomes in RSV, 'I testify to him too, and you know my testimony is true.' Or is John, as C.H. Dodd believes, identifying himself with the whole Church? Or again, is he, as has been traditionally accepted, distinguishing himself from the Church at large and associating himself with the other apostles as if to say that, although they were dead and he alone survived, yet he was declaring the one, common apostolic message based upon the one, common apostolic eyewitness experience? 'St. John . . . uses the plural . . . as speaking in the name of the apostolic

body of which he was the last surviving representative'
(Westcott). True, he often abandons the 'we' and uses the
more direct first person singular, but there does not seem to be
any change of subject between the 'these things write *we* unto
you' of i. 4 and the 'these things write *I* unto you' of ii. 1.

Certainly the use of the first person plural as an indication
that his message was not his alone but the apostolic faith has
parallels in the Pauline Epistles (e.g. 1 Cor. xv. 11 and
Gal. ii. 14–16). C. H. Dodd, however, after a lengthy excursus
on the identity of the 'we' in i. 1–4 (pp. 9–16), concludes that
the author speaks 'not exclusively for himself or for a restricted
group, but for the whole Church, to which the apostolic
witness belongs by virtue of its *koinōnia* . . .'. The corollary is
that 'this kind of language . . . is not in itself sufficient to prove
authorship by an eyewitness'. His argument is persuasive and
deserves careful consideration. He points out that elsewhere
in the Epistle 'the first person plural . . . is very frequently used
in a way which includes author and readers in one class. It is
what we might call the preacher's "we" '. But, he continues,
its use is occasioned by more than tact and humility. 'It
belongs to the language of the Church as a fellowship.' So far
we must agree. The author does clearly identify himself with
his readers in many parts of the Epistle, as the preacher does
with his congregation in a sermon, both in confession (e.g.
i. 6–ii. 2), in affirmation (e.g. ii. 3, iii. 2, 14, 19–24, iv. 19 and
v. 18–20) and in exhortation (e.g. iii. 11, iv. 7, 11). In these
(and other) 'we' sentences the author is neither speaking
editorially nor associating himself with the other apostles but
identifying himself with the whole Christian community, or at
least with his readers. In each case 'we' introduces a general
statement of appeal applicable to all Christian people alike.
In such passages the antithesis to 'we' is not 'you' but 'they',
meaning 'the world' of non-Christians, to which group the
heretics properly belong, e.g. ii. 19 ('they went out from us,
but they were not of us') and v. 19 ('we know that we are of
God, and the whole world is in the power of the evil one',
RSV).

The problem is more difficult, however, in three passages

which C. H. Dodd goes on to discuss, and in which the anti-thesis is not between 'we' and 'they' but between 'we' and 'you': iv. 4–6, 14 and i. 1–5. In the first passage the crucial question is whether there is any difference of subject in the expressions 'ye are of God' (verse 4) and 'we are of God' (verse 6). C. H. Dodd says there is not and concludes that the test of knowing God or being of God, viz. whether people listen to 'us', means whether they listen to 'the Church . . . proclaiming the Gospel'. Certainly the sequence of thought in these verses is complicated, since at least five persons or groups are mentioned, and possibly six, namely 'you' (the church), God, 'they' (the false teachers), 'he' (the devil), 'the world', and the controversial 'we'. As the argument unfolds, it seems more natural that the statements 'ye are of God' (verse 4) and 'we are of God' (verse 6) refer to different groups ('ye' to the Christian community, 'we' to the apostolic body), since they lead to different conclusions. 'Ye are of God . . . and have overcome them' (verse 4). That is, your divine birth has enabled you to resist the false teaching. 'We are of God. Whoever knows God listens to us' (verse 6, rsv). That is, just as the world listens to the message of the false teachers who are themselves of the world (verse 5), so those who know God and are of God will listen to the apostolic faith because the apostles' message and commission were themselves of God. The contrast in verse 4 is between the false teacher and the Christian *hearer*; in verse 6 between the false teacher and the Christian *teacher*. 'The hearer discerns the true message. The teacher discovers the true disciple' (Westcott on verse 6). This is an application of Christ's word to the twelve apostles 'he who receives you receives me, and he who receives me receives him who sent me' (Mt. x. 40, rsv).

The next verse C.H. Dodd examines is iv. 14: 'we have seen and do testify that the Father sent the Son to be the Saviour of the world.' He again refers the 'we' to the Christian community, particularly because the verse is embedded in a paragraph (verses 7–19) in which 'we' does plainly refer to Christians in general. He claims this as 'an example of a type of argument which recurs all through the Epistle, in which the validity of certain propositions is tested by reference to the common Christian faith and experience'. He continues, 'it is difficult to accept a sudden shift of meaning so radical that whereas all through the passage "we" has meant Christians in general, it now means a group of eyewitnesses sharply distinguished from Christians in general.' The solution he proposes is derived from the New Testament, and not least Johannine, view of *koinōnia*, 'which connotes a sharing of life and experience so deep and thoroughgoing that what is predicated of the whole community can in some real sense be predicated of each member, and vice versa'. He cites as Old Testament parallels the 'I' of the Psalms, which sometimes 'expresses the solidarity of the Psalmist with the Israel of God'—a solidarity extending to 'the successive generations of Israel', as is plain from Amos ii. 10 and Joshua xxiv. 7, where the redemption from Egypt is said to have been experienced and seen by a generation who had themselves personally neither seen nor experienced it. Similarly, C. H. Dodd suggests, the author of the First Epistle could write of the whole Christian community 'seeing' and therefore testifying to 'the mighty acts of the Lord' by which they had been redeemed, even if they had not individually been eyewitnesses of them.

This is an impressive argument, containing undoubtedly much truth, and comment on it will be reserved until we have considered the conclusion which C.H. Dodd reaches as he now returns to the Preface (i. 1–4). He agrees that 'here certainly a distinction is made . . . between the author and his readers', which is expressed by 'we—you' at least in verses 3 and 4, although even here he refers the 'our' of 'our fellowship' (verse 3) and 'our joy' (verse 4, rsv) to the whole Church. As for the 'we' of verses 1 and 2, although conceding that 'this kind of language would be very natural from the Apostle John or the Presbyter John . . . or some other eyewitness . . . , it is not in itself sufficient to prove authorship by an eyewitness'. The emphasis, he argues, is on the literal hearing, seeing and touching, and not on the identity of those who heard, saw and touched, nor on 'the direct knowledge of some

Christians over against the secondhand knowledge of others'.

All this is plausibly argued, but leaves the critical reader of C. H. Dodd's Commentary uneasy, particularly with regard to the Epistle's Preface. Approaching this paragraph *de novo*, there are some points to which insufficient weight has been given. First, the author distinguishes himself from those he is addressing more clearly than C. H. Dodd allows, not only as writer to readers, but as eyewitness and authoritative teacher to taught. The Preface contains seven verbs in the first person plural, describing both the empirical experience and the announcement, before the writer adds the 'you' to whom the announcement is made. Who is this 'you' to whom 'we declare' the gospel, if the 'we' who declare it includes the whole Christian community? It is certainly not 'the world'. But how can it be the Church? Neil Alexander's note hardly makes sense: 'the *you* in verses 2, 3 and 4 (John's readers) are not over against, but included in the *we*. *You* and *we* alike are the Church.' Are we then to understand that preaching the gospel is a kind of self-proclamation, the Church talking to itself? No. The sequence of thought in the parenthesis of verse 2 is that the life which was with *the Father* was made manifest to *us*, that *we* might declare it to *you*. And the purpose of the declaration is that *you* (of a subsequent generation) may have fellowship with *us* (the original eyewitnesses of the Word made flesh). We desire this for *you* because *our* fellowship is so privileged and precious; it is with *the Father* and with *His Son Jesus Christ* (verse 3).

Nor does it seem fair to say that the emphasis of the first verse is on the empirical experience itself as a fact rather than on the identity of those who had it. On the contrary, the author seems to stress not only the material reality of what was heard, seen and felt, but the persons who had the experience also, because he mentions that it was 'our eyes' which saw and 'our hands' which handled. Moreover, the first person plural is used not only of the verbs describing the historical experience, but also of the verbs describing the proclamation of it. The persons who make the announcement are the persons who had the experience. The natural interpretation of these verses is, therefore, not merely of an empirical experience in general, nor of the original eyewitnesses with whom the Christian community is identified in the *koinōnia*, but of the personal experience of the very ones who are now making the proclamation. It is they whose eyes have seen, ears heard and hands handled, whose mouths are opened to speak.

This is particularly clear from the author's use, in addition to 'we declare' (*apangellomen*), of the verb 'we bear witness' or 'testify' (*marturoumen*) preceded by 'we have seen' (*heōrakamen*). Although it is true that *martureisthai* is commonly employed in the Acts for preaching, which is a public testimony to the facts of the gospel, yet the compound expression 'see and testify' is used exclusively of eyewitnesses, especially by John. The two form 'a compacted pair of ideas' (Ebrard). Thus John the Baptist 'bore witness', saying, 'I saw the Spirit descend . . . on him. . . . And I have seen and have borne witness that this is the Son of God' (Jn. i. 32, 34, RSV). The same combination is used of the teaching of Jesus Himself (Jn. iii. 11, 32), and of the Evangelist's own testimony in the Gospel, in connection with the spear thrust, 'He who saw it has borne witness' (xix. 35, RSV). Cf. Acts xxii. 14–16. In all these occurrences of the linked 'see and bear witness', it is plain that the seeing qualified the witness. He could only testify to what, and because of what, he had seen.

In view of this consistent New Testament (and especially Johannine) usage, we must respectfully dissent from C. H. Dodd's interpretation of the 'we' both in the Preface and, with a little less conviction, in iv. 14. To interpret these words of 'a spiritual vision', writes Brooke, would be 'forced and unnatural in the extreme'. The kind of second-hand vision of the Christian community is unconvincing also. Alford is nearer the truth when he writes of the emphatic 'we' of iv. 14: 'this *hēmeis* brings up in sharp relief the apostolic body whom Christ appointed His witnesses, Jn. xv. 27, Acts i. 8. The assertion is of the same kind as that in chapter i. 1.' The whole difficulty arises because the writer (if an apostle) was a man holding two positions. In one sense, associated with his fellow-apostles, he was unique; in another sense, associated with his readers, he was just a common Christian. We see this same tension in the apostle Paul who could style himself at the beginning of an Epistle both 'slave of Jesus Christ', a title shared by all Christians, and 'called to be an apostle' or 'an apostle of Jesus Christ', which set him apart from his readers (Rom. i. 1; Tit. i. 1). So John can call those to whom he writes both his 'little children', which indicates his authority as well as his age, and his 'brethren', on an equal footing with them. He can begin by writing 'we have seen and testify, and declare to you' (i. 1–5), distinguishing himself from them, and immediately continue, 'if we say that we have no sin' (verse 6), including himself with them. Again, 'my little children, these things write I unto you, that ye sin not' is followed at once by 'if any man sin, we have an advocate . . .' (ii. 1).

Only the context can guide us as to whether his 'we' is uniquely apostolic or commonly Christian. It appears that when doctrine is at stake, he retains the 'we—you' mode of address. This is so in iv. 1–6. The change comes abruptly with verse 7, 'Beloved, let us love one another.' Although he and they were distinct in the teaching-learning relationship, they were one in ethical responsibility. Certainly when he is teaching them, or referring to the apostolic faith which they have received from him 'from the beginning', he slips into direct 'I (or we)—you' speech (e.g. ii. 7, 18, 21, 24). iii. 11 is a particularly interesting example, because it begins 'this is the message which *you* have heard from the beginning' (RSV) and continues 'that *we* should love one another'. It is 'I—you' in the issuing of the message, but 'we' in the receiving and obeying of it. It is for this reason, no doubt, that the only exception to the rule mentioned above is 2 John 5, where he at first describes the commandment as one 'which we had from the beginning, that *we* love one another', since the commandment applies to him as much as to them and he does not exempt himself from it. But in the next verse he is back to direct speech, 'this is the commandment, as *you* have heard from the beginning, that *you* follow love' (RSV). All these examples of the author's use of 'we' may enable us to agree with Calvin: 'As the words are in the plural and the matter applies equally to all the apostles, I interpret it of them; especially as it deals with the authority of witness.'

f. The author's self-conscious authority

The author's authoritative tone is particularly evident in the 'I—you' passages and appears the more striking when viewed in contrast to the humble way in which he associates himself with his readers in some 'we' passages. There is nothing tentative or apologetic about what he writes. He does not hesitate to call certain classes of people liars, deceivers or antichrists. He supplies tests by which everybody can be sorted into one or other of two categories. According to their relation to his tests they either have God or have not, know God or do not, have been born of God or have not, have life or abide in death, walk in the darkness or in the light, are children of God or children of the devil. This dogmatic authority of the writer is seen particularly in his statements and in his commands. For some of his pronouncements see i. 5, ii. 1, 2, ii. 8, ii. 17, ii. 23, iii. 6, 9, iv. 8, 16, iv. 18, v. 12. For positive commands see ii. 15, ii. 28, iv. 1, v. 21. More striking than the general ethical commands of the First Epistle are the personal and particular directions of the Second and Third: 'if anyone comes to you and does not bring this doctrine, do not receive him into the house or give him any greeting' (2 Jn. 10, RSV); and in the Third Epistle the instruction to entertain itinerant Christian missionaries, an instruction which Diotrephes had disobeyed in defiance of the Elder's authority (verses 5–10).

But who is this who presumes to make such dogmatic affirmations and to issue commands which are reminiscent of what James Denney called the 'sovereign legislative authority' of Jesus Himself? True, in statement and command, John is sometimes quoting or echoing the teaching of Jesus, which he has himself recorded in the Gospel (e.g. 1 Jn. ii. 25, iii. 13), but he goes much further than this. He dares to instruct and to direct in matters beyond the boundaries of the Lord's teaching. Moreover, in doing so he gives no hint that he regards one kind of teaching as less authoritative than the other. Some of the commandments of which he writes are God's (e.g. iii. 23,

24, v. 3), some are Christ's (e.g. ii. 7; 2 Jn. 5), and some are his own (e.g. 2 Jn. 10, 11 and 3 Jn. 9 ff.). But he does not distinguish between them; he expects them all to be obeyed. Compare Paul's commands and requirements of obedience in 2 Thessalonians iii. 4, 6, 10, 12, 14.

All this 'would have been impossible for any lesser personage than an Apostle' (Smith). It is entirely consistent with the unique position occupied by the apostles of Jesus in view of the promises and commission which He gave them. They were to teach others to observe whatever He had commanded them (Mt. xxviii. 20), but He would by His Spirit continue to teach and command through them (Jn. xiv. 26, xvi. 12, 13; cf. Acts i. 1). It is the bestowal of this authoritative commission and message, together with their eyewitness experience, which constituted the uniqueness of the apostles; and John lays claim to both in the first chapter of the First Epistle. It was what he had 'seen' of Christ which qualified him to 'witness', and what he had 'heard' from Christ which qualified him to 'declare' an authoritative message to others. If John's claim to this twofold qualification is a true claim, then his identity is John the apostle.

g. *The title 'elder'*

But in the Second and Third Epistles the title he gives himself is not 'apostle' but 'elder'. Why is this? It is becoming increasingly common for commentators to answer this question by saying that there were in fact two Johns (who may or may not both have lived in Ephesus), John the apostle and John the presbyter (or 'elder'), and that it is the latter who wrote these Epistles. Some add that he wrote the Fourth Gospel also. What is the evidence that such a person existed? It is to be found in Eusebius' *Ecclesiastical History*, at the end of Book III, in which he has been describing some of the outstanding personalities of the subapostolic period. The last chapter (39) is concerned with Papias, Bishop of Hierapolis, who is quoted as saying that 'if anyone chanced to come who had actually been a follower of the elders', he (Papias) would enquire about (or into) 'the discourses of the elders, what Andrew or what Peter said, or what Philip, or what Thomas or James, or what

John or Matthew or any other of the Lord's disciples; and the
things which Aristion and John the elder, disciples of the Lord,
say' (iii. 39. 4). Eusebius goes on immediately to draw attention to the double mention of John, once with the apostles and
once with Aristion. He concludes that Papias was referring to
two separate Johns, the apostle and the presbyter. On the
strength of this, and in spite of his quotation from Irenaeus that
Papias was 'a hearer of John and a companion of Polycarp, a
man of primitive times' (iii. 39. 1), he goes on to assert
categorically that Papias 'was in no sense a hearer and eyewitness of the holy Apostles', but only learned from 'their
pupils' (iii. 39. 2).

But was Eusebius right in his interpretation? He was
writing a century later, and he had a poor opinion of Papias
who, he said, judging from his writings, 'was a man of exceed-
ingly small intelligence' (iii. 39. 13). Papias was not only
unintelligent, but 'an uncommonly clumsy writer' (Dodd).
Certainly his statement about 'the elder John' is ambiguous.
Brooke refers to 'the Elder John whom Papias so carefully
distinguishes from the Apostle', while other commentators
have doubted whether it was Papias' intention to distinguish
between two Johns at all. They rightly point out that the seven
apostles who are named in the quotation are themselves called
'elders' just like 'the elder John' (iii. 39. 4 and cf. 39. 7), and
maintain 'it is impossible that the term should bear different
meanings within the compass of a single sentence' (Smith).
Not only are the seven apostles and 'the elder John' alike
'elders', but they are both termed 'disciples of the Lord' as
well. In this case, it may be asked, if the two Johns are the
same person, why is he mentioned twice?

The ambiguity seems to be due to the fact that Papias has
three categories in mind, according to whether they were
'disciples' in general or 'apostles' ('elders') in particular, and
whether they were dead or still alive. What was common to the
three categories is that they were all 'disciples of the Lord',
who had known Him in the days of His flesh. The seven were
apostles or 'elders' as well as disciples, but were dead. Aristion
was alive as well as a disciple, but not an apostle. John was in

a category of his own because only he possessed the three qualifications, being a disciple and an apostle/elder and alive. This is why he is mentioned twice: first with Andrew, Peter, Philip and the others who, though not alive, were like him apostles or elders, and secondly with Aristion who, though not an apostle/elder, was like him still ,alive.

This interpretation is suggested by the change of tense, to which Plummer, Smith and others have drawn attention, from what the apostles/elders 'said' (*eipen*) to what Aristion and the elder John 'say' (*legousin*). They argue cogently that Papias was claiming to draw his materials from two sources; one was second-hand, namely the 'followers' of the apostles/elders who had heard them during their lifetime, and the other first-hand, namely living eyewitnesses, whether disciples like Aristion or the only surviving apostle/elder, John. Since Papias had heard the teaching of John in both ways, from others by report and from his own lips, he mentions him twice. If it cannot be proved that this, and not Eusebius' interpretation, is the correct one, it must at least be conceded with C. H. Dodd (who believes that the author of the three Epistles was a 'presbyter John' distinct from the apostle) that Papias 'expresses himself so loosely in the crucial passage that it would be possible to hold that he intended to include apostles in the wider class of presbyters'.

Irenaeus, Bishop of Lyons, is also quoted in support of the theory of two Johns. He himself had come from Asia and was familiar with the writings of Papias. In his famous *Adversus Haereses* (v. 33, 36) he refers several times to a group of people whom he names 'the presbyters, disciples of the Apostles'. He seems to be referring to 'those who had companied with Apostles, and had perhaps been placed in office by them' (Brooke), who thus 'formed a link between the apostles and the next generation' and 'transmitted . . . the apostolic traditions' (Dodd). He also sometimes mentions such a presbyter in the singular (iv. 47, 49, i. 8, 17 and *Ecclesiastical History*, v. 8. 8, 'a certain apostolic elder, whose name he bequeaths to silence'), but there is no indication that he means the presbyter John whom in fact he does not mention. He does, however, refer to the apostle John, and calls him a 'disciple of the Lord', which is the same title used by Papias for the seven apostles/elders, Aristion and 'the elder John'.

Dionysius of Alexandria in the third century was quoted by Eusebius (iii. 39. 6 and vii. 25. 16) in confirmation of his theory that there were two Johns: 'since it is said both that there were two tombs at Ephesus, and that each of the two is said to be John's.' This statement needs to be treated with considerable caution. To begin with, Eusebius does not appear to have any personal knowledge of these two tombs; he is merely quoting Dionysius. Dionysius claims no personal knowledge of them either, but only that 'it is said' there were two tombs and it 'is said' that both were John's. Further, Dionysius had a reason for wanting to distinguish two Johns: he was determined to find a John other than the apostle to whom he could attribute the Book of Revelation, which he did not like. Finally, even if there were at one time two tombs at Ephesus bearing John's name, it is more likely that they were rival claimants for the tomb of the same John than separate tombs of two distinct Johns. Certainly Polycrates, who was Bishop of Ephesus at the end of the second century, and who sent to Bishop Victor of Rome a list of earlier Christian celebrities who had been buried in Asian cities, does not mention 'the elder John'; he does, however, mention the apostle John and Polycarp as having their graves in Ephesus. It is not until Jerome (d. 420) that a second tomb was said to be either an alternative site for the same John's grave, or the grave of another John 'the elder', who according to the opinion of many was the author of the shorter Epistles (*De Viris Illustribus* 9).

It is probable that Eusebius adopted the theory of two Johns for the same reason as Dionysius, namely that he disapproved of the Revelation for its supposed millenarian views and wanted to ascribe it to an author other than the apostle John. He therefore proposed 'John the elder' and quoted Papias and Dionysius in support of such a person.

It must be admitted that grounds for believing in a second John, 'the presbyter', are extremely scanty. Plummer does not hesitate to write: 'there is no independent evidence of the existence of a second John. Papias, as interpreted or mis-interpreted by Eusebius, is our sole witness. . . . We, therefore, give up the second John as unhistorical.'

Turning now from the vexed question of the historicity of a distinct 'presbyter John', let us suppose for a moment that such a person existed, and ask: could he be the author of these Epistles? Scholars find themselves in difficulties here because some want him as the author of the Epistles, while others want him as the author of the Gospel, and yet others as the author of the Apocalypse. Leaving aside this rather unseemly scramble for the shadowy presbyter John, in order to attribute to him writings for which it is desired to relieve the apostle John of responsibility, is there any evidence that this presbyter wrote the Epistles? Westcott describes such a view as 'purely conjectural' and adds that 'there is not the least direct evidence external or internal in its favour'.

We agree, of course, that the author of the two short Epistles called himself 'the elder'. He must have done so, without adding his name, because his identity was so well known and his authority so well recognized that he could use the title without needing to qualify or amplify it. Moreover, since the two Epistles were written to different churches, he was evidently known and acknowledged in a wide area of the province of Asia. It is plain, as we read his letters, that he is intimately acquainted with their affairs, and accepts responsibility for their spiritual oversight. He loves them, exhorts them, teaches them, warns them, commands them. Is it possible that a man of such prominence, who exercised such authority and wrote three Epistles which are included in the New Testament canon, should have left no more trace of himself in history than one dubious reference by Papias? It seems far more probable that this widespread authority was that of the apostle John who, according to well-attested tradition, lived to a ripe old age in Ephesus. Eusebius says (iii. 23. 1, 3, 4) that 'he whom Jesus loved, apostle alike and evangelist, even John' lived on in Asia, 'directing the churches there', according to Irenaeus 'until the time of Trajan' (reigned AD 98–117). Such was his far-flung 'diocese' that, in words of Clement of Alexandria also quoted by Eusebius, 'he used to go off, when requested, to the neighbouring districts of the Gentiles also, to appoint bishops in some places, to organize whole churches in others. . . .' (iii. 23. 6).

If the author was the apostle John, we still have to ask why he styled himself 'the elder'. There is nothing strange about an apostle calling himself an 'elder'. The title had been taken over from the Jewish eldership, and elders were appointed in Christian churches at least from the time of Paul's first missionary journey (Acts xiv. 23). The apostle Peter used the title of himself, calling himself a 'fellow elder' of those he was addressing in his First Epistle (v. 1, RSV). And we have seen that the Papias quotation, whichever way it is interpreted, calls the apostles 'elders' also. But why did John use the absolute title '*the* elder'? Of course the word literally means an 'old man', 'senior' or 'veteran', and it is possible that John assumed, or was given, the title in his old age, much as Paul called himself 'Paul the aged' in his letter to Philemon (verse 9; although there the word is the similar *presbutēs*, not *presbuteros*). It is not necessary to speak of the title as an 'affectionate nickname', like our 'The Old Man' (Dodd), which John would be unlikely to use in a formal and solemn pastoral letter. But as a serious title, it would be particularly appropriate to the apostle who had outlived the other apostles. He would not have dreamed of calling himself 'the apostle', for all the apostles shared the same special divine commission. He was only '*an* apostle', as Paul and Peter also styled themselves (e.g. Rom. i. 1; 1 Pet. i. 1). But he could be called '*the* elder' *par excellence*. There were other elders in Ephesus, but he was unique among them because he was an apostle as well and a veritable patriarch in age. It is even conceivable that the later technical use of the title 'elders' for 'disciples of the apostles' was derived from John, who as the last surviving apostle and 'the elder' was the link between the apostolic and the subapostolic periods. As 'the elder', whose leadership was accepted, he exercised a widespread supervision of the Asian churches surrounding Ephesus, perhaps especially the six others named in the seven letters of Revelation ii and iii.

We conclude, therefore, that although we can only guess how and why the writer came to be called 'the elder' in this anonymous and absolute way, the use of the title tends to confirm the unique position of the person who held it. Such an exceptional position, together with the author's authoritative tone and claim to have been an eyewitness, are fully consistent with the early tradition of the Church that these three Epistles were in fact written by the apostle John.

II. OCCASION

A number of authors have argued that the Epistles of John are to be regarded rather as pastoral than polemical writings. There is some truth in this assertion. John exhibits a tender, pastoral care for his readers. His first concern is not to confound the false teachers, whose activities form the background of the Epistles, but to protect his readers, his beloved 'little children', and to establish them in their Christian faith and life. Thus, he defines his own purpose in writing as being 'that your joy may be full', 'that ye sin not', and 'that ye may know that ye have eternal life' (i. 4, ii. 1, v. 13). Joy, holiness, assurance. These are the Christian qualities the pastor desires to see in his flock. The First Epistle is 'a masterpiece in the art of edification' (Findlay).

Nevertheless, he has also a polemical purpose. It is not a theological treatise written in the academic peace of a library, but a tract for the times, called forth by a particular and urgent situation in the Church. This situation concerns the insidious propaganda of certain false teachers. 'These things have I written unto you concerning them that seduce you' (ii. 26), or 'those who would deceive you' (rsv). Again, 'little children, let no man deceive you' (iii. 7). The apostle Paul's prophecy to the Ephesian elders about 'grievous wolves' (Acts xx. 29, 30), later repeated to Timothy (2 Tim. iii. 1 ff., iv. 3, 4), has evidently come true. John describes them by three expressions, which draw attention to their diabolical origin, evil influence and false teaching. First, they are 'false prophets' (iv. 1). A prophet is a teacher who speaks under the inspiration of a supernatural power. The true prophet is the mouthpiece of the Spirit of truth, the false of the spirit of error. This is why examining the teaching of prophets is called 'testing the spirits' (iv. 1–6). Secondly, they are 'deceivers' (2 Jn. 7), because they are leading people astray. Thirdly, they are 'antichrists' (ii. 18, cf. verse 22, iv. 3; 2 Jn. 7), because the substance of their teaching is to deny the divine-human Person of Jesus Christ. In each case they are 'many'—'many false prophets', 'many deceivers', 'many antichrists'. They once passed as loyal members of the church, but now they have seceded (ii. 19) and 'gone out into the world' (iv. 1; cf. 2 Jn. 7) to spread their pernicious lies. It seems probable that their secession was due to their failure to convert the rest of the congregation, who by their loyalty to the truth had 'overcome them' (iv. 4). Yet some who remained must have been left in a wavering and insecure state, so that John needs to write to reassure and strengthen them. His great emphasis is on the differences between the genuine Christian and the spurious, and how to discern between the two.

The internal evidence furnished by the Epistles discloses not only the existence and activity of the false teachers but to some extent the nature of their perverted system as well. We can learn it both from John's direct references to their teaching which he contradicts and from the positive emphasis he feels it is necessary to make in order to counteract it. The context of his double mention of deceivers shows that their error was both theological (ii. 26; cf. 2 Jn. 7) and ethical (iii. 7).

Their theological error concerned the Person of Jesus. They denied that Jesus was the Christ (ii. 22). This does not mean, however, that they disbelieved in Jesus of Nazareth as the Christ of Old Testament expectation. John's argument has little in common with the earliest apostolic reasoning with the Jews that Jesus was the Christ (e.g. Acts ix. 22, xvii. 3, xviii. 5).[1] What John's opponents denied was not the Messiahship, but the incarnation of Jesus. In their case to deny that

---

[1] Brooke and Barclay, however, think that John did have Jews in mind, who, especially after the destruction of Jerusalem in AD 70, were even more vigorous in their rejection of the Messiahship of Jesus.

He was 'the Christ' was equivalent to a denial that He was 'the Son' (ii. 23, iv. 15; 2 Jn. 9). Similarly he 'who believes that Jesus is the Christ' is identical with him 'who believes that Jesus is the Son of God' (v. 1, 5, RSV, and cf. verses 9, 13). It is the same in the Gospel (Jn. xx. 31). In two important verses John is more precise. The heretical teaching was a denial either that 'Jesus Christ had come in the flesh', or that 'Jesus was the Christ come in the flesh' (iv. 2; 2 Jn. 7, see notes *ad loc.*). But whether John uses this more elaborate expression or the very simplest, namely to 'confess Jesus' (iv. 3), he means the same thing. He is asserting the reality of the incarnation, the coming in flesh of Jesus Christ, which the heretics denied. Moreover, although they thus denied the incarnation, they evidently claimed to be progressive thinkers (2 Jn. 9, RSV) and still to have the Father without the Son (ii. 22, 23; 2 Jn. 9). Against these false teachers John emphasizes the historical manifestation of 'that which was from the beginning' to the ears, eyes and hands of witnesses (i. 1–3, iv. 14). He also appeals against the 'progressive' thought of the heretics to the original apostolic gospel which his readers received 'from the beginning' (ii. 7, 24).

We are not told explicitly what the ethical error of the false teachers was, but the implication is plain. Their claims appear to be in view wherever John uses the formulae 'if we say' and 'he who says'. The three 'if we say' sentences of i. 6 ff. are a denial either that sin exists in our nature and our behaviour, or that sin matters since it does not interfere with our fellowship with God. Those who make such assertions, John says bluntly, either lie or deceive themselves or make God a liar (i. 6, 8, 10). God's self-revelation is ethical, and there can be no fellowship with Him without righteousness. Similarly, 'he who says' he knows God is a liar if he disobeys His commandments; while 'he who says' he abides in Christ ought to give evidence of it by walking as Christ walked (ii. 4, 6). And what do the commandments of God and the walk of Christ involve? In a word, love. 'He who says' he is in the light and yet hates his brother is still in the darkness (ii. 9; cf. iv. 20). John does not mince his words. The false teachers were claiming to 'know God', to 'abide in Him', to 'be in the light' (perhaps their very expressions or catchphrases), while living themselves in unrighteousness and uncharitableness. Such people are 'liars'. They cannot claim to 'be' righteous unless they actually 'do' righteousness (ii. 29 to iii. 10).

John does not rest content with negatives. The First Epistle is a great positive affirmation that 'God is light' (i. 5) and 'God is love' (iv. 8, 16), and that therefore the darkness of sin and hatred is incompatible with any claim to know God. It is only if we obey God's commandments and love the brethren that we can know that we know Him (ii. 3, iii. 14). Further, Jesus Christ appeared to put away sin and to destroy the works of the devil. Therefore sin and lovelessness are as much at variance with the mission of Christ as they are with the nature of God (iii. 4–10). All sin is 'lawlessness' and 'unrighteousness' (iii. 4, RSV, v. 17) and wholly inconsistent with the profession and conduct of a Christian. The Epistle expounds in successively profound and elaborate arguments the indispensable necessity of righteousness and love in the child of God. Moreover, John appeals against the heretics' ethical error, as he does against their Christological error, to the original apostolic teaching which his readers had 'heard from the beginning', namely 'that we should love one another' (iii. 11).

From this internal evidence it emerges that, if we are to identify the heresy against which John writes, we must find a system which both denied that Jesus was the Son or the Christ come in the flesh and viewed righteousness and love as indifferent. Some writers have argued that this system is the doctrine known as 'Docetism'. The name is derived from the Greek verb *dokein*, to seem, and describes the view that Jesus was not a man in reality but only in appearance. He 'seemed' to the eyes of witnesses to be truly human, but it was a disguise similar to that of the Old Testament theophanies when God (or the angel of the Lord) appeared in the form of a man. We know of this error from several patristic writers, who also used the Johannine Epistles to refute it. It was condemned, for instance, by Ignatius, Polycarp and Tertullian.

But a careful study of the phraseology of John shows that he is concerned not just with the reality of the 'flesh' of Jesus, but with the relation between the human 'Jesus' and the divine 'Son' or 'Christ'. 'The emphasis is not upon the real humanity of Jesus so much as upon the personal identity of the pre-existent Divine Christ with Jesus' (Law).

This has led a majority of commentators to discover the heretics in the ranks of the Gnostics whose preoccupation was with deliverance from the 'flesh', which they regarded as the soul's material imprisonment. 'Gnosticism' is a broad term embracing various pagan, Jewish and semi-Christian systems. It was pagan in origin, combining elements of 'Western intellectualism and Eastern mysticism' (Law). Thoroughly syncretistic in its genius, a 'theosophical hotchpotch' (Dodd), it did not hesitate to fasten upon and to corrupt first Judaism and then Christianity. Plummer sums up its two main principles as 'the impurity of matter' and 'the supremacy of knowledge'. The notion that matter is inherently evil was both oriental and Greek. It led to speculations about the origin of the material universe and how it could in any sense have been created by the Supreme Being who is Good. The Gnostics posited a series of 'aeons' or emanations from the Supreme, each more removed from Him than its predecessors, until one emerged sufficiently remote to create the material world.

The controversy which John's Epistles reflect, however, concerns the doctrine not of the creation, but of the incarnation. Gnostics who believed that matter was evil were obsessed with the problems raised not just by the world in general but by the body in particular. They were immediately in difficulties with the Christian religion because it is such an essentially 'material' religion. It asserts that the Son of God clothed Himself with a body, and that the Christian's body is the temple of the Holy Spirit. What could they make of the body of Christ and of the body of Christians? We have already seen that they denied the former. Their denial was not that the man Jesus had a body, but that the Christ was to be personally identified with the bodily man Jesus. They could not conceive how the 'aeon' Christ could become incarnate, still less assume a body subject to suffering and pain. As for the

Christian's body, it was fundamental to their thought that the body was a base prison in which the rational or spiritual part of man was incarcerated, and from which it needed to be released by *gnōsis*, knowledge. They believed in salvation by enlightenment. This enlightenment could come by the imparting of an esoteric knowledge in some secret initiation ceremony. The initiated were the *pneumatikoi*, the truly 'spiritual' people, who despised the uninitiated as *psuchikoi*, doomed to an animal life on earth. The better Gnostic systems combined these views of spiritual enlightenment and release with a strict asceticism; the worst systems asserted that evil could not harm the enlightened spirit, that morality was therefore a matter of indifference, and that the grossest forms of licence were quite permissible. Such *pneumatikoi* claimed also to be *dikaioi*, 'righteous', irrespective of their behaviour.

The earliest traditions associate the Johannine Epistles with Asia, especially Ephesus, and it is clear from other parts of the New Testament (e.g. the Epistles to the Colossians and Timothy, and those to Pergamum and Thyatira in Revelation ii) that Gnostic views had begun to infiltrate the churches of Asia. One Gnostic resident in Ephesus was a certain Cerinthus, who is known to have been both a contemporary and an opponent of John. We learn about him chiefly from Irenaeus and Eusebius. Irenaeus records in *Adversus Haereses* the famous anecdote told by Polycarp, Bishop of Smyrna, that 'John, the disciple of the Lord, going to bathe at Ephesus, and perceiving Cerinthus within, rushed out of the bath-house without bathing, exclaiming "Let us fly, lest even the bath-house fall down, because Cerinthus, the enemy of the truth, is within" '![1] Irenaeus has already given an account of the heretical views of Cerinthus in Book I of this same great work *Against Heresies*. He says that Cerinthus 'represented Jesus as having not been born of a virgin, but as being the son of Joseph and Mary according to the ordinary course of human generation, while he nevertheless was more righteous, prudent and wise than other men. Moreover, after his baptism, Christ descended

---

[1] iii. 3. 4. Eusebius also records the story in the *Ecclesiastical History*, both in iii. 28. 6 and in iv. 14. 6.

upon him in the form of a dove from the Supreme Ruler, and that then he proclaimed the unknown Father, and performed miracles. But at last Christ departed from Jesus, and that then Jesus suffered and rose again, while Christ remained impassible,[1] inasmuch as he was a spiritual being'.[2] Epiphanius' account of the heresy in his *Refutation of All Heresies* is substantially the same, except that he identifies the divine aeon descending upon the man Jesus as 'the Spirit' rather than 'Christ'.[3] The essence of Cerinthus' error was this severance of the man Jesus from the divine Christ or Spirit. Irenaeus refers to it again later when he alludes to those 'who separate Jesus from Christ, alleging that Christ remained impassible, but that it was Jesus who suffered',[4] and again 'the Son of the Creator was, forsooth, one, but the Christ from above another, who also continued impassible, descending upon Jesus, the Son of the Creator, and flew back again into His Pleroma'.[5]

John's arguments are most readily to be understood as directed against Cerinthianism. He defines it as a denial 'that Jesus is the Christ' (ii. 22), a denial that the two are to be identified. More precisely, it is a denial that Jesus is 'the Christ come in the flesh' (iv. 3; 2 Jn. 7). An ancient reading of iv. 3 renders the heretical position not as 'denying' but as 'loosing' Jesus Christ. See Note on p. 156. It is mentioned in the RV margin. Irenaeus evidently knew this variant, for he quotes iv. 3 as 'every spirit which *separates* Jesus Christ is not of God'.[6] The Vulgate has *solvit*. Although the reading is not original, it bears witness to an early recognition that the Gnostic rejection of the incarnation was a sundering or 'loosing' of Jesus from Christ. John goes further in his refutation of Cerinthus when he describes Jesus (v. 6, RSV) as 'he who came by water and blood, Jesus Christ, not with water only but with the water and the blood'. See the notes on this verse, where it is argued that 'water' here refers primarily to the baptism of Jesus Christ,

[1] I.e. 'not liable to pain or injury' (*O.E.D.*).
[2] i. 26. 1.
[3] *Haereses* xxviii. 1.
[4] *Op. cit.*, iii. 11. 7.
[5] *Op. cit.*, iii. 11. 1.
[6] iii. 16. 8.

47

and 'blood' to His death. Cerinthus taught that the Christ descended upon Jesus *after* His baptism and departed from Him *before* His death; John asserts that on the contrary 'Jesus Christ', one Person, passed *through* both baptism and death.

Irenaeus and Eusebius tell us about the ethical, as well as the Christological, leanings of Cerinthus. According to Irenaeus the error of Cerinthus had been 'disseminated among men . . . a long time previously by those termed Nicolaitans',[1] and these Nicolaitans are mentioned in Revelation ii. 6, 14, 15 as having been guilty of immorality. Both Tertullian and Clement of Alexandria said that they were unrestrained in their dissolute ways. This is further confirmed by two passages in the *Ecclesiastical History* of Eusebius, who had strong anti-millenarian views and criticized Cerinthus for the thoroughly sensual millennium he seems to have been anticipating.[2]

There is no clear evidence in the Johannine Epistles that the false teachers John is opposing held such extreme carnal views, but there is abundant evidence, as we have already seen, that they regarded righteousness of conduct as a matter of indifference. So John lays repeated emphasis on the necessity of holy living and obedience to the commandments of God. He shows that the practice of sin is wholly inadmissible in the Christian. He also denies the possibility of a dual standard of morality by which the *élite* are spared the moral obligations demanded of the common herd. '*Every one* who hopes in Christ purifies himself', he writes. Again, '*No one* born of God practises sin . . .' (see iii. 3, 9). The *dikaioi*, the self-styled 'righteous' ones, can show themselves worthy of the title only by *doing* righteousness (iii. 7). If they sin, they show that, whatever they may claim, they have neither seen nor known God (iii. 6).

A third characteristic of the Gnostics, Cerinthus no doubt included, seems to have been their lovelessness. Claiming to be a spiritual aristocracy of the enlightened, who alone had come to know 'the depths', they despised the ordinary run of Christians. John cuts across this dangerous outlook by asserting

---

[1] *Op. cit.*, iii. 11. 1.
[2] iii. 28. 1, 2, vii. 25. 2, 3.

that there are not two categories of Christians, the enlightened and the unenlightened, for 'God is light', continuously revealing Himself to all. 'You all know', he writes (see ii. 13, 14, 20, v. 20). His readers have all received the same 'unction' and the same message 'which you heard from the beginning' (see ii. 20–27). It is argued in the notes on this paragraph that John is referring to the Spirit and the Word. If all Christians have received both the Word of God and the Spirit of God, there is no room for cliques claiming a superior illumination.

Nor is there any justification for an unloving spirit among the brethren, such as characterized the Gnostics. Bishop Ignatius of Antioch describes them in his letter to the Smyrnaeans. Having quoted the 'new commandment . . . that ye love one another', he goes on: 'Do ye, therefore, notice those who preach other doctrines, how they affirm that the Father of Christ cannot be known, and how they exhibit envy and deceit in their dealings with one another. They have no regard for love. . . .' St. Paul had written in 1 Corinthians of the dangers of knowledge without love (viii. 1–3, xiii. 2). It is very apparent in the Johannine Epistles. So John affirms that God is in His very being love, and that we know love because God sent His Son to be our Saviour and because Christ laid down His life for us (iv. 8, 10, 14, iii. 16). Since God is love and has loved, and since all love is of God, he reasons, 'beloved, let us love one another'; 'he who does not love does not know God' (iv. 7, 8, RSV).

In his commentary on Galatians vi. 10 Jerome tells a famous story of 'blessed John the evangelist' in extreme old age at Ephesus. He used to be carried into the congregation in the arms of his disciples and was unable to say anything except 'little children, love one another'. At last, wearied that he always spoke the same words, they asked: 'Master, why do you always say this?' 'Because', he replied, 'it is the Lord's command, and if this only is done, it is enough.'[1]

We may conclude, then, that against the Christological heresy, the moral indifferentism and the arrogant lovelessness of Cerinthian Gnosticism, John lays his emphasis on three

---

[1] Longer Version, Chapter VI.

marks of authentic Christianity, namely belief in Jesus as the Christ come in the flesh, obedience to the commandments of God and brotherly love.

III. MESSAGE

The mid-twentieth century is an epoch of fundamental insecurity. Everything is changing; nothing is stable. New nations are constantly coming to birth. New social and political patterns are continually evolving. The very survival of civilization is in doubt before the threat of a nuclear war. These external insecurities are reflected in the world of the mind and of the spirit. Even the Christian Church, which has received 'a kingdom which cannot be moved' and is charged to proclaim Him who is 'the same yesterday, and today, and for ever' (Heb. xii. 28, xiii. 8) now speaks its message softly, shyly and without conviction. There is a widespread distrust of dogmatism and a preference for agnosticism or free thought. Many Christians are filled with uncertainty and confusion.

Against this background, to read the Epistles of John is to enter another world altogether, whose marks are assurance, knowledge, confidence and boldness. The predominant theme of these Epistles is Christian certainty. Their characteristic verbs are *ginōskein*, 'to perceive' (15 times), and *eidenai*, 'to know' (25 times), while the characteristic noun is *parrēsia*, 'confidence of attitude' or 'boldness of speech'. The Christian's certainty is twofold—objective (that the Christian religion is true) and subjective (that he himself has been born of God and possesses eternal life). Both are expounded by John, who takes it for granted that this double assurance is right and healthy in all Christian people. His teaching about these certainties, their nature and the grounds on which they are built, urgently needs to be heard and heeded today.

a. Certainty about Christ

It can be asserted of Christians, as a result of the anointing which we have received, that we 'all know' (ii. 20, RSV), absolutely. This does not mean, of course, that we know all things, as the AV mistakenly suggests, for some things God has not yet revealed (e.g. iii. 2). Nevertheless, we 'know the truth' (ii. 21; cf. 2 Jn. 1 and iv. 6), which includes the truth about the world and its condition (v. 19; cf. ii. 18, iii. 15), and about ourselves, our duty and destiny (ii. 10, 11, 29, iii. 2, v. 18). Above all, we know the truth about God and Christ. 'We know that the Son of God has come and has given us understanding, to know him who is true' (v. 20, RSV). We thus know both God (ii. 13, 14, iv. 6, 7) and Christ (iii. 6; cf. iii. 1). We know, moreover, that the cause of Christ's coming was love (iii. 16, iv. 16) and its purpose 'to take away our sins' (iii. 5).

But how do we know these things, especially who Jesus Christ is and why He came? John's clear answer is in three stages. First, there is the historical event, Christ's being 'sent' (iv. 9, 10, 14), His 'coming' (v. 20), His 'manifestation' or 'appearing' (*ephanerōthē* in i. 2, iii. 5, 8, iv. 9). His coming was 'in the flesh' (iv. 2; 2 Jn. 7) and 'through water and blood' (v. 6). That is, it was real, and involved Him in the definite historical experiences of birth, baptism and death. Next, there is the apostolic witness. The event did not pass unnoticed. The One who came in the flesh was seen, heard and touched, so that those who saw could testify from their own first-hand experience (i. 1–3, iv. 14). Thirdly, there is the 'anointing' of the Holy Spirit, by whom we are taught and therefore know (ii. 20, 27; cf. iii. 24, iv. 13). This testimony of the Spirit is within the believer (v. 10) and corroborates the external witness of 'the water and the blood' (v. 6, 8, 9).

The ground of our certainty about Christ has not changed. The fact that we read the Epistles of John in the twentieth century rather than the first makes no difference. The Christian religion is still tethered to the historical event of Christ and the witness which the apostles bore to it. In this 'doctrine of Christ' we must 'abide' (2 Jn. 9). To advance beyond it will inevitably lead us into error and therefore into ruin. The duty of Christian ministers today is to follow the apostle John, not the false teachers. We are not to lead the congregation into novel doctrines, but to recall them to what they heard 'from the beginning' (ii. 7, 24, iii. 11; 2 Jn. 5). Further, those who believe in the historical Jesus on the unique testimony of the apostolic eyewitnesses, which is now preserved in the New Testament and expounded by the Church, are granted the contemporary and confirmatory witness of the Spirit within themselves.

b. Certainty about eternal life

The kind of Christian knowledge which is distinctively treated in these Epistles, however, is subjective rather than objective. It concerns not so much the truth about God and Christ as about our own Christian standing, which John describes by four favourite expressions. First, we know 'that we know him' (ii. 3; cf. v. 20). Secondly, we know 'that we are in him' and 'that we dwell in him and he in us' (ii. 5, iv. 13; cf. iii. 24). Thirdly, we know 'that we are of God' (v. 19; cf. iii. 19 'of the truth'). Fourthly, we know 'that we have passed from death unto life' and that therefore we have eternal life (iii. 14, v. 13). To be a Christian, then, in the language of John, is to have been born of God, to know God and to be in Him, enjoying that intimate, personal communion with Him which is eternal life (v. 20; cf. Jn. xvii. 3). Of this heavenly birth and life-giving relationship we have no doubt. Indeed, John declares that his purpose in writing the First Epistle is that those who 'believe' might also 'know' (v. 13).

John's argument is double-edged. If he seeks to bring believers to the knowledge that they have eternal life, he is equally at pains to show that unbelievers have not. His purpose is to destroy the false assurance of the counterfeit as well as to confirm the right assurance of the genuine. He is conscious throughout the Epistles of these two companies, 'you' and 'they' (e.g. ii. 18–20, iv. 4, 5). The same two groups exist today. Some are cocksure and boast of what they may well not possess; others are conventional churchgoers who have no assurance of salvation, and even say it is presumptuous to claim any. But there is a true Christian assurance, which is neither arrogant nor presumptuous, but is on the contrary, as these Epistles show, the plainly revealed will of God for His people (v. 13). So John urges his readers to examine themselves, and he supplies tests by which they (and we) may do so.

Robert Law called his studies in the First Epistle *The Tests of Life* (1885) because in it are given what he terms 'the three cardinal tests' by which we may judge whether we possess life eternal or not. The first is theological, whether we believe that Jesus is 'the Son of God' (iii. 23, v. 5, 10, 13), 'the Christ come in the flesh' (iv. 2; 2 Jn. 7). No system of teaching which denies either the eternal divine pre-existence of Jesus or the historical incarnation of the Christ can be accepted as Christian. 'No one who denies the Son has the Father' (ii. 23, RSV). The second test is moral, whether we are practising righteousness and keeping the commandments of God. Sin is shown to be wholly incompatible with the nature of God as light (i. 5), the mission of the Son to take away sins (iii. 5) and the new birth of the believer (iii. 9). Now, as then, any claim to mystical experience without moral conduct is to be rejected (i. 6). The third test is social, whether we love one another. Since God is love and all love comes from God, it is clear that a loveless person does not know Him (iv. 7, 8).

It is important to see that John's three tests are not arbitrarily selected. On the contrary, they possess an inner coherence, which he particularly unfolds in the second half of chapter iv in relation to the gospel. This in brief is that 'the Father sent the Son to be the Saviour of the world' (iv. 14), an affirmation which implies the divine-human Person of the Son who was sent, the love of the Father who sent Him, and the righteousness of those who receive His salvation. The three tests belong to each other also, because faith, love and holiness are all the works of the Holy Spirit. It is only if God has given us His Spirit that we are able to believe, to love and to obey (iii. 24, iv. 13). So everyone who believes that Jesus is the Christ, and loves, and does righteousness, thereby gives evidence that 'he has been begotten of God'. This identical expression occurs in the Greek text of ii. 29, iv. 7 and v. 1. 'The tenses sufficiently show', writes Law, referring to the change from the present to the perfect, 'that in each case the Divine Begetting is the necessary antecedent to the human activity.' Further, if belief, holiness and love betray a birth of God, they are marks also of the continuing reciprocal indwelling of God and His people (iii. 24, iv. 12, 13, 16, and iv. 15).

To fail to pass these tests is to stand self-exposed. We may still claim to be Christian, to know God and to have life, but John insists that our verbal profession is negatived by the facts (e.g. i. 6, 8, 10, ii. 4, 6, 9, iv. 20). Indeed, 'he who says' he knows and loves God, while disobeying His commandments and hating his brother, like him who denies that Jesus is the Christ, is 'a liar' (ii. 4, iv. 20; cf. ii. 22). On the other hand, 'by this we know' that we know God, are in Him and have life, if we keep His commandments, love the brethren and believe in Jesus Christ (ii. 3, 4, iii. 14, 18, 19, 24).

A fresh certainty about Christ and about eternal life, based upon the grounds which John gives, can still lead Christian people into that boldness of approach to God and of testimony to men, which is as sorely needed as it is sadly missing in the Church today.

ANALYSES

The First Epistle of John

I. THE PREFACE (i. 1–4).

II. THE APOSTOLIC MESSAGE AND ITS MORAL IMPLI-
CATIONS (i. 5–ii. 2).

    a. The denial that sin breaks our fellowship with God
(i. 6, 7).

    b. The denial that sin exists in our nature (i. 8, 9).

    c. The denial that sin shows itself in our conduct (i. 10–ii. 2).

III. FIRST APPLICATION OF THE TESTS (ii. 3–27).

    a. Obedience, or the moral test (ii. 3–6).

    b. Love, or the social test (ii. 7–11).

    c. A digression about the Church (ii. 12–14).

    d. A digression about the world (ii. 15–17).

    e. Belief, or the doctrinal test (ii. 18–27).

IV. SECOND APPLICATION OF THE TESTS (ii. 28–iv. 6).

    a. An elaboration of the moral test: righteousness (ii. 28–
iii. 10).

    b. An elaboration of the social test: love (iii. 11–18).

    c. A digression about assurance and the condemning heart
(iii. 19–24).

    d. An elaboration of the doctrinal test: belief (iv. 1–6).

V. THIRD APPLICATION OF THE TESTS (iv. 7–v. 5).

    a. A further elaboration of the social test: love (iv. 7–12).

    b. A combination of the doctrinal and social tests (iv. 13–21).

    c. A combination of the three tests (v. 1–5).

VI. THE THREE WITNESSES AND OUR CONSEQUENT
ASSURANCE (v. 6–17).

    a. The three witnesses (v. 6–12).

    b. Our consequent assurance (v. 13–17).

VII. THREE AFFIRMATIONS AND A CONCLUDING EX-
HORTATION (v. 18–21).

The Second Epistle of John

The Third Epistle of John

I JOHN: COMMENTARY

I. THE PREFACE (i. 1-4)

The opening of the Epistle is remarkable in that it lacks any salutation or personal reference. In this it differs from all the other New Testament Epistles except Hebrews. For the bearing of this on the question of authorship see Introduction, p. 13. All commentators have found this first paragraph involved in syntax and abstruse in meaning. It is, in fact, a 'grammatical tangle' (Dodd). It is necessary that we should try to disentangle it. The main verb, which does not occur until verse 3 (*apangellomen, declare we* or 'we proclaim'), shows that the Preface is concerned essentially with the apostolic proclamation of the gospel—what it was, and why it was made. In outline the first sentence begins with four relative clauses in apposition to each other (*that which was from the beginning, which we have heard, which we have seen with our eyes, which we have looked upon, and our hands have handled*), followed by the phrase *of the Word of life*. Verse 2 is a parenthesis, explaining how that which was from the beginning could have been heard, seen and handled, namely because *the life was manifested*, and elaborates what is meant by *life* in the expression *Word of life*. This parenthesis so interrupts the flow of the sentence that verse 3 opens with the resumptive, relative clause *that which we have seen and heard* before we finally reach the main verb, *declare we unto you*. The rest of verse 3, and verse 4, describe the purposes, immediate and ultimate, of the apostolic proclamation, *that ye also may have fellowship with us* and *that your joy may be full*. In brief, therefore, and omitting the parenthesis of verse 2, the sentence might be paraphrased: 'We proclaim to you, concerning the word of life, what was from the beginning, which we have seen, heard and touched, and the objects of our proclamation are fellowship and joy.'

Before considering the Preface in detail, two questions concerning the phrase *of the Word of life* (*peri tou logou tēs zōēs*) need to be discussed. The first is whether *logos* is here personal or impersonal, whether it is the semi-technical designation of the Son found in the Prologue to the Fourth Gospel or whether it is rather a synonym for 'the word of the gospel' (Acts xv. 7). The second question is whether the clause introduced by *peri* is in apposition to the four relative clauses which precede it, or whether it qualifies them (or they it). For a detailed consideration of these questions see Additional Note, 'The Word of life' (i. 1) (p. 66). The conclusion there reached is that *the Word of life* is not a title for the Son, the Word or *Logos* of the Fourth Gospel Prologue, but an expression for the gospel, the message of life; and, secondly, that this 'word of life' is the general subject of the apostolic proclamation, the particular emphasis of which concerns *that which was from the beginning, which we have heard . . . seen . . . and . . . handled.* In other words, what the apostle stresses in his proclamation of the gospel is the historical manifestation of the Eternal.

We are now in a position to approach the Preface as a whole. Its noble sweep unfolds the purpose of God from eternity to eternity, from *that which was from the beginning* (1) to the fullness of *joy* (4) experienced by Christian believers, which will not be finally consummated until the end. Five stages are discernible in the unfolding of this divine purpose, indicated by the words *beginning* (*archēs*, 1), *was manifested* (*ephanerōthē*, twice in verse 2), *declare we* (*apangellomen*, 3), *fellowship* (*koinōnia*, twice in verse 3) and *joy* (*chara*, 4).

a. The eternal pre-existence

C. H. Dodd interprets the opening phrase of the beginning of the gospel. The author is announcing, he says, 'what has always ("from the beginning") been true about the word of life'. He is not introducing 'any innovation or afterthought' but proclaiming 'the unchanged, original content of the Gospel, over against novel forms of doctrine'.[1] Now, it is true

---

[1] C. H. Dodd adds in a footnote, however, that it is not necessary to decide between this and 'the absolute Beginning of the universe', since 'the Gospel is by its nature, as the Word of God, an "eternal Gospel" (Rev. xiv. 6)'.

that 'the beginning' is used in the Fourth Gospel with reference
to the beginning of Christ's ministry (Jn. vi. 64, xv. 27, xvi. 4)
which was virtually the beginning of the Christian era, and in
the Epistles with reference to the individual's Christian
experience (ii. 7, 24, iii. 11; 2 Jn. 6).

Nevertheless, the similar expression at the beginning of the
Prologue to the Gospel ('In the beginning was the Word')
suggests that here too the beginning of all things is meant.
The phrase is so used of the Eternal God in ii. 13, 14 and, with
a less clear time reference, to the devil sinning 'from the
beginning' in iii. 8. Moreover, since the words precede the
clauses *which we have heard . . . seen . . . handled*, we should expect
the meaning to precede them logically too. The Eternal Son
was before His historical manifestation; the preaching of the
gospel came after. Finally, the expression is parallel to that in
the parenthesis of verse 2 *that eternal life which was with the
Father*. In both phrases the verb is imperfect (*ēn*) and expresses
the Son's eternal pre-existence. The first says that He *was from
the beginning*; the second that He *was with the Father*, just as in
the Gospel Prologue it is written first 'in the beginning was the
Word', and secondly, 'and the Word was with God'. Since
life eternal is to know God (Jn. xvii. 3), He who is Eternal
Life does not enjoy immortal solitude but conscious, continuous, intimate communion as Son with the Father.

b. The historical manifestation

The contrast between the first and the next three relative
clauses with which the Epistle begins is dramatic. The Eternal
entered time and was manifested to men. The Word became
flesh and thus presented Himself to the three higher senses of
men (hearing, sight and touch). The four relative clauses
proceed 'from the most abstract to the most material aspect
of divine revelation' (Westcott). To have *heard* was not enough;
men 'heard' God's voice in the Old Testament. To have *seen*
was more compelling. But to have *handled* was the conclusive
proof of material reality, that the Word was 'made flesh, and
dwelt among us'. This word *handled* (*epsēlaphēsan*), the climax
of the four relative clauses, means more than to 'touch'.

' "*Psēlaphān*" is to *grope* or *feel after* in order to find, like a blind man or one in the dark; hence to *handle*, *touch*. . . . It may also be used in the sense of "examine closely" ' (Brooke). Although the 'handling' is the climax of the sentence, the emphasis is on 'seeing' (which is repeated four times in the first three verses), presumably because it is sight in particular which qualifies men to witness (2). Two verbs are used for sight, *horan* three times and *theasthai* once. 'If *blepein* is to "look", and *horan* to "see", *theasthai* is to "behold" intelligently, so as to grasp the meaning and significance of that which comes within our vision' (Brooke). This is the verb used in the fourth clause, where it is associated with *our hands have handled* by one relative (*ho*). Whereas the two earlier verbs *have heard* and *have seen* are in the perfect tense, suggesting the abiding possession which results from the hearing and seeing, these two are both aorists, and seem to refer to a particular time, perhaps after the resurrection, when the apostles had an opportunity both to gaze thoughtfully upon the Lord Jesus and to handle Him (cf. Lk. xxiv. 39; Jn. xx. 26–29). These two verbs express a 'definite investigation by the observer' (Westcott). The latter is also used in John i. 14, 'the Word was made flesh and dwelt among us, and we *beheld* his glory'.

The proclamation of what had been heard, seen and felt was part of *the Word of life*, the gospel of Christ. It would seem most natural to take the genitive *of life* as indicating the content of *the Word*, as in Philippians ii. 16. The gospel announces and offers life in Christ. Compare 'the word of the kingdom' (Mt. xiii. 19), 'the word of this salvation' (Acts xiii. 26), 'the word of reconciliation' (2 Cor. v. 19), and similar expressions used in the New Testament to describe the gospel. Nevertheless, the genitive *of life* in the Fourth Gospel means 'life-giving' (e.g. 'light of life', 'bread of life' in viii. 12, vi. 35, 48; cf. 'living water' in Jn. iv. 10, 11 and 'water of life' in Rev. xxi. 6, xxii. 1, 17). Perhaps it is not necessary to choose between these alternatives since 'the revelation proclaims that which it includes; it has, announces, gives life' (Westcott).

This audible, visible and tangible apprehension of that which was from the beginning was only possible to men because (*for*) *the life was manifested*. The aorist verb *ephanerōthē*, indicating the historic fact of the incarnation, is repeated twice, at the beginning and end of the parenthesis. First it occurs absolutely; and then *unto us* is added. We could not have seen the One who was eternally with the Father unless He had taken the initiative deliberately to manifest Himself. Men can apprehend only what God is pleased to make known.

This stress on the material manifestation of Christ to men's ears, eyes and hands is of course directed primarily against the heretics who were troubling the Church. The followers of Cerinthus are shown that *the Word of life*, the gospel of Christ, is concerned with the historical incarnation of the Eternal Son. He who is from the beginning is He whom the apostles heard, saw and touched. It is impossible to distinguish between Jesus and the Christ, the historical and the eternal. They are the same Person, God and man. Such an emphasis on the historical revelation of the invisible and intangible is still needed today, not least by the scientist trained in the empirical method, the radical who regards much in the Gospels as 'myths' (but you cannot 'demythologize' the incarnation) and the mystic who tends to become preoccupied with his subjective religious experience to the neglect of God's objective self-revelation in Christ.

c. The authoritative proclamation

The historical manifestation of the Eternal Life was proclaimed, not monopolized. The revelation was given to the few for the many. They were to dispense it to the world. The manifestation *unto us* (2) becomes a proclamation *unto you* (3). John desires his readers to enjoy 'the same advantageous position which he himself and his fellow-apostles enjoyed, as regards the knowledge of God in Christ' (Candlish).

John uses two verbs to describe the apostolic announcement, *we . . . bear witness* (*marturoumen*, 2) and *we declare* (*apangellomen*, 2 and 3). The apostolic ministry involved both a testimony and a proclamation. Both words imply an authority, but of a different kind. *Martureisthai* indicates the authority of experience. To witness is an activity which belongs properly to an eyewitness. He must *be* a witness before he is competent to *bear* witness. (Compare Luke xxiv. 48, RSV, 'you are witnesses of these things' with Acts i. 8, RSV, 'You shall be my witnesses'.) The true witness speaks not of what he has gathered second-hand from others, but of what he has himself personally seen and heard. It is for this reason that the verbs to 'see' and to 'testify' are so commonly associated with each other in the New Testament, as they are in verse 2. (For the bearing of this on the authorship of the Epistle see Introduction, pp. 26 ff.) Since John introduces the Epistle with relative clauses describing what had been heard, seen and felt, concerning the word of life, it is natural that the first verb he uses for the apostolic preaching is the word *we . . . bear witness.*

If *martureisthai* is the word of experience, *apangellein* indicates the authority of commission. The experience is personal; the commission is derived. In order to witness, the apostles must have seen and heard Christ for themselves; in order to proclaim, they must have received a commission from Him. It is true that, although *apangellomen* occurs in verses 2 and 3, the verb in verse 5 is *anangellomen*, and that *apangellein* means strictly 'to report with reference to the source from which the message comes' while *anangellein* is 'to report with reference to the persons addressed' (Law, Brooke). But it is also significant that in verse 5 where *anangellein* is used, the phrase 'which we have heard of him' (*ap' autou*) is added. The verbs in both passages, therefore, the one from its own prefix and the other from its explicit additional clause, seem to direct the reader's attention to the source from which the message was derived, namely Christ Himself (cf. 1 Cor. ii. 13, xi. 23, xv. 3). He not only manifested Himself to the disciples to qualify them as *eyewitnesses*, but gave them an authoritative commission as *apostles* to preach the gospel. The author insists that he possesses these necessary credentials. Possessing them, he is very bold. Having heard, seen and touched the Lord Jesus, he bears witness to Him. Having received a commission, he proclaims the gospel with authority, for the Christian message is neither a philosophical speculation, nor a tentative suggestion, nor a modest contribution to religious thought, but a dogmatic affirmation by those whose experience and commission qualified them to make it.

d. The communal fellowship

The proclamation was not an end in itself; its purpose, immediate and ultimate, is now defined. The immediate is *fellowship* (*koinōnia*, 3), and the ultimate *joy* (*chara*, 4). The fellowship created by Christ in the days of His flesh within the apostolic band, and deepened by the coming of the Spirit at Pentecost, was not to be limited to them. It was to extend to the next generation (*that ye also may have fellowship with us*), and so on down the ages. 'The last of the apostles points to the unbroken succession of the heritage of Faith' (Westcott).

The purpose of the proclamation of the gospel is, therefore, not salvation but *fellowship*. Yet, properly understood, this is the meaning of salvation in its widest embrace, including reconciliation to God in Christ (*fellowship . . . with the Father, and with his Son Jesus Christ*), holiness of life (see verse 6), and incorporation in the Church (*ye . . . with us*). This fellowship is the meaning of eternal life (Jn. xvii. 3). As the Son, who is *that eternal life*, was (eternally) with the Father (2), so He purposes that we should have fellowship with Them and with each other (cf. Jn. xvii. 21, 22, RSV). 'Fellowship' is a specifically Christian word and denotes that common participation in the grace of God, the salvation of Christ and the indwelling Spirit which is the spiritual birthright of all Christian believers. It is their common possession of God, Father, Son and Holy Spirit, which makes them one. So John could not have written *that ye also may have fellowship with us* without adding *and truly our fellowship is with the Father, and with his Son Jesus Christ*, since our fellowship with each other arises from, and depends on, our fellowship with God.

This truth, although expressed in different language, is an echo of our Lord's prayer 'that they may all be one . . . , that they also may be in us' (Jn. xvii. 21, RSV). As there our oneness depends on our being in Them, so here our fellowship with each other is impossible without fellowship with the Father and the Son. John does not here mention the fellowship of the

Holy Spirit, which is a characteristic expression in the Pauline Epistles (2 Cor. xiii. 14; Phil. ii. 1), no doubt because the false teachers against whom he is writing make him concentrate on the Son, whom their heresy dishonoured, and the Father whom they thereby forfeited. He here states not just that our fellowship is with the Father through the Son, and that we may have the Father only by confessing the Son (ii. 23), but that our fellowship is both *with the Father and with his Son*. The phrase 'marks emphatically the distinction and equality between the Son and the Father' (Plummer). The use of the full title *his Son Jesus Christ* (as in iii. 23, v. 20, and 2 Jn. iii) also, perhaps, contains a side-glance at the heretics, who denied that the man Jesus was the Christ, the Son of God. (Cf. 1 Cor. i. 9.)

This statement of the apostolic objective in the proclamation of the gospel, namely a human fellowship arising spontaneously from a divine fellowship, is a rebuke to much of our modern evangelism and Church life. We cannot be content with an evangelism which does not lead to the drawing of converts into the Church, nor with a Church life whose principle of cohesion is a superficial social camaraderie instead of a spiritual fellowship with the Father and with His Son Jesus Christ. The doctrine and behaviour of the heretics were threatening to disrupt the Church; the true *angelia* ('message', 5), on the other hand, produces a true *koinōnia*.

e. The completed joy

Verse 4, like verse 3, contains a final clause introduced by *hina*, *that*. . . . In verse 3 the clause depends on *declare*, and in verse 4 on *write*. Do these verbs refer to the same message, in one case oral and in the other written, or are they different messages? A majority of commentators seem to take the proclamation of verses 1–3 to refer to the author's 'whole apostolic ministry' (Westcott) and especially his written Gospel (Ebrard), and the writing mentioned in verse 4 to his present Epistle. 'The preceding verses have reference to the writer's habitual oral proclamation of the Gospel, or to its literary embodiment. These words now introduce the Epistle itself' (Law). Westcott also adds that, whereas the relative *ho* (*that which*) in verses 1 and 3 denotes 'the apostolic message . . . in its unity', *tauta* (*these things*) in verse 4 points by contrast to certain special aspects of it. At the same time, the distinction can be over-pressed. Verse 4 is the first occasion in the Epistle when the adjective *houtos* ('this') occurs. It comes frequently later in such expressions as 'this is' (*houtos estin* and *touto estin*) and 'by this we . . .' (*en toutō, ek toutou* and *dia touto*, etc.). In nearly every case it is uncertain whether these phrases point back-wards to what has just been written or forwards to what is about to be written. According to Brooke 'the reference forward would seem to be his prevailing custom' (e.g. i. 4, ii. 3, iii. 8, 10, 16, 23, 24, iv. 2, 9, 13, 17, v. 4, 11, 14). But it is not always so (e.g. ii. 22, iv. 6, v. 20, and especially ii. 26 and v. 13, where the similar phrase *these things I have written* occurs and in each case refers to the previous paragraph). And when the reference is forward, it points to what *immediately* follows. It is possible, therefore, and seems to me more natural, to take *these things* as referring not to the whole Epistle which follows but to the statements just made in the Preface about the apostolic proclamation. In this case 'declare we' (3) and 'write we' (4) refer to the same message.

The purpose of the writing is now given. It is difficult to decide whether 'your' (*humōn*) or 'our' (*hēmōn*) joy is the correct reading. Indeed, since both are well supported, Westcott declares that 'a positive decision on the reading here is im-possible'. However, it seems preferable with the RV and RSV to choose 'our'. This need not be understood as referring exclusively to the author and those associated with him, but may well include the readers, 'you . . . with us' as in verse 3. Brooke quotes John iv. 36 in this connection where Jesus spoke of the sower and reaper rejoicing together.

And what is the secret of fullness of joy, 'the complete and perfect felicity which we obtain from the Gospel' (Calvin)? It is in the fellowship which the proclamation creates; for if the immediate purpose of the proclamation is the establish-ment of fellowship, the ultimate purpose is the completion of joy. This is the divine order—*angelia, koinōnia, chara.*

The idea of fullness of joy is not uncommon in the Johannine literature (cf. Jn. iii. 29, xv. 11, xvi. 24, xvii. 13; 2 Jn. 12), and it is significant that in each case there is some allusion to the subject of fellowship with God or with each other. Yet 'perfect joy' is not possible in this world of sin, because perfect fellowship is not possible. So verse 4 must be understood also to look beyond this life to the life of heaven. Then consummated fellowship will bring completed joy. 'In thy presence is fullness of joy; at thy right hand there are pleasures for evermore' (Ps. xvi. 11). It is to this ultimate end that He who *was from the beginning was manifested* in time and that what the apostles heard, saw and touched they have proclaimed to us. The substance of the apostolic proclamation was the historical manifestation of the Eternal; its purpose was and is a fellowship with one another, which is based on fellowship with the Father and the Son and issues in fullness of joy.

Additional Note: 'The Word of life' (i. 1)

a. The meaning of 'logos'

The Greek word *logos* can be translated either as 'reason' or as 'word' or 'speech'. It is used in the Prologue to the Fourth Gospel as a designation of the Son who is the revelation of the Father.[1] That the word is also a descriptive title of the Eternal Son in the Preface to the First Epistle has been held by many commentators. Thus, Moffatt transliterates the Greek word into English and coins the expression 'Logos of Life'. There is certainly a parallel to be drawn between the Gospel and the Epistle, although the Prologue is considerably longer and more elaborate than the Preface. Both open with a reference to the beginning (verses 1, 2: verse 1); both speak of the Logos in connection with the Father and, with life (verses 1, 4: verses 1, 2); both declare that the Eternal entered history (verses 10, 11, 14: verse 2); both add that the divine manifestation was seen by men (verses 14, 18: verses 1, 2, 3); both mention testimony resulting from what men saw (verses 7, 8, 15:

[1] See R. V. G. Tasker, *The Gospel According to John* (Tyndale New Testament Commentary, pp. 41 f.).

verse 2); both speak of Christ as the Father's Son (verses 14, 18: verse 3); both describe the result of responding to Christ in terms of a new relationship with God (verses 12, 13: verse 3). And yet the similarity between the two passages can be overdrawn. The general sequence of thought is the same, and there are verbal echoes, but Westcott is right in saying that 'the two passages are complementary and not parallel'. Two differences must be mentioned:

First, in the Prologue 'the Word' is used absolutely four times (three times in verse 1 and once in verse 14), while in the Preface the phrase is 'the Word of life'.

Secondly, it is plain from the parenthesis which immediately follows the use of this expression (verse 2) that the emphasis in it in the author's mind is not on 'Word' but on 'life', for the word *logos* is not used again in the Preface, or indeed in the whole Epistle, whereas 'life' is repeated twice in verse 2 and five times more in the rest of the Epistle (ii. 25, iii. 14, v. 11, 12, 20). It is significant that what the author writes is not 'concerning the word of life—the word was made flesh' but 'concerning the word of life—the life was made manifest'. What he means by 'that eternal life, which was with the Father' is clear: it is a plain personification of the Son. It cannot be otherwise because the expression 'with the Father' (*pros ton Patera*) implies personal communion. Besides, both Gospel and Epistle declare not only that life is in Christ (Jn. i. 4; 1 Jn. v. 11, 12) but that He is Himself the Life (Jn. xi. 25, xiv. 6; cf. v. 26; 1 Jn. v. 20). It is this Life, he says, which was eternally in communion with the Father and was historically manifested to us, which we proclaim.

Now what is stated briefly in verse 2 as the subject of the proclamation is stated more elaborately in verses 1 and 3. John is concerned to make known what is eternal ('that which was from the beginning') and historical ('that which we have heard . . . seen . . . handled') concerning 'the word of life'. What then does 'the word of life' mean? Westcott renders it 'the revelation of Life' and understands it as referring generally to 'the whole message from God to man, which tells of life, or, perhaps, out of which life springs, which beginning to be spoken by the prophets, was at last fully proclaimed by one who was His Son'. With this Brooke agrees. C. H. Dodd is more particular and translates the phrase 'the Gospel', since 'the word of life' in Philippians ii. 16 (although without the definite article), 'the words of this life' in Acts v. 20 and 'the words of eternal life' (Jn. vi. 68) are similar expressions for the gospel. But in view of the personal meaning given to 'life' in verse 2, we desire to be more particular still, and say that 'the word of life' means 'the gospel *of Christ*'. What John proclaims is Christ, who is the Life (2), and in this proclamation concerning the word of life he lays his emphasis on His eternal being and historical manifestation (1, 3).

b. *The meaning of* 'peri'

In discussing the precise meaning of the expression 'the Word of life' we have already begun to solve the second problem which concerns the relation of the phrase 'of the Word of life' to the whole paragraph in which it is embedded. Moffatt and other commentators have taken the phrase *peri tou logou tēs zōēs* as being in apposition to the four preceding relative clauses and as adding another aspect of the proclamation to the four already mentioned. The proclamation would then be concerned equally with 'that which was from the beginning', with that which was 'heard', 'seen' and 'handled' and with 'the Word of life'. But this is very awkward and is rejected by Westcott, Law, C. H. Dodd and others, both because it would bring four neuter relative pronouns into apposition to the masculine *logos*, and because it pays no attention to the change of construction from relative clauses to the use of the preposition *peri*.

The alternative is to take *peri tou logou tēs zōēs* as an independent adverbial clause. In this way, 'the Word of life' becomes the 'subject' (Westcott, Law) of the announcement, while the four relative clauses 'declare the substance' of it (Law). Similarly, 'the clause "concerning the word of life" indicates the *theme* of the announcement, and the clauses "that which was from the beginning . . . our hands felt" state the *contents* of the announcement' (Dodd). It is essentially about eternal life

in Christ that John is concerned (Jn. xx. 31; 1 Jn. v. 12, 13).
What he seems to be saying here is: 'In our proclamation
concerning the message of life in Christ we concentrate on the
historical manifestation of the Eternal. We do this partly
because we are uniquely qualified to be witnesses to the
incarnation. Our own eyes have seen, and our own hands
have handled Him. We have heard and beheld Him for ourselves. Or, to put it otherwise, the very Life itself (with which
our message is concerned), the Eternal Life which was
eternally with the Father, was made manifest to us, and we
saw it. So we testify to it. Our announcement is a testimony.
We also make this our particular emphasis because of the false
teaching of the heretics who deny the truth of the incarnation
either by affirming that the body of Jesus was not real (the
Docetists) or by distinguishing the divine *Logos* or Spirit or
Christ from the man Jesus upon whom He came at the
baptism and from whom He departed before the cross. In
contradiction of these errors we stress both that His body was
real (because we heard, saw and touched Him) and that this
historical Jesus was the same person as the Eternal Word.'
This apostolic purpose would explain the clumsy syntax which
leaves the main verb to near the end of the sentence and
begins with the emphatic clauses 'that which was from the
beginning, which we have heard . . . seen . . . and . . . handled'.
It is these aspects of the Word of Life that the proclamation
underlines. 'St. John employs the neuter (*that which . . .
which . . .*) as the most comprehensive expression to cover the
attributes, words and works' (Plummer) of the incarnate Life.

II. THE APOSTOLIC MESSAGE AND ITS MORAL IMPLICATIONS (i. 5–ii. 2)

5. The link between this paragraph and the foregoing Preface
is in the word *message*. John has already used the verb *apangellomen* ('declare we', verse 3); he now uses the similar verb
anangellomen, we . . . declare, in conjunction with the noun
angelia, message. This message has not been invented by himself

or the other apostles, but is what they *have heard of him*. It is unlikely that he is quoting any specific saying of Jesus that *God is light*, as no such saying has survived. Rather is he summarizing the Lord's teaching according to the emphasis he gives to it in his own Gospel. 'The Word of life' (verse 1), with which his proclamation is concerned, can be condensed into the single great affirmation *God is light, and in him is no darkness at all* (cf. Jn. i. 4). The statement is absolute and anarthrous. The Logos is 'the light' (*to phōs*); but God is *light* (*phōs*), just as He is 'love' and 'spirit' and 'consuming fire'. In none of these statements is the article used (1 Jn. iv. 8, 16; Jn. iv. 24; Heb. xii. 29).

Of the statements about the essential Being of God, none is more comprehensive than *God is light*.[1] It is His nature to reveal Himself, as it is the property of light to shine; and the revelation is of perfect purity and unutterable majesty. We are to think of God as a personal Being, infinite in all His perfections, transcendent, 'the high and lofty One that inhabiteth eternity, whose name is Holy' (Is. lvii. 15), who yet desires to be known and has revealed Himself. The miserable errors of the heretics were due to their ignorance of God's ethical self-revelation as Light. They could never have laid claim to a private, esoteric *gnōsis* into which they had been initiated if their conception of God had been of One who is Light, diffusive, shining forth and manifesting Himself, in whom *is no darkness at all*, no secrecy, no hiding in the shadows. And if God is also light in the sense of possessing an absolute moral perfection, their claim to know Him and have fellowship with Him despite their indifference to morality is seen to be sheer nonsense, as the author goes on to demonstrate.

Additional Note: The symbolism of light in Scripture (i. 5)

The categories of light and darkness belong to the universal language of religious symbolism. They are common to most

---

[1] For the symbolic use of 'light' in Scripture, and particularly in the Johannine literature, see Additional Note on this page.

religions, not least the revealed religion of the Bible.[1] They are used metaphorically in Scripture in several senses. Intellectually, light is truth and darkness ignorance or error. Morally, light is purity and darkness evil. One or two examples will suffice to illustrate this double use. God's self-revelation through the law and the prophets is described in terms of light. The 'commandment is a lamp; and the law is light'; 'Thy word is a lamp unto my feet, and a light unto my path'; and the 'more sure word of prophecy' is 'a light that shineth in a dark place' (Pr. vi. 23; Ps. cxix. 105, 130; 2 Pet. i. 19). God said He would make His servant 'a light of the Gentiles' and His 'salvation unto the end of the earth' (Is. xlii. 6, xlix. 6), phrases which are applied by Simeon to the infant Jesus (Lk. ii. 30, 32; cf. Lk. i. 79), and by Paul and Barnabas to their own ministry (Acts xiii. 46, 47; cf. Acts xxvi. 18, 23). The apostle Paul also wrote to the Corinthians of 'the light of the knowledge of the glory of God in the face of Jesus Christ' which had shone in their hearts (2 Cor. iv. 4, 6).

The second use of light, namely to symbolize righteousness, is already plain in Isaiah v. 20, where the inhabitants of Judah are so morally perverse that they 'call evil good, and good evil. . . . put darkness for light, and light for darkness'. In the ethical instruction contained in his Epistles Paul several times employs this metaphor (see Eph. v. 8–14, RSV; Rom. xiii. 11–14; cf. 1 Thes. v. 4–8; 1 Cor. iv. 5).

This double use of the symbolism of light and darkness is found in the Fourth Gospel, particularly in four passages. In three of these the emphasis is undoubtedly on light as the revelation of truth. See the Prologue to the Gospel, especially verses 4, 5 and 9,[2] John viii. 12, a passage which is related to the healing of the man born blind (cf. Jn. ix. 4, 5), and John xii. 35, 36, 46 (cf. also xi. 9, 10). In this last passage,

[1] See, e.g., Ex. xl. 34–38; Ps. civ. 2; 1 Tim. vi. 16; 1 Pet. ii. 9; Jas. i. 17, RSV; Rev. xxi. 23; cf. Rev. xxii. 5. See also Mt. viii. 12, xxii. 13, xxv. 30.
[2] In the Prologue the Logos is distinguished from John the Baptist. John 'was not that Light, but was sent to bear witness of that Light' (8). True, in v. 33–36, John's witness to the truth is described in terms of light, in which men 'were willing for a season to rejoice'; yet he was himself not the light, but 'a burning and shining *lamp*' (verse 35, RSV).

however, a moral element is also discernible. The effect of the light is not just to make men see, but to enable them to *walk*. Right conduct, not just clear vision, is the benefit which light bestows. This brings us to John iii. 19–21, where the relation between light and purity, darkness and evil, is made explicit. In this passage the good man, opposed to him 'that doeth evil', is actually described as 'he that doeth truth'. Truth, like light, in Scripture has a moral content. Men are not just to *know* the truth, but to *do* it, just as they are not only to *see* the light, but to *walk* in it. So it is not uncommon, as here, for 'truth' to be contrasted not with 'error' but with 'wickedness' or 'unrighteousness' (cf. Rom. i. 18, RSV and 2 Thes. ii. 12).

The moral implications of light are apparent also in 1 John ii. 8–11. Here the statement is made that 'the true light now shineth' (8). This light diffuses righteousness, and in particular love. A man's claim to be 'in the light' (9) can be credited only if he is walking in love, for 'he that loveth his brother abideth in the light', while 'he that hateth his brother is in darkness' and is so blind that he does not know where he is going (10, 11).

(End of Additional Note)

In i. 6–ii. 2 three of the spurious claims of the false teachers are exposed and contradicted. Each is introduced by the formula *if we say* (6, 8, 10). C. H. Dodd thinks the writer is 'alluding all through to certain maxims which were used as watchwords by heretical teachers'. Whether or not he is quoting their actual slogans, he is certainly representing some of their pernicious teaching, and, having stated it, he immediately proceeds to brand it as deceitful error. A man's verbal profession is not necessarily to be believed. It must be tested both in itself, in its relation to the fundamental truth that God is light, and in its bearing upon his behaviour. Similar expressions are used in ii. 4, 6, 9 (*he that saith*) and in iv. 20 (*if a man say*). Cf. James ii. 14–18. This is the dominant theme of the Epistle. John supplies searching tests by which to judge one who professes and calls himself Christian. The supreme question is whether his teaching and behaviour are consistent with each other and with the apostolic proclamation that God is light. This affirmation is still the test of the truth and reality of our Christian profession.

The symmetry of the seven verses is evident. First, he introduces the false teaching with the words *if we say*. Next, he contradicts it with an unequivocal *we lie* or a similar expression. Finally, he makes a positive and true statement corresponding to the error he has refuted, *but if we . . .*, although in the last of the three examples the ending is different (cf. verses 7, 9 with ii. 1, 2).

The introductory phrase *if we say* is noteworthy because with it the identity of the *we* has subtly changed. See Introduction, p. 43. The we—you relationship of the authoritative apostle to his readers seen in i. 1–5 has faded; John now humbly identifies himself with them. Naturally, he is not suggesting that he has ever himself said or thought the errors he is rebutting. He uses the first person plural only because he is stating general principles which are applicable to all men equally.

The three errors he treats concern the fact of sin in our conduct, its origin in our nature, and its consequence in our relationship to God. They are the misconceptions of men who want fellowship with God on easy terms. They have never learned the indissoluble marriage of religion and ethics; they are seeking a divorce between them. They have a thoroughly inadequate doctrine of sin and its sinfulness in relation to God who is light. So, in each of the three examples he gives, John faces the fact and the problem of sin before proceeding to state the solution. He not only denies the erroneous view, but indicates the divine remedy which is offered if men will only acknowledge their need of it. Each time he describes the cleansing and forgiveness which God has made possible through the death of Jesus Christ His Son (7, 9 and ii. 1, 2). Christianity is the only religion which, by emphasizing that God is light, first insists on taking sin seriously and then offers a satisfactory moral solution to the problem of sin. The way to have fellowship with a God who is light is not to deny the fact or effects of sin, but to confess our sins and thankfully appropriate God's provision for our cleansing.

a. The denial that sin breaks our fellowship with God (i. 6, 7)

6. The false claim here is the assertion that we have fellowship with God, while at the same time we *walk* (that is, habitually live) *in darkness* (cf. ii. 11; Is. ix. 2; Jn. viii. 12; Rom. ii. 19). Some of the early Gnostics were guilty of such blatant anti-nomianism. They thought of the body as a mere envelope covering the human spirit and maintained that man's spirit was inviolable; it could not be contaminated by the deeds of the body. Others, according to Irenaeus, taught that if a man had become truly 'spiritual', he had progressed beyond the possibility of any defilement. You could, they said, *be* righteous without necessarily *doing* righteousness (cf. iii. 7, where John denies this), and consequently spiritual communion with God was independent of physical morality. Still today, although Gnostic notions are outmoded, it is not uncommon for people to claim fellowship with God who see no necessity either first to go to the cross of Christ for cleansing and forgiveness or thereafter to lead a consistently holy life. We are right to be suspicious of those who claim a mystical intimacy with God and yet 'walk in the darkness' (lit. as RV) of error and sin, paying no regard to the self-revelation of an all-holy God. Since God is light, such claims are ludicrous. Religion without morality is an illusion. Sin is always a barrier to fellowship with God (cf. Ps. v. 4, lxvi. 18; Is. lix. 1, 2), for 'what communion hath light with darkness?' (2 Cor. vi. 14).

If we make such a claim *we lie*, deliberately, knowingly, self-evidently, *and do not the truth*. That is, we not only contradict the truth in our words, but deny it by our inconsistent lives. We 'do not live according to the truth' (RSV). 'Our words and our lives are a lie' (NEB).

7. The error having been refuted, John now affirms a complementary truth. He has shown the consequence of walking in darkness; he now describes what happens *if we* *walk in the light.* Any interpretation of this phrase must be consistent both with the symbolic meaning of light and with the following phrase *as he is in the light.* God *is* eternally and necessarily in the light because He *is* Himself light; men are called to walk in the light. God is in the light because He is always true to Himself and His activity is consistent with His nature. 'He cannot deny himself' (2 Tim. ii. 13). We must walk in the light of His holy self-revelation, and in His presence, without deceit or dishonesty in our mind or consciously tolerated sin in our conduct. 'Walking in the light' describes 'absolute sincerity . . . to be, so to speak, all of a piece, to have nothing to conceal, and to make no attempt to conceal anything'.[1] Two results of this are given. First, *we have fellowship one with another.* Since in verse 6 John has declared that to walk in darkness prevents fellowship with God, one would have expected him in verse 7 to express the opposite truth that if we walk in the light, we enjoy fellowship with God. This is no doubt true, but characteristically he moves one step further, and states that walking in the light leads to that fellowship with each other which, as he has already said in verse 3, is grounded upon our fellowship with the Father and the Son.

The second result of walking in the light is that *the blood of Jesus Christ his Son cleanseth us from all sin.* The verb suggests that God does more than forgive; He erases the stain of sin. And the present tense shows that it is a continuous process. But what sin needs to be cleansed *if we walk in the light?* Alford, aware of this difficulty, insists that here and in verse 9, cleansing indicates 'sanctification distinct from justification'. Ebrard also thinks this interpretation 'conclusively decided by the ninth verse'. But it would be unusual to ascribe this benefit to *the blood of Jesus.* Law, to whom 'light' means revelation rather than holiness, sees nothing inconsistent about the presence of sins in those who 'walk in the light'. He goes further and writes: 'to "walk in the light" is, first of all, to confess sin; to walk in the darkness, to ignore or to deny sin.' But if 'light' signifies holiness as well as revelation, to walk in it is to live not only in honesty, but, at least to some degree, in purity also.

[1] Stephen Neill, *Christian Holiness*, p. 35.

So the reference here must be to cleansing not from deliberate sins but either from 'every sin' (NEB), even those committed unconsciously, or, as may be suggested by the use of the singular *sin*, from the defilement of our fallen nature. What is clear is that if we walk in the light, God has made provision to cleanse us from whatever sin would otherwise mar our fellowship with Him or each other. This provision is *the blood of Jesus Christ his Son*, that is to say, the virtue of His death for our sins.[1] This is the only explicit reference in the Epistle to the saving power of the death of Jesus Christ, although an allusion is implied when it is written that the Son came 'to be the Saviour of the world' (iv. 14), 'to be the propitiation for our sins' (iv. 10; cf. ii. 2, where see note) and 'that we might live through him' (iv. 9). The efficacy of this death for our sins is due to the unique Person of Him who died. He was both man (*Jesus*; 'Christ' should be omitted, as in RV, RSV), and God (*his Son*). The condition of receiving cleansing through the blood of Christ and of enjoying fellowship with each other is to walk in the light, to be sincere, open, honest, transparent.

b. The denial that sin exists in our nature (i. 8, 9)

8. The second claim of the heretics was one stage worse than the first, namely to *have no sin*, 'to be sinless' (NEB). The first heretical claim at least appeared to concede the existence of sin, while denying that it had the effect of estranging the sinner from God. Now the very fact of sin is denied. These men cannot benefit from the cleansing effects of the blood of Jesus because they say *we have no sin*. 'Sin' is again in the singu-

---

[1] Bishop Westcott argues in an Additional Note that 'by the outpouring of the Blood the life which was in it was not destroyed, though it was separated from the organism which it had before quickened'. Thus, 'participation in Christ's Blood is participation in His life . . . the simple idea of the Death of Christ, as separated from His Life, falls wholly into the background in the writings of St. John'. With this Brooke agrees, describing the blood of Christ as 'the power of Christ's life . . . set free by death for wider service than was possible under the limitations of a human life in Palestine at a definite date'. But this view has been seriously challenged by A. M. Stibbs in *The Meaning of the Word 'Blood' in Scripture* (Tyndale Press, 1948), where he clearly shows that 'blood' in the Bible (e.g. Lv. xvii. 11) signifies not 'life' merely, but 'life violently ended; it is a sign of life either given or taken in death' (p. 33).

lar and refers to the inherited principle of sin or self-centredness. The heretics are now saying that, whatever their outward conduct may be, there is no sin inherent in their nature.[1] Perhaps they asserted that in those enlightened with *gnōsis* the sinful nature was eradicated, and claimed a kind of sinless perfection which some do today. Alternatively, John is referring to the Gnostic subtlety that sin was a matter of the flesh and did not touch or defile the spirit. Whatever their exact pretension, John repudiates it. To say that we have no sin means that *we deceive ourselves*, that is, we are self-deceived rather than deliberate liars, and *the truth is not in us*. Not only do we fail to do the truth (verse 6); we are void of it. For if it did indwell us we should inevitably be aware of our sinfulness. John's affirmation is equally applicable today to those who deny the fact or guilt of sin by seeking to interpret it solely in terms of physiological, psychological or social causes.

9. The proper Christian attitude to sin is not to deny it but to admit it and so to receive the forgiveness which God has made possible and promises to us. *If we confess our sins*, acknowledging before God that we are sinners not only by nature (*sin*) but by practice also (*our sins*), God will both *forgive us our sins and . . . cleanse us from all unrighteousness*. In the first phrase sin is a debt which He remits and in the second a stain which He removes. In both He is said to be *faithful and just*. The first word may mean that He is faithful to His nature and character (cf. 2 Tim. ii. 13). But the faithfulness of God in Scripture is constantly associated with His covenant promises (e.g. Ps. lxxxix; Heb. x. 23). He is true to His word and faithful to His covenant. Since the new covenant includes the pledge, 'I will forgive their iniquity, and I will remember their sin no more' (Je. xxxi. 34, RSV), it is not difficult to see why God is said to be 'faithful' in forgiving our sins. But how can He also be described as *just to forgive us our sins*? Some commentators relate

[1] Other commentators argue that to 'have sin' in the Johannine literature means to 'have guilt' or 'be guilty'. It is thus translated by RSV in Jn. ix. 41 (cf. Jn. xv. 22, 24, xix. 11), and Moffatt translates 1 Jn. i. 8: 'If we say "we are not guilty". . .' Law urges that in the Fourth Gospel the phrase 'specifically denotes the guiltiness of the agent'. In this case the denial here would not be so much of sin itself as of responsibility for it.

God's justice to His faithfulness and suggest that it is by being faithful to His promises that God is just to forgive. Even so it is a strange adjective to use. Justice is associated in our minds with punishment, not forgiveness. If God visits upon the sinner his sin and 'will by no means clear the guilty' (Ex. xxxiv. 7), how can He forgive sins? This is the divine dilemma. The Judge of all the earth cannot lightly remit sin. The cross is, in fact, the only moral ground on which He can forgive sin at all, for there the blood of Jesus His Son was shed that He might be 'the propitiation' for our sins (ii. 2). Cf. Romans iii. 25, another passage in which the justice of God is related to the propitiation of Christ. So we may say that in forgiving our sins and cleansing us from them God displays loyalty to His covenant—His faithfulness because of the word which initiated it and His justice because of the deed which ratified it. More simply, He is *faithful* to forgive because He has promised to do so, and *just* because His Son died for our sins.[1]

This forgiveness and cleansing, issuing from the faithfulness and justice of God, are conditional upon confession. There are many warnings in Scripture about the danger of concealing our sins, and many promises of blessing if we confess them. Moreover, what is required is not a general confession of sin but a particular confession of *sins*, as we deliberately call them to mind, confess and forsake them (cf. Ps. xxxii. 1–5; Pr. xxviii. 13).

c. The denial that sin shows itself in our conduct (i. 10–ii. 2)

10. The third heretical claim is indicated by the words *if we say that we have not sinned*. We may concede in theory that sin

---

[1] Some commentators interpret differently the relation between the faithfulness and the justice, or righteousness, of God, drawing attention to the fact that in the Old Testament God's righteousness is often not an attribute but an activity equivalent to 'salvation' (e.g. Is. li. 5). Thus C. H. Dodd writes: 'For "John" as for Paul . . . the mercy or forgiveness of God is a function of His righteousness. . . . If we confess our sins, . . . God forgives, . . . because no other course would be consistent with the perfectly good will by which the whole universe is created and sustained.' But God's righteousness (*dikaiosunē*) is also displayed against sin, and 'the perfectly good will' of God does not exclude His 'wrath' or antagonism to sin and the consequent need of a 'propitiation'. See note on ii. 2.

would break our fellowship with God if we did sin, and that sin does exist in our nature as an inborn disposition, and yet deny that we have in practice sinned and thus put ourselves out of fellowship with God. This is the most blatant of the three denials. The heretics maintained that their superior enlightenment rendered them incapable of sinning. But John is as clear about the outbreak of sin in our behaviour as he is about its origin in our nature and its consequences in preventing our fellowship with God. To say that we have not sinned is not just to tell a deliberate lie (6), or to be deluded (8), but actually to accuse God of lying, to *make him a liar* and to reveal clearly that *his word is not in us*, because His word frequently declares that sin is universal (e.g. 1 Ki. viii. 46; Ps. xiv. 3; Ec. vii. 20; Is. liii. 6, lxiv. 6), and the word of the gospel, which is a gospel of salvation, clearly assumes the sinfulness of man.

ii. 1. The symmetrical construction of this paragraph now changes, lest it should be thought that the frank admission and full forgiveness of our sins (i. 9, 10) allowed us to think lightly of them. On the contrary, the author's purpose is 'to prevent sin, not to condone it' (Brooke). So instead of adding 'if' as on the two previous occasions, John begins a new sentence in order to enlarge on the subject of sin in the Christian. He does this first negatively (*that ye sin not*) and then positively (*And if any man sin*). It is important to hold these two statements in balance. It is possible to be both too lenient and too severe towards sin. Too great a lenience would seem almost to encourage sin in the Christian by stressing God's provision for the sinner. An exaggerated severity, on the other hand, would either deny the possibility of a Christian sinning or refuse him forgiveness and restoration if he falls. Both extreme positions are contradicted by John.

The phrase *my little children* is suggestive both of the author's advanced years and of the affectionate, tender relationship which existed between him and his readers. They are simply *paidia*, 'children' (RSV), in ii. 13, 18, or *teknia*, 'little children', in ii. 12, 28, iii. 7, 18, iv. 4, v. 21, but here alone he adds the possessive adjective. Both words occur in the Gospel on the lips of Jesus Himself, *teknia* in xiii. 33 and *paidia* in xxi. 5. The purpose of his Epistle, he says, is to keep them from sinning. His references to the cleansing blood of Jesus (i. 7) and to the forgiveness of God (9) are not intended to give them a light view of the gravity of sin. Far from it. 'Horror, hatred, fear, repudiation of sin pervade the whole Epistle' (Law). He longs that they shall be preserved from the evil teaching of the heretics and that they shall not fall into sin. The Christian may never escape the specific command of Jesus 'sin no more (Jn. v. 14, viii. 11). But, on the other hand, he adds that, *if any man sin*, God has graciously made provision for his restoration. The clause is significant. It clearly indicates the author's conviction that acts of sin (the aorist *hamartē* implies this), as opposed to the continuous sinful habit, are possible in the Christian, which some have thought denied in iii. 9 and v. 18. 'The thought is of the single act (*hamartē*) into which the believer may be carried against the true tenor of his life, as contrasted with the habitual state (*hamartanei*, iii. 6, 8, 9, v. 18)' (Westcott).

The provision which God has made for the sinning Christian is now unfolded. It is in One, who is described first as *an advocate with the Father*, secondly as *Jesus Christ the righteous*, and thirdly (in verse 2) as *the propitiation for our sins*.

In form the word *advocate* in both its Latin and Greek equivalents (*advocatus* and *paraklētos*) is passive not active. It means literally not 'comforter' but 'called alongside' and describes anybody summoned to the assistance of another. It was particularly used in the law courts of a barrister, whose responsibility it is, as counsel for the defence, to plead the cause of the person on trial. Although the verb *parakalein*, to encourage, to exhort or to comfort, is used quite frequently in the New Testament, the noun *paraklētos* occurs only in the Johannine literature. Indeed, apart from this verse its use is restricted to the upper room discourses in the Fourth Gospel where Jesus made it a title for the Holy Spirit (Jn. xiv. 16, 26, xv. 26, xvi. 7). A comparison of the two uses is instructive. If we have an advocate in heaven, Christ has an advocate on earth. The Holy Spirit is Christ's Paraclete, as the Lord Jesus is ours. But whereas the Holy Spirit pleads Christ's cause before a hostile world, Christ pleads our cause against our 'accuser' (Rev. xii. 10) and *with the Father*, who loves and forgives His children. He is not now to be regarded as our Judge. The person who believes in Christ already 'has eternal life; he does not come into judgment, but has passed from death to life' (Jn. v. 24, RSV; cf. 1 Jn. iii. 14, v. 12 and Rom. viii. 1, 33, 34). Once the sinner has been justified by God his Judge, he has entered the family of God and become related to God as his Father. If he should sin, he does not need another justification from the divine Judge. He is a child of God; he needs the Father's forgiveness. This is assured to him through the advocacy of *Jesus Christ the righteous*, a composite expression indicating His human nature (*Jesus*), Messianic office (*Christ*) and righteous character. In the picture of a righteous Advocate standing before the Father on our behalf, 'the case is not that of love pleading with justice'. Rather the opposite: 'Justice pleads with love for our release!' (Findlay).

This reference to Christ being *righteous*, like the description of God in i. 9 as being 'just' (the adjective is *dikaios* in both cases), is unexpected. Yet the similarity between the two verses can be exaggerated. The righteousness, purity and sinlessness of Christ's character are mentioned several times, directly or indirectly, in this Epistle (ii. 6, 29, iii. 3, 5, 7). It is self-evident that only through a *righteous* Saviour could we be cleansed from 'all unrighteousness' (i. 9). Cf. 2 Corinthians v. 21 and 1 Peter iii. 18. For the relation between Christ's intercession and His holiness see Hebrews vii. 25, 26. There are many similarities between the teaching of this Epistle and of the Epistle to the Hebrews on the subjects of propitiation and intercession. In both books the doctrines are closely linked, although in Hebrews Christ intercedes as Priest, in this Epistle as Paraclete.

2. John now proceeds to describe our righteous Advocate as *the propitiation for our sins*, since it is this alone which qualifies Him for the position. 'Our Advocate does not plead that we are innocent, or adduce extenuating circumstances. He acknowledges our guilt and presents His vicarious work as the ground of our acquittal' (Smith). 'Christ's intercession is the continual application of His death to our salvation' (Calvin). In pagan writings this noun *propitiation* (*hilasmos*) and its cognate verb (*hilaskesthai*) were commonly used for the appeasement of an angry deity by offerings. So base and corrupt was this heathen conception that many modern scholars have altogether rejected the notion of a Christian *propitiation*. It is incompatible, they say, with the revelation of God through Jesus Christ. They argue that the barrier to fellowship with God is not in Him but in us and our sin, and that the 'propitiation' removes the barrier by dealing with our sin. They point out, in support of their view, that the verb *hilaskesthai* is very seldom used in the Old Testament with God as its object (only Zc. vii. 2, viii. 22; Mal. i. 9), and never in the New Testament. It is not God who is the object of the *propitiation* but men's sin and defilement, which is thereby 'covered' (the probable root meaning of the Hebrew word *kipper*, translated by *hilaskesthai* in the LXX), 'neutralized' (Westcott), even 'sterilized' (Dodd). For this reason they propose to translate the word by 'expiation' (RSV), and assume that what is meant is not the placating of the wrath of God but the annulling of the guilt of sin. Thus 'He is himself the remedy for the defilement of our sins' (NEB). But this is too summary a dismissal of the idea of *propitiation*. It is true that the New Testament phrase is that Christ is *the propitiation for our sins* and that nowhere is God explicitly said to be propitiated. But this does not settle the matter, for there are other biblical words and phrases which indicate that in some senses God does need to be propitiated. His 'wrath' abides upon all sin and must somehow be averted or appeased if the sinner is to be forgiven.

The notion of the propitiation of God by the death of His Son is not at all inconsistent with the revelation we have been given of His character in His Son and in His Word, if it is rightly understood. It needs to be safeguarded, and distinguished from heathen conceptions, in two particulars.

First, God's wrath is not arbitrary or capricious. It bears no resemblance to the unpredictable passions and personal vengefulness of the pagan deities. Instead, it is His settled, controlled, holy antagonism to all evil. Secondly, the means by which His wrath is averted is not a bribe, either from us or from a third party. On the contrary, the initiative in the propitiation is entirely God's. In the LXX frequently He is Himself the subject of the verb to 'propitiate'—a usage unknown in pagan writings. Similarly, in this Epistle the whole initiative is ascribed to God. 'The action of which, in some sense, God is Himself the object, has God Himself as its origin' (Law). This origin is His love, the spontaneous, uncaused love of Father and Son together. We must not imagine either that the Father sent His Son to do something which the Son was reluctant to do, or that the Son was a third party intervening between the sinner and a reluctant God. Both these views are excluded by the teaching of this Epistle. It is not reluctance but love which is attributed to both Father and Son. 'Herein is love, not that we loved God, but that he loved us, and sent his Son to be the propitiation for our sins' (iv. 10, AV). 'By this we know love, that he laid down his life for us' (iii. 16, RSV).[1]

Having distinguished between the pagan and Christian concepts of propitiation in these two major respects, we must now ask: what was or is the propitiation? John's answer is that it is 'Jesus Christ the righteous' Himself (ii. 2), the Father's sent Son (iv. 10). In both verses He is described not as the 'propitiator', but as the 'propitiation'. This is significant because it emphasizes 'the thought that He is Himself the propitiatory offering. . . . A propitiator might make use of a means of propitiation outside Himself. But Christ is our propitiation. . . .' (Westcott), which is implied by the prominent *he* (*autos*). But in what sense is He *the propitiation for our sins*? No direct answer is given in this verse, but if John writes of 'propitiation' here and in iv. 10, and of forgiveness in i. 9, it is because he has stated in i. 7 that what cleanses sinners

[1] See Additional Note, p. 84, for a fuller discussion of the linguistic and theological questions involved in the word *propitiation*.

from their guilty stains is the blood of Jesus, God's Son, that is the laying down of His life in a violent death. 'In these passages we have a concatenation of ideas—propitiation, blood, cleansing, forgiveness—which are directly derived from the sacrificial system of the Old Testament, which are expressed, indeed, in technical Levitical terms' (Law; cf. Lv. xvi. 30; Heb. ix. 22 and notes on i. 7).

Moreover, Christ still *is* the propitiation, not because in any sense He continues to offer His sacrifice, but because His one sacrifice once offered has an eternal virtue which is effective today in those who believe. And the propitiation for our sins is *not for ours only, but also for the sins of the whole world*. This cannot be pressed into meaning that all sins are automatically pardoned through the propitiation of Christ, but that a universal pardon is offered for (the sins of) the whole world and is enjoyed by those who embrace it; cf. iv. 9, 14 and John i. 29, iii. 16, v. 24. 'For no man in the whole world is there any other way of being reconciled than that of the propitiation of Christ' (Ebrard).

Thus, the Father's provision for the sinning Christian is in His Son, who possesses a threefold qualification: His righteous character, His propitiatory death and His heavenly advocacy. Each depends on the others. He could not be our advocate in heaven today if He had not died to be the propitiation for our sins; and His propitiation would not have been effective if in His life and character He had not been Jesus Christ the righteous.

Additional Note: The biblical concept of propitiation (ii. 2)

The only two occurrences in the New Testament of the noun *hilasmos*, 'propitiation', are in this Epistle (ii. 2 and iv. 10). The verb *hilaskesthai* occurs twice also (Lk. xviii. 13; Heb. ii. 17), while *hilastērion* is found in Hebrews ix. 5 for the 'mercy seat', and in Romans iii. 25 either in the same sense or, more probably, signifying 'a means of propitiation'.

The AV translation of *hilasmos* as 'propitiation' comes from the Vulgate, but is regarded by many modern writers as 'infelicitous' (Dodd). Thus the RSV prefers 'expiation' and the NEB the rather clumsy periphrasis 'the remedy for the defilement of'. The main contemporary objection to the vocabulary of 'propitiation' is theological. It is said to conjure up notions of an irritable and capricious deity who needs to be appeased with bribes. Such ideas are rightly dismissed as pagan and inconsistent with the revelation of God in Jesus Christ. Apparently unwilling to concede that there may be a biblical and Christian concept of propitiation quite distinct from crude pagan views, some scholars proceed to support their theological rejection of propitiation with linguistic arguments.

It is quite true, they say, that in pagan Greek from Homer onwards the verb *hilaskesthai* meant to make somebody propitious to oneself, to propitiate or pacify an offended person, and especially to placate the angry gods by gifts or sacrifices. This is incontrovertible. But, the argument goes, secular Greek had a rarer, secondary use of the same verb, meaning 'to perform an act by which defilement (ritual or moral) is removed; to "expiate" ' (Dodd). In these cases the object is not personal (God) but impersonal (sin's defilement). It was, in fact, a universal belief of the ancient world that certain rituals acted as a 'powerful disinfectant' (*ibid.*). Further, it is maintained, this second, expiatory meaning of the verb is found in the Greek Old Testament. It is true that on three occasions, God Himself is the object of *exilaskesthai* (Zc. vii. 2, viii. 22; Mal. i. 9, where RSV renders the Hebrew 'entreat the favour of the Lord'; cf. Gn. xxxii. 20 of Jacob and Esau), but nowhere else. The commonest use of the verb is with an impersonal object, translating the Hebrew *kipper*, to 'cover' and so to 'make atonement' or 'expiate'. Indeed, so far from being the object of the verb in the LXX, God is frequently its subject, a usage unknown in pagan Greek. Similarly, in the LXX of Psalms lxv. 3, lxxviii. 38 and lxxix. 9 God is the subject of the non-compound verb *hilaskesthai*, while its object is the sins or ungodliness of men (in the accusative in the first case and the dative in the other two). In these verses the AV translation is 'forgive' or 'purge away', so that C. H. Dodd can write, 'the meaning is virtually indistinguishable from "to forgive"; the defilement of sin can be removed, in the last resort, only by divine forgiveness'. Therefore, in 1 John ii. 2, to say that Jesus is 'the propitiation for our sins' is just another way of saying that through Christ God both 'cleanses' and 'forgives' us, as has already been stated in i. 7, 9 (cf. Lv. iv. 20, xii. 7). We have thus come full circle. The notion conveyed by *hilasmos* and its cognates, we are told, is not an action by which God is propitiated, but by which man is cleansed and his sin 'neutralized' (Westcott, Dodd). The thought is 'not that of appeasing one who is angry . . . against the offender; but of altering the character of that which from without occasions a necessary alienation, and interposes an inevitable obstacle to fellowship' (Westcott). The *hilasmos* changes man not God; it annuls his sin and thus removes the barrier to fellowship with God.

Dr. Leon Morris has subjected to a close and critical analysis the linguistic arguments by which this reconstruction is buttressed.[1] He shows that the only two possible secular Greek passages in which *exilaskesthai* is said to mean to 'expiate' are quite capable of being translated in a propitiatory sense; that the eleven occurrences of *hilaskesthai* in LXX, which are all in the middle or passive, with God as the subject, either must or may convey the sense 'propitiate' or 'be propitious to'; that the compound verb *exilaskesthai* (commoner in LXX, but not found in New Testament) translates the Hebrew *kipper* eighty-three times, and that the latter from its context normally means either 'to avert punishment, especially the divine anger, by the payment of a *kopher*, a ransom', or in its cultic use 'to accomplish reconciliation between God and man' by sacrifice; and that, contrary to what has often been asserted, this compound verb *exilaskesthai* 'is never followed by an accusative of sin in the canonical Scriptures of the Old Testament', but most commonly (fifty-eight times) by *peri* with a genitive of person, meaning 'to make propitiation concerning a person'. Dr. Morris's conclusion from this linguistic study, briefly summarized here, is that 'it would seem impossible for anyone

[1] *The Apostolic Preaching of the Cross* (Tyndale Press, 1955), pp. 125–185.

in the first century to have used one of the *hilaskomai* group
without conveying to his readers some idea of propitiation'.

Turning from linguistics to theology, and in particular to
the two Johannine verses in which the noun *hilasmos* occurs
(ii. 2 and iv. 10), three points may be made. The first concerns *the need for the propitiation*. This is indicated in the words
'the propitiation for our sins' common to both verses. If what
John had in mind was in reality an expiation, of which our
sins were the object, the construction would surely have been
a simple genitive, 'the expiation of our sins'. Instead he uses
the preposition *peri*. The need for a *hilasmos* is seen not in 'our
sins' by themselves but 'concerning our sins', namely in God's
uncompromising hostility towards them. The pagan was
wrong to see the need for propitiation in the wrathful character
of his god, arbitrary and without ethical cause. Some modern
commentators, in their proper reaction against this travesty,
are equally wrong to see it in sin and its taint alone. Christ
'has made possible the removal of the sin which keeps men
from God', writes Brooke. But what is this 'removal' of sin
which takes no account of the divine judgment upon sin? The
need for propitiation is constituted neither by God's wrath in
isolation, nor by man's sin in isolation, but by both together.
Sin is 'lawlessness' (1 Jn. iii. 4), a defiant disregard for the law
of God which deserves the judgment of God. It is this divine
judgment upon human rebellion which makes the barrier to
fellowship with God; and there can be no expiation of man's
sin without a propitiation of God's wrath. God's holy antagonism to sin must somehow be turned away if sin is to be forgiven
and the sinner restored. These concepts are not foreign to
John, the apostle of love. Although he does not mention God's
wrath in these Epistles, he does in the Gospel, where he writes
that 'the wrath of God abides' upon the disobedient unbeliever
(Jn. iii. 36). And in the First Epistle the concept is implied.
The condition of the unbeliever is 'death', which is the result
of sin (iii. 14, v. 16); and 'life', which is fellowship with God,
is available only in Christ who came to win it for us (iv. 9,
v. 11, 12). Moreover, the fact that Jesus Christ the righteous is
our Advocate in heaven, implies the need for His advocacy. It

is on the ground of His propitiation that His advocacy is effective.

Secondly, both verses indicate that *the nature of the propitiation* is Jesus Christ Himself. God 'sent his Son to be the propitiation for our sins' (iv. 10). 'He (*autos*) is the propitiation . . .' (ii. 2). No direct mention is made in either verse of His death, but John has already written that what cleanses from sin is the blood of God's Son (i. 7), that is, the virtue of His sacrificial death. He died the death which was the just reward of our sins. And the efficacy of His death abides, so that He is today Himself the propitiation. 'Christ is said to be the "propitiation" and not simply the "propitiator" (as He is called the "Saviour", iv. 14), in order to emphasize the thought that He is Himself the propitiatory offering as well as the priest (cf. Rom. iii. 25)' (Westcott).

Thirdly, *the source of the propitiation* is clearly taught in iv. 10, namely the love of God. This was so in Old Testament days, since the propitiatory offerings were divinely instituted and prescribed as the means by which the sinner might be forgiven. 'The life of the flesh is in the blood: and I have given it to you upon the altar to make an atonement for your souls . . .' (Lv. xvii. 11). The sacrifices were not a human arrangement, but a divine gift. So with the sacrifice of Christ. God gave His Son to die for sinners. This gift was not only the result of God's love (Jn. iii. 16), nor only the proof and pledge of it (Rom. v. 8, viii. 32), but the very essence of it: 'Herein is love . . . that he loved us, and sent his Son to be the propitiation for our sins' (1 Jn. iv. 10). There can, therefore, be no question of men appeasing an angry deity by their gifts. The Christian propitiation is quite different, not only in the character of the divine anger but in the means by which it is propitiated. It is an appeasement of the wrath of God by the love of God through the gift of God. The initiative is not taken by man, nor even by Christ, but by God Himself in sheer unmerited love. His wrath is not averted by any external gift, but by His own self-giving to die the death of sinners. This is the means He has Himself contrived by which to turn His own wrath away (cf. Pss. lxxviii. 38, lxxxv. 2, 3, ciii. 8–10; Mi. vii. 18, 19).

III. FIRST APPLICATION OF THE TESTS
(ii. 3-27)

So far John has given a general introduction to his theme of Christian consistency. He has been defining the nature of the apostolic proclamation concerning the word of life in Christ. It centres first on the historical manifestation of the Eternal, and secondly on the fact that God is light. These two truths are fundamental and must control and condition our lives if we call ourselves Christian. Indeed, all Christian profession may be judged in relation to these truths. No thought or action can be condoned which is inconsistent either with God's nature as light, pure and self-giving, or with His historical, palpable self-disclosure in Christ.

This general introduction to the essential relation of man's life to God's truth is now particularized in three tests—moral (the test of obedience), social (the test of love) and doctrinal (the test of belief in Christ). The rest of the Epistle contains three successively elaborate expositions and applications of these tests.

a. Obedience, or the moral test (ii. 3-6)

In the preceding section the author has recorded three false claims of the heretics, each introduced by the phrase 'if we say that we have'; he now expresses two right and positive assurances which the true Christian may have, introduced by the formula *en toutō ginōskomen hoti* (*hereby we do know that* (3), and *hereby know we that* (5)). Each of these statements in the first person plural, *we know*, is followed by an application in the third person singular, *he that saith* (4 and 6), the first illustrating a spurious claim and the second the obligation which alone can prove a claim to be true.

3. *Hereby we do know* is a characteristic phrase of the Epistle. Sometimes, as here, the word is *ginōskomen*, a present tense meaning 'we come to know' or 'we perceive' (twenty-five times in this Epistle, in present, aorist and perfect tenses); sometimes it is *oidamen*, the perfect tense of the verb *eidenai*, and means 'we know as a fact', not by perception but as something self-evident (fifteen times in this Epistle). The repetition of these expressions in the Epistle shows that the author's purpose is to supply tests by which the genuine Christian may be discerned from the spurious and vice versa (cf. v. 13). 'Here is the test by which we can make sure that we know him' (NEB). The Gnostics in particular laid claim to the knowledge of God. They had been enlightened with the true *gnōsis*. John does not deny the possibility of knowing God since both the Old Testament and the Gospel promise it (e.g. Je. xxxi. 34; Jn. xvii. 3). But he insists that no religious experience is valid if it does not have moral consequences (cf. Tit. i. 16). It is not the person who claims to be a Christian and to know God who is presumptuous, but he whose claim is contradicted by his conduct. He is a *liar* (4).

How may we 'be sure that we know him' (RSV)? By his answer John gives the first test, which he has already adumbrated in the first chapter and now forcefully clarifies. It is the test of moral obedience. We may know that we have come to know Him (perfect tense, *egnōkamen*) only *if we keep his commandments*. Only if we obey Him can we claim to *know* Him, not to have accurate information about Him merely, but to have become personally acquainted with Him. If it is objected that in this case no-one knows God because no-one is perfectly obedient, we may reply with Calvin: 'he does not mean that those who wholly satisfy the Law keep His commandments (and no such instance can be found in the world), but those who strive, according to the capacity of human infirmity, to form their life in obedience to God.' The word for *keep* (*tērein*) 'expresses the idea of watchful, observant obedience' (Law).

4. The positive principle of the previous verse is illustrated by a negative example. A man's words must be tested by his works. If he disobeys God's commandments, his claim to have come to know God is a lie (cf. i. 6). His conduct contradicts his profession and proves it to be false.

5. On the other hand, *whoso keepeth his word* (observing not only His commandments in particular but His word in general, regarded as a single and complete revelation of His will), he is shown by his obedience to be indeed a true Christian, whether he lays claim to be one or not. In him is *the love of God*, and that so completely as to be described as *perfected*. The genitive in the expression *the love of God* could be subjective (God's love for him), qualitative (love like God's love) or objective (his love for God). The RSV is almost certainly right to take it in the latter sense here and to render the phrase 'love for God', although various commentators have questioned whether obedience really supplies evidence of a love for God that is *perfected*. True love for God is expressed not in senti-mental language or mystical experience but in moral obedience (cf. v. 3 and our Lord's teaching in Jn. xiv. 15, 21, 23, xv. 10). The proof of love is loyalty. Such love is 'perfected'. For perfect love as expressed in confidence towards God rather than obedience to Him, see iv. 17, 18. For perfected joy, see i. 4, and for faith perfected by works, James ii. 22.

John now states the same general principle in a slightly different form, and adds another and more positive illustration of it. The whole context, and especially verse 6, suggests that the phrase *in him* again refers to Christ. To be 'in Christ' is Paul's characteristic description of the Christian. But John uses it too. To be (or to 'abide' verse 6) 'in' Him is equivalent to the phrase to 'know' Him (3, 4) and to 'love' Him (5). Being a Christian consists in essence of a personal relationship to God in Christ, knowing Him, loving Him, and abiding in Him as the branch abides in the vine (Jn. xv. 1 ff.). This is the meaning of 'eternal life' (Jn. xvii. 3; 1 Jn. v. 20).

6. It is never easy in this Epistle to decide whether expres-sions like 'hereby know we' look back to what precedes or forward to what follows. Usually the look is forward; once or twice it is clearly backward; while sometimes the expression is what Neil Alexander calls a 'swing-door' because it appears to move in both directions! In this case the AV is probably wrong. The symmetry between verses 3, 4 and 5, 6 suggests that the RSV punctuation is preferable, making the reference a forward one, namely 'By this we may be sure that we are in him: he who says . . .' A second time the author adds a more specific example to the general principle he has stated. This time the formula *he that saith* introduces not a false claim but an obligation to righteous conduct which alone can make the claim credible. It is not enough to keep *his word* (5); we must *walk, even as he walked*. We are not told explicitly who *he* is, but in this Epistle the pronouns *ekeinos* (here, iii. 3, 5, 7, 16, iv. 17) and *autos* (ii. 8, 12, 27, 28, iii. 2, 3, iv. 21) refer to Christ. Christian conformity is to the example of Christ as well as to His commandments (cf. ii. 29, iii. 3, 7; Jn. xiii. 15; 1 Pet. ii. 21). We cannot claim to abide in Him unless we behave like Him.

b. Love, or the social test (ii. 7–11)

7. John now applies to professing Christians his second test, which is not moral but social. As he is about to write of brotherly love, he appropriately addresses them as his 'beloved' (AV *brethren* is a less well supported reading). His 'little children' (1) are dear to him. In urging them to love one another, he assures them of his love for them. See also iii. 2, 21, iv. 1, 7, 11; and 3 Jn. 2, 5, 11. He has been writing about the Christian obligation to keep His commandments (3, 4); he now singles out one of them which in one sense is *old* (7) and in another is *new* (8). He does not explicitly reveal what the nature of this commandment is; but since the subject of verses 9–11 is love, and since the 'new commandment' which Jesus gave was 'that ye love one another; as I have loved you' (Jn. xiii. 34; cf. xv. 12, 17), it is plain that the commandment concerns brotherly love. Cf. 2 John 4–6. John has told them they must walk as Christ walked (6); and that was a walk in love.

Is this commandment new or old? It is both. In one sense, as they read John's Epistle, it was *no new commandment . . . but an old commandment*. They had learned it before. Indeed, they had known it from the outset of their Christian life (cf. ii. 24, iii. 11, and 2 Jn. 6 for this meaning of *from the beginning*). It was part of the ethical instruction they received from the day of their conversion. So basic was it to the teaching they received that John could even equate it with *the word which ye have heard,* literally 'which you heard' (*ēkousate*, aorist; *from the beginning* is not repeated in the better MSS). Brotherly love was part of the original message which had come to them. John was not now inventing it. It was not an innovation such as the heretics claimed to teach. It was as old as the gospel itself.

8. Nevertheless (AV, *again*, is better rendered 'yet' as RSV), what was old to them, because they had heard it before, was in itself *new, which thing* (neuter *ho*, referring not to the commandment, but to the newness of it) *is true in him and in you.* That is, its novelty was a fact when He first called it 'a new commandment' (Jn. xiii. 34) and Himself exemplified it, and it remains a fact for you, who are required to obey it. The idea of love in general was not new, but Jesus Christ invested it with a richer and deeper meaning. It was new in the emphasis He gave it, bringing Deuteronomy vi. 5 and Leviticus xix. 18 together and declaring that the whole teaching of law and prophets hung upon them. It was new in the quality He gave it. A disciple was to love others not just as he loved himself but in the same measure as Christ had loved him, with selfless self-sacrifice even unto death. It was new in the extent He gave it, showing in the Parable of the Good Samaritan that the 'neighbour' we must love is anyone who needs our compassion and help, irrespective of race and rank. It was also to continue new by their fresh apprehension of it, 'for though doctrinal Christianity is always old, experimental Christianity is always new' (Candlish). In these ways it was 'a new commandment', and would always remain new. It was new teaching for the new age which had dawned, new . . . *because the darkness is past* (*paragetai*, present tense, 'is passing away', RSV), *and the true light now shineth.*

All Jews were familiar with the division of history into 'the present age' and 'the age to come' (cf. e.g. Mt. xii. 32), and the New Testament teaches that 'the age to come' came with Jesus. He inaugurated it, so that the two ages overlap one another. Christians have been delivered out of this present evil age (Gal. i. 4) and have already begun to taste the powers of the age to come (Heb. vi. 5; cf. 1 Cor. x. 11). *The darkness* is the present age or the 'world' which in verse 17 is also said to be passing away (*paragetai*). The *true light* is Jesus Christ, with whom light came 'into the world' (Jn. iii. 19; cf. Is. ix. 2; Mt. iv. 16 and Lk. i. 79). He is *true* (*alēthinos*) not in the sense in which a statement is true as opposed to false (*alēthēs*, the word used at the beginning of this verse), but in the sense in which the real differs from the unreal, the substance from the shadow and the prototype from the type. The adjective is a favourite of John's. Christ is the true, or real, light, of which physical light is but a reflection, just as He is the true bread and the true vine (Jn. i. 9, vi. 32, xv. 1). The true idea of light, vine, bread, etc., is the heavenly reality; the earthly material things which we call 'light', 'vine', 'bread' are copies of the true (cf. Heb. viii. 5, ix. 23, 24, x. 1). So the new commandment remains new because it belongs to the new age which has been ushered in by the shining of the true light.

9. John now shows that Jesus Christ, the true light, is the light of love, and that therefore to be, or to abide, or to walk *in the light* (9, 10; cf. i. 6) is to walk in love. Light and love, darkness and hatred belong together. In verses 3 to 6 the general principle preceded the specific example. Here the example comes first. The Gnostic claim was as much to have been 'enlightened' as to possess the 'knowledge' of God. The falsity of the claim to *be in the light* is betrayed not now by disobedience, but by hatred. The true Christian, who knows God and walks in the light, both obeys God and loves his brother. The genuineness of his faith is seen in his right relation to both God and man.

10, 11. Now follows the general principle, stated first positively and then negatively. The contrast is stark and absolute. Love and hatred are set in opposition to each other with no alternative, just as we are said to be either *in the light* or *in darkness*, and there is no twilight. The first part of the contrast is simple. What follows shows, however, that our love and hatred not only reveal whether we are already in the light or in the darkness, but actually contribute towards the light or the darkness in which we already are. Thus, of the man of love who abides in the light it may be said that *there is none occasion of stumbling in him.* (RSV 'in it there is no cause for stumbling, *en autō,* could refer either to the man or to the light in which he abides.) The light shines on our path, so that we can see clearly and so walk properly. If we love people, we see how to avoid sinning against them. The man with hatred in his heart, however, because he *is in darkness,* also *walketh in darkness.* He *knoweth not whither he goeth, because that darkness hath blinded his eyes* (11; cf. Pr. iv. 19). Hatred distorts our perspective. We do not first misjudge people and then hate them as a result; our view of them is already jaundiced by our hatred. It is love which sees straight, thinks clearly and makes us balanced in our outlook, judgments and conduct. Cf. John viii. 12, xi. 9, 10, xii. 35.

c. A digression about the Church (ii. 12–14)

12. John has abruptly concluded his exposition of his second test. He does not mean to give his readers the impression that he thinks they are in darkness or that he doubts the reality of their Christian faith. It is the false teachers whom he regards as spurious, not the loyal members of the Church. So he digresses to tell them his view of their Christian standing. His purpose in writing is as much to confirm the right assurance of the genuine Christian as to rob the counterfeit of his false assurance. They are in the new age all right and are enjoying the forgiveness, the knowledge of God and the power to overcome which had been prophesied (e.g. Je. xxxi. 33, 34) of the new covenant. So John makes six statements about them, the first three introduced by the words *I write unto you* (*graphō humin,* present tense) and the second three by *I have written unto you* (*egrapsa humin,* aorist). (The AV's fourth *I write unto you,* at the end of verse 13, is due to an inferior reading.)

Some commentators have thought the aorist verbs refer either to a former Epistle (and the present verbs to this) or to the first part of the Epistle already written (and the present verbs to the whole letter). Law makes the ingenious suggestion that 'the author was interrupted' at the end of verse 13 and that, when he resumed, he repeated what he had just written, changing the tense of the verbs from the present to the aorist! But this is pure conjecture. The aorist of the second trio is probably an epistolary aorist referring to the present Epistle, in which case there is really no difference in meaning between the two tenses. He first 'writes' and then confirms what he 'has written'. His message is sure and steadfast; he does not change his mind; this is his 'full and final testimony' (Candlish).

The author divides his readers into three groups, whom he names *little children, fathers* and *young men* and addresses each group twice. He is indicating not their physical ages, as some have thought, but stages in their spiritual development, for God's family, like every human family, has members of different maturity. In view of John's use of the title 'little children' elsewhere in this Epistle to embrace all his readers, many (including the Greek fathers, Calvin and Luther) have thought that here the phrase has the same inclusive reference to all church members who are subsequently divided into two two groups only, *fathers* and *young men*, the mature and the immature, corresponding to the familiar Pauline 'babes in Christ' and 'full grown in Christ' (e.g. 1 Cor. iii. 1 and Col. i. 28). Certainly the order (children, fathers, young men) may also suggest this. But the distinctive content of the message addressed to the three groups favours the view of some ancient Latin commentators such as Augustine that they represent three different stages of spiritual pilgrimage. The little children are those newborn in Christ. The young men are more developed Christians, strong and victorious in spiritual warfare; while the fathers possess the depth and stability of ripe Christian experience. Since the description of each group is similar on both occasions when it is addressed, it will be simplest to take the corresponding pairs together. The repetition of the three groups and of the messages addressed to them, which if not the same are similar, is no doubt intended for emphasis.

12, 13c. The *little children* are first called *teknia* (12) and then *paidia* (13c). If any distinct flavour is preserved between them, *teknia* emphasizes the community of nature between the child and its parent (from *tekein*, to beget or bring forth), while *paidia* refers to the child's minority as one under discipline (*paideuein*, to train or chastise). *Paidia* differs from *teknia* 'by emphasizing the idea of subordination and not that of kinsmanship' (Westcott). By being born of God John's readers had become children of God. Their *sins are forgiven . . . for his name's sake* (12), that is, they have been and remain forgiven (perfect tense, *apheontai*) because of the name of Christ, our propitiation and advocate (verses 1, 2), whose *name* represents both His divine Person and His saving work (cf. Acts iv. 12). Further, they *have known the Father* (13c), literally, 'have come to know' (another perfect tense) God as their Father. These are the earliest conscious experiences of the newborn Christian. He rejoices in the forgiveness of his sins through Christ and in his consequent fellowship with God. The Holy Spirit within him makes him aware of his sonship and causes him to cry 'Abba! Father!' (Rom. viii. 15, 16; Gal. iv. 6).

13a, 14a. The *fathers*, to whom John now addresses himself, are the spiritually adult in the congregation. Their first flush of ecstasy in receiving forgiveness and fellowship with the Father was an experience of long ago. Even the battles of the young men, to which he will next refer, are past. The fathers have progressed into a deep communion with God. Both times he addresses them, John uses identical words: *ye have known him that is from the beginning*. The verb is the same as that used of the little children. All Christians, mature and immature, have come to know (*egnōkate*) God. But their knowledge of Him ripens with the years. The little children know Him as *the Father*; the fathers have come to know Him as *him that is from the beginning*, which is probably a reference, not to the Logos (though see i. 1 and Jn. i. 1), but to the immutable eternal God who does not change, as men change, with advancing years, but who is for ever the same. Time hurries on, but in all generations they find a refuge in Him who from everlasting to everlasting is God (Ps. xc. 1, 2; cf. Mal. iii. 6). They are already consciously living in eternity.

13b, 14b. In between the little children and the fathers are the *young men*, busily involved in the battle of Christian living.

The Christian life, then, is not just enjoying the forgiveness and the fellowship of God, but fighting the enemy. The forgiveness of past sins must be followed by deliverance from sin's present power, justification by sanctification. So in both messages to the *young men* it is asserted that they *have overcome* (NEB 'mastered') *the wicked one*. Their conflict has become a conquest. Possibly John uses a deliberate assonance: *neaniskoi . . . nenikēkate* (13b). It is significant that in each of these six messages the verb is in the perfect tense, which indicates the present consequence of a past event. John is laying emphasis on the assured standing into which every Christian has come, whatever his stage of spiritual development. A hint is given as to the secret of the young men's victory. *Ye are strong*, he says, and your strength is due to the fact that *the word of God abideth in you* (14b). They have grasped the Christian revelation. They are seeking to conform their lives to its ethical demands, for 'wherewithal shall a young man cleanse his way?' Even 'by taking heed thereto according to thy word' (Ps. cxix. 9; cf. verse 11). Alternatively, the reference may be to their overcoming of the antichrists' false teaching which was diabolical (cf. iv. 1–4, v. 4, 5).

d. A digression about the world (ii. 15–17)

John turns now from a description of the Church to a description of the world and instruction about the Church's attitude to it. In so doing he changes from affirmations about the Christians' standing to warnings about their behaviour. The characteristic tense of this paragraph is not the perfect indicative but the present imperative: *love not the world*. Christian people have entered into a great inheritance in the forgiveness of sins, fellowship with God and the conquest of the wicked one, but their temptations have not come to an end.

What is *the world*? John here mentions it for the first time, but he refers to it many times later. His teaching about it in the Epistle, supplemented by our Lord's recorded teaching on this subject in the Fourth Gospel, is summarized in an Additional Note (p. 101). Suffice it to say here that sometimes he simply means 'the universe' (Jn. i. 10) or 'life on earth' (iii. 17,

iv. 17), but usually he is referring to 'the life of human society as organized under the power of evil' (Dodd), 'the order of finite being regarded as apart from God' (Westcott). In these verses in which the world is mentioned six times, the sequence of thought is clear. The command not to love the world is grounded on two arguments, first the incompatibility of love for the world and love for the Father (15, 16) and secondly, the transience of the world as contrasted with the eternity of him who does God's will (17).

15. *Love not the world.* Some people have been puzzled as to how this command not to love the world can be reconciled with the statement of God's love for the world in John iii. 16. There are two possible explanations. The first is that *the world* has a different connotation in these verses. Viewed as people, the world must be loved. Viewed as an evil system, organized under the dominion of Satan and not of God, it is not to be loved. The second explanation is that it is the verb 'to love', not its object 'the world', which has a different shade of meaning. In the one it is 'the holy love of Redemption'; in the other it is 'the selfish love of participation' (Alford). The first aims 'to save the sinner's person'; the second, 'to share his sin' (Ebrard). So NEB: 'Do not set your hearts on the godless world.' Perhaps there is a subtle change of emphasis in both words. The commandment is uncompromising. The Christian is to love God (5) and his brother (10), but he is not to love the world. And love is a fit subject for such commandment and prohibition because it is not an uncontrollable emotion but the steady devotion of the will. The reason why we are enjoined not to love the world is because 'love for the Father' (RSV) and love for the world are mutually exclusive. If a man is engrossed in the outlook and pursuits of the world which rejects Christ, it is evident that he has no love for the Father. 'The friendship of the world is enmity with God' (Jas. iv. 4). 'No man can serve two masters' (Mt. vi. 24; Lk. xvi. 13), and if we cannot serve God and mammon, neither can we love the Father and the world.

16. If there were some things *in the world* (in the technical sense in which John uses this phrase) which were *of the Father*, that is, which owed their origin and existence to Him, we might love them. But since *all that is in the world . . . is of the world*, we may not love any of it. John selects for special mention *the lust of the flesh, the lust of the eyes, and the pride of life*. These appear to him 'the essential marks of the pagan way of life' (Dodd). The first describes the desire of our fallen and sinful nature. It may be said to be 'in the world', because the world, where the devil rules, is the sphere of its free operation. It is noteworthy that within the space of three verses, John mentions the world, the flesh and the devil (14–16). The second seems to indicate temptations which assault us not from within, but from without through *the eyes*. This is 'the tendency to be captivated by the outward show of things, without enquiring into their real values' (Dodd). Eve's view of the forbidden tree as 'a delight to the eyes', Achan's covetous sight among the spoil of a 'goodly Babylonish garment', and David's lustful looking after Bathsheba as she bathed, are obvious examples (Gn. iii. 6; Jos. vii. 21; 2 Sa. xi. 2). It will include 'the love of beauty divorced from the love of goodness' (Law). *The pride of life (hē alazoneia tou biou)* is the most difficult of these three expressions. While *zōē* means 'life in its essential principle', *bios* is 'life in its present concrete manifestation' (Westcott). It occurs again in iii. 17 in the expression *ton bion tou kosmou*, translated *this world's good*. The *alazōn* was a braggart (Rom. i. 30; 2 Tim. iii. 2; Jas. iv. 16), 'a conceited, pretentious humbug' (Dodd), who seeks 'to impress everyone he meets with his own non-existent importance' (Barclay). *The pride of life* is, therefore, an arrogance or vainglory relating to one's external circumstances, whether wealth or rank or dress, 'pretentious ostentation' (Plummer), 'the desire to shine or outshine others' in luxurious living (Ebrard).

Some commentators have seen 'this trinity of evil' (Plummer, Findlay) exemplified in our Lord's three temptations in the wilderness, and even in the threefold attraction of the forbidden fruit to Eve (Gn. iii. 6). But neither parallel is sufficiently close to suppose a deliberate allusion to be intended. Nor is there a very obvious correspondence between these aspects of the world and the 'three master vices which occupy a prominent place in ancient and medieval ethics' (Westcott), namely *voluptas*, *avaritia* and *superbia*. Findlay summarizes John's three as 'two lusts and one vaunt, two forms of depravation arising from our needs and one from our possessions—unholy desire for things one has not, and unholy pride in things one has'. C. H. Dodd's summary is 'base desires, false values, egoism'.

17. The second reason for not setting our love on the world is that the new age has arrived, and the present age is doomed. The world, like the darkness that is in it, is already disintegrating (*paragetai* is used both here and in verse 8). Cf. I Corinthians vii. 31. And men with a lust that is worldly will pass away with it. Only one class of people will remain: *he that doeth the will of God abideth for ever.* Jesus had said that 'whosoever shall do the will of God' was His 'brother, and . . . sister, and mother' (Mk. iii. 35). John draws the logical conclusion, that those thus related to Christ abide as He abides (cf. Jn. viii. 35, xii. 34). The same choice between God and the world, or more particularly between the lust of the world and the will of God, still confronts Christians. We shall more readily obey the command to 'love not the world' if we remember that while *the world . . . and the lust thereof* are transient, God's will and he who does it are alike eternal (cf. 2 Cor. iv. 18).

Additional Note: The meaning of 'the world' (ii. 15–17)

1. *The world and Satan.* 'The world' is under the dominion of Satan. He is 'the prince of this world' (Jn. xii. 31, xiv. 30, xvi. 11), and 'the whole world lieth in wickedness' (v. 19), that is, in, or under the power of, the evil one. Indeed, the devil is entitled 'he that is in the world' (iv. 4). The world is his sphere of influence. Similarly, the 'spirit of antichrist' which is coming, is 'now already . . . in the world' (iv. 3), and 'many false prophets are gone out into the world' (iv. 1). 'The world', therefore, is an inclusive term for all those who are in the kingdom of darkness and have not been born of God. Though 'the whole world lieth in wickedness, we know that we are of

God' (v. 19). Because we are the sons of God, 'the world knoweth us not, because it knew him (Christ) not' (iii. 1, 2), nor the Father (Jn. xvii. 25). The world and the Church are thus portrayed in sharp contrast to each other, two entirely separate and distinct groups of people, the one under the dominion of Satan, the other born of God and knowing God. Since the world's prince is 'cast out' and 'judged' (Jn. xii. 31, xvi. 11), it stands to reason that the world itself is doomed. Indeed already it is passing away (ii. 17).

2. *The world and God.* This sinful 'world', ruled by Satan, is nevertheless the object of God's love and saving activity. Not, of course, that He condones its materialism and sin, but His compassion embraces the poor creatures the devil has enthralled. 'God so loved the world, that he gave his only begotten Son . . .' (Jn. iii. 16). 'God sent his only begotten Son into the world, that we might live through him' (iv. 9). 'The Father sent the Son to be the Saviour of the world' (iv. 14), and Jesus Christ died to be 'the propitiation for our sins: and not for ours only, but also for (the sins of) the whole world' (ii. 2).

3. *The world and the Christian.* Christians know themselves to have been chosen 'out of the world' (Jn. xvii. 6) in such a way that they no longer belong to it. They are still 'in this world' (iv. 17; cf. Jn. xvii. 11, 15), yet distinct from it, so that we and the world are set over against each other. For this reason John writes: 'Marvel not, my brethren, if the world hate you' (iii. 13; cf. Jn. xv. 18, 19, xvii. 14). Hatred is characteristic of the world, as love is of the Christian (iii. 14). The world not only hates us but will not listen to us. It listens to false prophets. 'They are of the world: therefore speak they of the world, and the world heareth them.' But 'we are of God', and not 'of the world' (Jn. xvii. 14, 16), and so 'he that knoweth God heareth us', whereas 'he that is not of God heareth not us' (iv. 5, 6; cf. Jn. xv. 19). Though the world hates the Christian, the Christian must not hate the world. Nevertheless, he must 'love not the world, neither the things that are in the world' (ii. 15). He is to be neither conformed to, nor contaminated by, the world. What then is to be the Christian's attitude to the

world? He is not to escape out of it; he is to remain in it. He is to be 'unworldly' without becoming 'otherworldly', living 'in' it without being 'of' it. Indeed he is 'sent into the world' as Jesus was (Jn. xvii. 18), and, above all, 'whatsoever is born of God overcometh the world'. Not only does he resist the allurements of the world (ii. 15, 16), but he positively overcomes it; 'and this is the victory that overcometh the world, even our faith. Who is he that overcometh the world, but he that believeth that Jesus is the Son of God?' (v. 4, 5). The devil, through the spirit of antichrist, holds the world in unbelief; it is by faith in Jesus as the Son of God that we escape from the devil and thus overcome the world.

e. Belief, or the doctrinal test (ii. 18–27)

After his two brief digressions, John reverts to his principal thesis, namely discrimination between the true and the false by means of tests. To the moral and social tests which he has already expounded (3–11), he now adds his doctrinal test. He first draws a clear distinction between the heretics and the genuine Christians (18–21); then defines the nature and effect of the heresy (22, 23); and finally describes the two safeguards against heresy which his readers already have (24–27).

i. The heretics and the genuine Christians (ii. 18–21).

Twice he tells his *little children* that *it is the last time*, or 'hour' (RSV). Since the new age had dawned with the coming of Christ (see notes on verses 8 and 17), Christians knew themselves to be living 'in the last days'. The age to come had already come; the world and the darkness were already passing away (8, 17). John was convinced not only that it was the last time, but that within this end period 'the last hour' (*eschatē hōra*) had struck.[1]

The evidence for this was that *even now are there many antichrists*. The word 'antichrist' occurs in the Bible only in the Johannine Epistles (1 Jn. ii. 18, 22, iv. 3; 2 Jn. 7) but the conception is found elsewhere. The appearing of the anti-

---

[1] For a more detailed consideration of John's use of this term see Additional Note, p. 107.

christ was regarded as a sign of the approaching end. Daniel's prophecy of 'the abomination that maketh desolate' (Dn. xi. 31, xii. 11), which was partly fulfilled when Antiochus Epiphanes desecrated the Temple in *c.* 168 BC, was not thought to have been finally fulfilled even when the Temple was defiled and destroyed by the Roman army under Titus in AD 70, to which event Jesus had referred Daniel's phrase (Mk. xiii. 14; cf. Lk. xxi. 20, 21). Paul taught that a further outbreak of evil sacrilege would precede the end, but that even now 'the mystery of lawlessness is already at work' (see 2 Thes. ii. 1–12). In the same way John writes that, although *antichrist shall come, as ye have heard* (because this was part of the apostolic teaching; cf. 2 Thes. ii. 5), yet already *even now are there many antichrists*. They 'have come' (RSV).[1] The 'spirit of antichrist' is already at work in the world (iv. 3). It is not necessary to say that John 'rationalizes (demythologizes?) the myth and boldly identifies the heretics with the foretold Antichrist' (Alexander) or that to John 'antichrist is not so much a person as a principle' (Barclay); what John means is that the *many antichrists* are forerunners of the one still to come.

It is tempting to interpret the prefix 'anti' in the word 'antichrist' as meaning not 'against' but 'instead of', on the analogy of *antibasileus*, 'viceroy', and to regard the antichrist as being essentially a substitute-Christ, a lying pretender, rather than an opponent of Christ—'a kind of diabolical parody of God's Messiah' (Dodd), active 'not in the world, but in perversions of Christianity' (Law). Certainly Jesus warned the disciples of 'false Christs' (*pseudochristoi*, Mt. xxiv. 24; Mk. xiii. 22), and it is characteristic of the antichrist that he is described as he that *shall come*. He makes himself out to be 'the coming one', thus aping the Christ, of whose first coming in the flesh and second coming in glory John has much to say (e.g. iv. 2; 2 Jn. 7 and ii. 28). Nevertheless, the early commentators understood the word to signify an 'adversary' of Christ, and if John had meant a 'false' Christ, he probably would

---

[1] The verb (*gegonasin*) may be contrasted with *was* (*ēn*), which is used of the Eternal Son in i. 1. 'Christ the Word *was* from all eternity; antichrists have arisen, have come into existence in time' (Plummer on i. 1).

have used the term *pseudochristoi* as he does *pseudoprophētēs* in
iv. 1. Certainly the antichrist's teaching is here recognized as
being fundamentally against Christ and a denial of Christ (22).
Perhaps both ideas are present in the word, 'counterfeiting
and opposing' (Plummer), as in the case of Paul's 'man of
lawlessness' (see especially 2 Thes. ii. 3, 4, RSV).

19. The many antichrists who have already come (in contrast to the one antichrist who shall come) are now identified
as human teachers. They are no doubt the same as the 'many
false prophets' of iv. 1 (cf. our Lord's combination of 'false
Christs and false prophets' in Mk. xiii. 22). They have left the
church to which John is writing, perhaps because they have
failed to win over the church leaders to their viewpoint. They
have excommunicated themselves. John distinguishes sharply
between the *they* who have left and the *us* who remain. By their
defection they have given clear evidence of their true character.
They were not of us. So certain is John of this fact that he adds
the hypothesis: *if they had been of us, they would no doubt have
continued with us.*

John not only relates the fact of their departure from the
fellowship, but discerns a purpose in it. The heretics went out
of their own volition, but behind the secession was the divine
purpose that the spurious should be *made manifest (phanerōthōsin)*
lest the elect should be led astray (Mt. xxiv. 24). Their
departure was 'their unmasking' (Law). What is counterfeit
cannot remain for ever hidden (cf. 1 Cor. iii. 13, iv. 5).
'Nothing is covered up that will not be revealed, or hidden
that will not be known' (Lk. xii. 2, RSV).

Light is shed by this verse upon two important doctrines:
the perseverance of the saints and the nature of the Church.
'He that shall endure unto the end, the same shall be saved'
(Mk. xiii. 13), not because salvation is the reward of endurance,
but because endurance is the hall-mark of the saved. If the
false teachers *had been of us, they would no doubt have continued with
us.* This is stated as a principle. Those who are of us stay with
us. Future and final perseverance is the ultimate test of a past
participation in Christ (cf. Heb. iii. 14). 'Those who fall

away', on the other hand, 'have never been thoroughly imbued with the knowledge of Christ but only had a slight and passing taste of it' (Calvin).

This verse also gives biblical warrant for some distinction between the visible and the invisible Church. Granted that God intends His Church to be visibly manifest in local worshipping, witnessing fellowships, this does not mean that all the professing baptized, communicant members of the Church are necessarily members of Christ. Only the Lord knows 'them that are his' (2 Tim. ii. 19). Perhaps most visible church members are also members of the invisible Church, the mystical body of Christ, but some are not. They are *with us* yet not *of us*. They share our earthly company but not our heavenly birth. Only on the final day of separation will the wheat and the tares be completely revealed. Meanwhile, some are *made manifest* in their true colours by their defection. Cf. iii. 10 for a manifestation in moral behaviour.

20. *Ye know all things.* RSV 'You all know' translates the better reading. The readers' loyalty to the truth is contrasted with the heretical teaching of those who have departed from the Church and is traced to the fact that they possess *an unction (chrisma) from the Holy One*, the latter title designating either God (e.g. Hab. iii. 3) or Christ (e.g. Jn. vi. 69). There seems to be here a deliberate play on words. Protection against the 'antichrist' is in the 'chrism' they had received. The word literally means an 'anointing', 'not the act of anointing, but that with which it is performed' (Westcott). This was commonly oil. When the Messiah ('the Lord's Anointed') came, however, in fulfilment of Isaiah lxi. 1 He was anointed at His baptism not with oil but with the Holy Spirit (Lk. iv. 18; Acts iv. 27, x. 38). It is likely, therefore, that the *unction* or anointing which we have received from God is the same Holy Spirit. If the false teachers were antichrists, there is a sense in which every Christian is a true 'Christ', having received the same spiritual 'chrism' as He received (cf. 2 Cor. i. 21, 22). It is through the illumination of the Spirit of truth that we know, as is elaborated in verse 27. Nor are we an esoteric, enlightened minority, such as the heretics claimed to be. It is probable that they used the word *chrisma* as a technical term for initiation into a special *gnōsis*. If so, it is in direct contradiction to their exclusive claim that John says *all* his readers have the same *gnōsis* because they have all received the same *chrisma*, the Spirit of truth (cf. Col. i. 28). 'You, no less than they, are among the initiated' (NEB).[1]

21. John emphasizes his assurance concerning their orthodoxy. His purpose in writing, he says, is not to inform them of new truth, but to confirm them in the truth they already know (cf. Rom. xv. 14, 15). Not only do they *know* . . . *the truth*, but they know the character of truth, that it is wholly true and self-consistent, and that *no lie is of* (that is, comes from) *the truth*. On the contrary, lies emanate from the devil (Jn. vii. 44). Cf. verse 27.

Additional Note: 'The last hour' (ii. 18)

The New Testament writers do not have an exact vocabulary to describe the chronology of the last time or the end, and it is not always easy to discern to what eschatological period or event they are alluding. What is clear is that they regarded the first coming of Christ as having inaugurated the new age and settled the doom of the old. 'The age to come' had come, and 'the present age' was therefore drawing to a close. It was not, of course, anticipated that this period would last for ever. It was a stage of transition called both the 'last days' (Mi. iv. 1; Acts ii. 17, RSV; cf. Joel ii. 28; Heb. i. 1, 2) and the 'last times' (1 Pet. i. 20; cf. 1 Cor. x. 11). The New Testament writers who describe its beginning are already looking forward to its consummation. The 'last days' will themselves have 'last days', a period of grievous moral and religious decadence (2 Tim. iii. 1 ff.; 2 Pet. iii. 3). Similarly, the 'last times' will have a 'last time' in which ungodly scoffers will arise (Jude 18; cf. 1 Tim. iv. 1). Nor is this all. The 'last time' of the 'last times' will have a culminating 'last time' when our eternal inheritance will be revealed (1 Pet. i. 5; cf. Jas. v. 3). In the same way, 'the

[1] See also Additional Note: The meaning of '*chrisma*', p. 109.

last days' of the 'last days' will themselves have a final 'last day' when Christ raises the dead and judges the world (Jn. vi. 39, 40, 44, 54, xi. 24, xii. 48).

In this progressive unfolding of the last things, to what does John's unique reference to a 'last hour' refer?

1. Some commentators are quite dogmatic about the proper interpretation. 'The "last hour" is the last period of the interval between the first and second coming of Christ' (Brooke). Those who hold this view (e.g. Dodd and Barclay) add logically that in this John has proved to be mistaken.

2. A second interpretation draws attention to the fact that *eschatē hōra* is anarthrous and that the phrase could or should be rather translated 'it is *a* last hour'. Westcott makes much of this and writes that the omission of the definite article 'seems to mark the general character of the period and not its specific relation to "the end". It was a period of critical change.' Other writers have endorsed this view. G. P. Lewis, after pointing out that 'in the history of Christendom there have been many last hours and new beginnings', goes on to suggest that the time of John's writing, with 'widespread heresy . . . massing its forces against the Christian faith and threatening its survival', was 'one of the ultimate crises in the history of Christendom'. Although Plummer is very scornful of such an interpretation, declaring roundly that 'there can be only one last hour', it cannot be lightly dismissed. Even C. H. Dodd, who is clear that John is mistaken, allows a secondary application to that greatest 'last hour', the crucifixion and resurrection of Jesus, into whose meaning, he writes, the Church was now entering.

3. There is a third possible interpretation, namely that John did mean the end of the old era and the consummation of the new, the last hour of the last days, but that he was not thereby dogmatizing that the end was imminent. He was expressing a theological truth rather than making a chronological reference. In view of our Lord's clear words about the uncertainty of the day and the hour (Mk. xiii. 32) and of 'times and seasons' (Acts i. 7), it is *a priori* most unlikely that the

apostles would have presumed to speculate precisely *when* the end would come.[1] John could state on theological grounds that the last hour had struck, but this was not the same as affirming chronologically when the last hour would end. It was generally believed, and Jesus had taught, that a period of tribulation and apostasy would precede the End, including the rise of 'false Christs and false prophets' (Mk. xiii. 22). It was because 'there are many antichrists' that John could affirm that he knew it was 'the last hour'. This is not 'a curious argument' (Dodd); it is sound reasoning. The powers of darkness were closing their ranks. The forces of evil were rallying. If the first coming of Christ evidenced the arrival of 'the last days', the coming of *many antichrists* proved that it was 'the last hour'. A last desperate stand on the part of Christ's enemies was expected before the consummation. This was taking place. The stage was now set for the end. 'No more remained but for Christ to appear for the redemption of the world' (Calvin). 'It is the last hour.' What John wrote was true. And it is still true. The fact that nearly 1,900 years have elapsed since he wrote these words does not invalidate his argument or contradict his affirmation. 'Nothing is so damaging in the study of New Testament prophecy . . . as to imagine that the Eternal God, who stands above and outside of time, is bound by the clocks and calendars of men' (Blaiklock). It is still 'the last hour', the hour of final opposition to Christ. Although there may yet be a special time of tribulation before the denouement, the whole Christian era consists of 'the great tribulation' through which all the redeemed must pass (Rev. vii. 14). We still await the end.

Additional Note: The meaning of 'chrisma' (ii. 20)

C. H. Dodd has a long passage about the interpretation of *chrisma* (pp. 58–64). He quotes from Hippolytus a document of the Gnostic 'Naassenes' sect in which reference is made to

---

[1] Compare John's references to the appearing of Christ in ii. 28 and iii. 2, where the Greek conjunction *ean*, translated 'when', strictly means 'if'. ' "If" implies no doubt as to the *fact*; it merely implies indifference as to the *time*' (Plummer).

an initiation by anointing into some esoteric mystery. From it he argues that the use of *chrisma* in these verses has a background of Hellenistic rather than Hebrew religion and signifies initiation not consecration. He also quotes a sentence from Ignatius' *Letter to the Ephesians* which speaks of anointing with 'doctrine'. He then refers to baptism as a rite of initiation 'which *all* Christians undergo', and concludes 'that the "chrism", which confers knowledge of God, and is also a prophylactic against the poison of false teaching, is the Word of God, that is, the Gospel, or the revelation of God in Christ, as communicated in the rule of faith to catechumens, and confessed in Baptism. This is the Christian's initiation, by water and the Word.' William Barclay appears to be in substantial agreement.

But this interpretation, attractive as it is in some respects, seems to confuse the relation between the *chrisma* and the *gnōsis*, the anointing or initiation and the knowledge into which the Christian is initiated. Is the knowledge the means by which, or the benefit into which, the Christian is initiated? In the Ignatius passage it is the former, the 'doctrine' being the actual oil of anointing. In C. H. Dodd's reconstruction, however, it is both, the gospel being the *chrisma* by which Christians are initiated into the knowledge of God. But would John's readers have appreciated this rather subtle distinction between the gospel and the knowledge of God? It seems more probable that John would have insisted on equating the gospel and the *gnōsis*, denying that there was a further knowledge into which the gospel initiated men. Otherwise, would he not be playing into the hands of the heretics? He makes it plain in the Second Epistle that his readers are to 'abide in the doctrine of Christ' and not 'go ahead' beyond it (2 Jn. 9, RSV). It is more likely, therefore, that, if the concept of initiation is present, the benefit into which Christians are initiated is the eternal gospel, which is itself the true *gnōsis*, while the *chrisma*, the means of initiation into it, is the Holy Spirit of truth.

ii. The nature and effect of the heresy (ii. 22, 23). The false teaching of those who have left the Church is now revealed. It is a denial *that Jesus is the Christ*. A study of these Epistles makes it plain that by this phrase John does not simply mean a denial that Jesus was the Messiah of Old Testament expectation (cf. Acts v. 42, ix. 22, xvii. 3, xviii. 28). In the second part of this verse and in verse 23 he refers to Jesus as *the Son*. For a similar linking of the two expressions see v. 1 and v. 5 and cf. John xx. 31; Matthew xvi. 16. In iv. 2, 3 and 2 John 7 the theological error he is combating is defined more precisely as a denial that 'Jesus Christ is come in the flesh', or, as perhaps these expressions should be translated, a denial that 'Jesus is the Christ come in the flesh'. The antichrists probably taught (as some later Gnostics certainly taught) that Jesus was born and died a man, and that 'the Christ', by which they meant a divine emanation, was within Him only during His public ministry, descending upon Him at His baptism and leaving Him before the cross. They thus denied that Jesus was or is (*estin*, verse 22) the Christ or the Son. They made Him a mere man invested for a brief period with divine powers or even adopted into the Godhead, but they denied that the man Jesus and the Eternal Son were and are the same Person, possessing two perfect natures, human and divine. In a word they denied the incarnation.

John's black and white contrasts are healthily clearsighted. Opposing views are not to him 'complementary insights' but 'truth and error' (cf. verses 21, 27). If we claim to enjoy fellowship with God while we walk in darkness 'we lie' (i. 6). He who says he knows God but disobeys His commandments 'is a liar' (ii. 4, *pseustēs*). But what shall be said of him who denies that Jesus is the Christ? We must pronounce him 'the' liar (22, RV, RSV, NEB, *ho pseustēs*), the liar *par excellence*. Indeed, you can tell that this is the arch-lie, because he who perpetrates it is none other than *the antichrist*, not the personal antichrist who is still to come (see verse 18), but a living embodiment of the spirit of antichrist (iv. 3; cf. 2 Jn. 7). The heretics' theology is not just defective; it is diabolical. The fundamental doctrinal test of the professing Christian concerns his view of the Person of Jesus. If he is a Unitarian or a member of a sect denying the deity of Jesus, he is not a

Christian. Many strange cults which have a popular appeal today can be easily judged and quickly repudiated by this test. The extreme seriousness of the lie is that a second denial is implicit in the first: *he denieth the Father and the Son.*

23. Having disclosed the nature of the heresy, John now elaborates its dread effect, which he has already mentioned at the end of the previous verse. He states the truth in absolute and unequivocal terms, first negatively, then positively. *Whosoever denieth the Son,* he declares, thereby forfeits even (*oude*) the Father, while *he that acknowledgeth the Son hath the Father also.*[1] John has in mind more than a private belief and disbelief. As when the words are used by Jesus, a public confession and denial of Him 'before men' are implied (cf. Mt. x. 32, 33; Jn. xii. 42 and Rom. x. 9, 10). On such a confession or denial depends not just our conception of, but our possession of, the Father. The verb *hath* (*echei*) is the same in both parts of the verse. Cf. v. 12; 2 John 9. We cannot possess, i.e. have fellowship with, the Father if we do not confess the Son. Only the Son can reveal the Father to men (Mt. xi. 27; Jn. i. 18, xii. 44, 45, xiv. 9); only the Son can represent and reconcile men to the Father (ii. 1, 2; Jn. xiv. 6; cf. 1 Tim. ii. 5).

iii. Safeguards against heresy (ii. 24–27). Having distinguished between the false teachers and the true believers, and having exposed the nature and consequences of the heresy, John now draws attention to the two safeguards which will protect his readers from being led astray. If they are to be proof against error two things must abide in them, first the word 'which ye have heard from the beginning' (24) and secondly 'the anointing which ye have received of him' (27).

24. That *which ye have heard from the beginning* is the gospel, the apostolic teaching, the original message which had been preached. It had not changed and would not change. They must *let* it *abide in* them. It would not do so automatically;

---

[1] It is strange that the AV prints the second part of verse 23 in italics as if its attestation were doubtful. Actually it is included in the best MSS and is certainly genuine.

they must allow it to do so. Christians should always be 'conservative' in their theology. To have 'itching ears', ever running after new teachers, listening to anybody and never arriving at a knowledge of the truth, is a characteristic of the 'perilous times' which shall come 'in the last days' (2 Tim. iii. 1, 7, iv. 3). The continuous obsession for 'some new thing' is a mark of the Athenian not the Christian (Acts xvii. 21). Christian theology is anchored not only to certain historical events, culminating in the saving career of Jesus, but to the authoritative apostolic witness to these events. The Christian can never weigh anchor and launch out into the deep of speculative thought. Nor can he forsake the primitive teaching of the apostles for the subsequent traditions of men. The apostolic testimony is directed essentially to the Son. That is why it will keep them true to Him if they remain true to it. Moreover, they will *continue in the Son, and in the Father*, in the sense of experiencing an intimate spiritual communion with Both. To *continue in* God (or 'abide in', RSV; Gk. *menein*) and to 'have' God (verse 23) are virtually identical in meaning.

25. As a result of such loyalty to and communion with the Son and the Father, we shall enjoy the promised *eternal life* (cf. v. 11, 12). The awful consequence of the heretical denial of the Son was a loss of life as well as of the Father.

26. But the apostolic teaching was not in itself enough to keep them in the truth. John does not underestimate the strength or the subtlety of the deceivers. The RV, RSV and NEB are doubtless right to render the present participle here (*planōntōn*) as those who 'would' deceive you. They have not succeeded, but they are in process of making the attempt. It is possible for Christians to be deceived by false teachers, as is implied here, by others (iii. 7) and by themselves (i. 8). The devil himself is the primary deceiver, for he is in his very nature 'a liar and the father of lies' (Jn. viii. 44).

27. Against such would-be deceivers they had a second safeguard, namely, *the anointing (chrisma) which ye have received of him* and which *abideth in you*. See notes on verse 20 and

Additional Note (p. 109), where it is argued that this is a reference to the Holy Spirit. Jesus Himself had promised that the Spirit once given would 'abide' with us for ever (Jn. xiv. 16). Possessing knowledge by the Holy Spirit's direct illumination, *ye need not that any man teach you.* (Cf. Je. xxxi. 34; 1 Thes. iv. 9.) It would not be difficult to exaggerate this statement in an incautious and unbalanced fashion. True, in the last resort the Holy Spirit is our absolutely adequate Teacher, and we maintain our right of private judgment by His illumination of the Word of God. But we must see this verse in the context of an Epistle in which John is, in fact, teaching those who, he says, have no need of human teachers! And other passages of the New Testament refer not only to the general ministry of teaching in the Church (e.g. Acts iv. 18, v. 28, 42; 2 Tim. ii. 24) but also to specially gifted 'teachers' (1 Cor. xii. 29; Eph. iv. 11).

The competence of the Holy Spirit to teach them is indicated in the next phrase, that the *same anointing . . . is truth* ('true', RSV), *and is no lie* (cf. verse 21). If our God is 'the true God' (e.g. 2 Ch. xv. 3; Je. x. 10; Jn. xvii. 3; 1 Thes. i. 9; cf. 1 Jn. v. 20) and Jesus Christ is 'the truth' (Jn. xiv. 6), the Holy Spirit also 'is true'. Indeed in v. 7 it is written, 'the Spirit is the truth' (RSV). Our Lord called Him 'the Spirit of truth' (Jn. xv. 26, xvi. 13). and promised that He would lead the apostles 'into all the truth' (Jn. xvi. 13). With this knowledge of His nature, and with the further assurance that *it hath taught you* in the past (*it*, neuter, because *chrisma*, anointing, is neuter, and not because the Holy Spirit is other than 'He', a Person), John looks confidently into the future and ends the paragraph either with the statement *ye shall abide in him* or perhaps (reading with the RSV *menete*, not *meneite*) with the command: 'abide in him', an imperative which certainly occurs in the following verse.

Here, then, are the two safeguards against error—the apostolic Word and the anointing Spirit (cf. Is. lix. 21). Both are received at conversion. 'You heard' (*ēkousate*, 24) the Word, he says, and 'you received' (*elabete*, 27) the Spirit, although indeed, he implies, the Word has come to you from us (i. 2,

3, 5), while you have received the Spirit direct *of*, that is from, *him*, 'the Holy One' (27, 20). The Word is an objective safeguard, while the anointing of the Spirit is a subjective experience; but both the apostolic teaching and the Heavenly Teacher are necessary for continuance in the truth. And both are to be personally and inwardly grasped. This is the biblical balance too seldom preserved by men. Some honour the Word and neglect the Spirit who alone can interpret it; others honour the Spirit but neglect the Word out of which He teaches. The only safeguard against lies is to have abiding within us both the Word that we *heard from the beginning* and the *anointing* that we *received* from Him. It is by these old possessions, not by new teachings or teachers, that we shall abide in the truth.

IV. SECOND APPLICATION OF THE TESTS
(ii. 28–iv. 6)

John now reverts to his cycle of tests, expanding and enforcing them: the moral test of obedience or righteousness (ii. 28–iii. 10), the social test of love (iii. 11–18) and, after a digression about the relation between our assurance and our condemning heart (iii. 19–24), the doctrinal test of truth concerning Christ (iv. 1–6).

It is now, in the second exposition of the three tests, that for the first time the believer is described as having been 'born' of God (ii. 29). Previously he has been delineated as one who knows God (ii. 3, 4, 13, 14), is in Christ (ii. 5, 6) and in the light (ii. 9, 10), and abides in the Father and in the Son (ii. 24, 27, 28). But now there comes to the fore that birth from God which alone makes it possible for men to know God and abide in Him. Such a spiritual 'birth' is due to a divine 'begetting', which is the imparting of the life of God. And it has manifest consequences in the life of the Christian, for he who has been begotten of God does not sin (iii. 9), but practises righteousness (ii. 29), loves his brother (iii. 10, 14; cf. iv. 7) and believes that Jesus is the Christ (v. 1; cf. iv. 1–6).

a. An elaboration of the moral test: righteousness (ii. 28–iii. 10)

The moral test again comes first. The proof of being a Christian is not merely orthodoxy, but righteous conduct as well. This time, in unfolding the moral test, John associates it closely with the Lord's 'manifestations' or 'appearings'. The thought of manifestation, either as a noun, adjective or verb, occurs in this passage six times, four of which refer to Christ, two to His future appearing which is treated first (ii. 28–iii. 2) and two to His past appearing (iii. 5 and 8; cf. i. 2). Such, then, is the theme of this paragraph. Unrighteous conduct is unthinkable in the Christian who has grasped the purpose of the two appearings of Christ. The fact of His first appearing and the hope of His second are both strong incentives to holiness.

i. Christ's future appearing (ii. 28–iii. 3). We have already seen that the command, *abide in him*, is probably a repetition of what he wrote at the end of the previous verse. But, whereas there the emphasis was upon abiding in Christ who is acknowledged as the incarnate Son, here the thought is rather of a mystical relationship with Christ which has wholesome moral consequences, so that (*hina*, the purpose of the abiding) *when he shall appear, we* (he includes himself) *may have confidence . . . before him.* There can be no mistaking this reference to our Lord's return. Some commentators on the New Testament have suggested that the vivid expectation of the Parousia in Paul's Epistles has been replaced in the later writings of John by the coming of the Spirit and the present enjoyment of eternal life. Such a theory ignores the teaching on the second coming which occurs in this Epistle or dismisses it as a concession to popular demand, which is a quite unwarrantable assumption. No. The doctrine of the Lord's return was part of the primitive apostolic faith. Four words (in verbal or substantive form) are used by Paul to describe it—His coming (*parousia*), His appearing (*phanerōsis*), His epiphany (*epiphaneia*), and His revelation (*apokalupsis*). Of these John uses the first two in this verse. There is ample evidence in the papyri that at the time in the East 'the word (*parousia*) was the usual expression for the visit of a King or Emperor' (Brooke). *Parousia* means literally 'presence', and the two words together imply that our Lord's return will involve the personal presence of one now absent, the visible appearing of one now unseen.

Men will react to His coming in one of two ways. Some will *have confidence*; others will *be ashamed before him*, or better 'shrink from him in shame' (RSV; Gk. *aischunthōmen ap'autou*). *Confidence* (*parrēsia*) is an interesting word and a favourite with John, nearly half its occurrences in the New Testament coming from his pen. In the AV the noun is translated either 'confidence' or 'boldness', while its adverbial use is rendered 'boldly', 'plainly' or 'freely'. It signifies literally 'outspokenness, frankness, freedom of speech' (Liddell and Scott) and is used to describe the Christian's boldness of approach both to men (as a witness) and to God (as a suppliant). But in this Epistle, as in the Epistle to the Hebrews (iv. 16, x. 19), the word indicates the confidence with which the Christian may draw near to God in prayer now (iii. 21, v. 14), at the *parousia* (ii. 28) and on the Judgment Day (iv. 17). But it is only if we *abide in him* now that we shall have confidence before Him and not shrink from Him on the last day. For a description of the shrinking of unbelievers from the presence of the divine Judge see Matthew xxii. 12 and Revelation vi. 15–17.

29. *Born of him* seems in this context to refer to Christ, but the consistent Johannine terms are to be born 'of God' or 'of the Spirit', and it is 'against the tenor of the New Testament to speak of Christians as "begotten of Christ" ' (Law). We must therefore suppose that there is an abrupt change of person between verses 28 and 29, the *he* and *him* referring in verse 28 to Christ and in verse 29 to God. This would certainly be a better transition to the next chapter. Law takes it thus and devotes a long chapter to the relation between the Johannine statements 'God is righteous' and 'God is love'. If you know as a fact (*eidēte*) that God is righteous, John says, then you will perceive as a logical consequence (*ginōskete*) *that everyone that doeth righteousness is born of him*. The child exhibits the parent's character because he shares the parent's nature. A person's righteousness is thus the evidence of his new birth, not the cause or condition of it. The Gnostics may have called their initiation into *gnōsis* a 'regeneration'; John shows that righteousness, not knowledge, is the mark of the regenerate.

iii. 1. The mention of being 'born of him' leads John to an outburst of wonder at God's love in making us His *sons*, or better 'children' (*tekna*, derived from *tekein*, 'to beget'), the allusion being to the divine nature we have received through being begotten of God rather than to our filial status. *What manner of* (*potapēn*) means originally 'of what country'. It is as if the Father's love is so unearthly, so foreign to this world, that he wonders from what country it may come. The word 'always implies astonishment' (Plummer). This love God has not only 'shown' us, but actually *bestowed upon us*; we have experienced it ourselves. Moreover, 'children of God' is no mere title; it is a fact. RV and RSV correctly add the phrase omitted by AV and not found in some MSS, 'and such we are' (*kai esmen*), not by nature, but by God's grace. And we are such, whatever men may say or think. The 'sons of God' and the 'world' are so different from each other, that in fact, *the world knoweth us not* (cf. 1 Cor. ii. 15, 16). The reason for this is that it *knew him not* which must surely here refer to Christ, as in verse 6. As His glory was veiled in flesh, so our 'life is hid with Christ in God' (Col. iii. 3). Our sonship, though real, is not yet apparent (Rom. viii. 19).

2. The author calls his readers *beloved* because those who are loved by the Father are loved by the apostle also. He then moves on from the reiteration *now are we the sons of God* (whether the world recognizes us or not) to a consideration of *what we shall be*, for 'we look . . . for an inheritance in virtue of that sonship' (Alford). At first he frankly admits that he does not know the precise character of this inheritance. What we are does not now appear to the world; what we shall be does not yet appear to us. It is important to note this apostolic confession of ignorance. His earlier statement that the 'anointing teacheth you of all things' (ii. 27) is not to be pressed literally.

The Christian is not omniscient. The New Testament apostles, like the Old Testament prophets, knew what it had been God's purpose to disclose to them, and no more (cf. Dt. iii. 24; 1 Cor. xiii. 8–12, RSV). So here John confesses that the exact state and condition of the redeemed in heaven had not been revealed to him. This being so, it is idle and sinful to speculate or to pry into things which God has not been pleased to make known. Indeed, it is implied, it will appear only when He shall appear.[1] The two revelations, of Christ and of our final state, will be made simultaneously. Then we shall be 'glorified together' (Rom. viii. 17; cf. Col. iii. 4).

This is, however, not to say that we know nothing about our future state. We do know this, *that, when he shall appear, we shall be like him; for we shall see him as he is.* The order of events is clear. First, He will appear; then, we shall see him as He is; and finally, we shall be like Him. (For references to 'seeing' God or Christ in heaven compare Mt. v. 8; Jn. xvii. 24; 1 Cor. xiii. 12; 2 Cor. v. 7; Heb. xii. 14; 1 Pet. i. 8; Rev. i. 7, xxii. 4.) Already the image of God, marred by the fall, has been stamped upon us again. The new man, which we assumed at our conversion, was 'created after the likeness of God in true righteousness and holiness' (Eph. iv. 24, RSV; cf. Col. iii. 10). And since that day, in fulfilment of God's pre-destinating purpose that we should be 'conformed to the image of his Son' (Rom. viii. 29), the Holy Spirit has been trans-figuring us 'into his likeness from one degree of glory to another' (2 Cor. iii. 18, RSV; cf. 1 Jn. ii. 6). In this latter passage the transformation is said to be due to the fact that we are 'with unveiled face beholding the glory of the Lord'; so it is under-standable that when we see Him as He is, and not our face only but His too is unveiled, we shall be finally and completely like Him, including our bodies (Phil. iii. 21; cf. 1 Cor. xv. 49). 'Vision becomes assimilation' (Law). This is all John knows about our final, heavenly state. Paul concentrates in his Epistles on the truth that in heaven we shall be 'with Christ'

---

[1] NEB ('when it is disclosed') follows RV margin and many commentators in taking as the subject of the verb *phanerothē*, as of the previous *ephanerothē*, not Christ but 'what we shall be'. It could be either. No subject is supplied in the Greek.

(2 Cor. v. 8; Phil. i. 23; Col. iii. 4; 1 Thes. iv. 17; cf. Lk. xxiii. 43; Jn. xiv. 3, xvii. 24). It is enough for us to know that on the last day and through eternity we shall be both with Christ and like Christ; for the fuller revelation of what we shall be we are content to wait.

3. John's reason for writing about the return of Christ and the final state is not theological but ethical. Like Paul he follows our Lord in teaching the practical implications of this glorious expectation. *In him* means 'in Christ', not 'in himself'. So RSV, 'every one who thus hopes in him'. The Christian 'hope' (the word is unique here in John's writings but common in Paul's and Peter's) has as its object or foundation (the preposition is *epi*, 'on', as in Rom. xv. 12; 1 Tim. iv. 10) the return of Christ and the glory which follows. It includes the three events already mentioned—His appearing, our seeing Him, and our becoming like Him. This is not an uncertain hope, like the hopes of men, because it is grounded upon the promise of Christ (cf. Heb. x. 23), and we know (verse 2) the truth for which we hope. Its very certainty adds to its challenge. The Christian who fixes his hope (his confident expectation) upon Christ's return, will purify himself, not ceremonially but morally. Purity (*hagneia*) is primarily 'freedom from moral stain' and so 'that element in holy character which is wrought out by the discipline of temptation' (Law). John has already emphasized that, since Christ is righteous, we must practise righteousness if we do not want to be ashamed at His coming (ii. 28, 29). Similarly, since He is pure, and when we shall see Him we shall be like Him, we must ensure that the process of purification is begun now and begin to purify ourselves. True, only the blood of Christ can cleanse us from the stain and guilt of sin (i. 7), but we have a part to play in purifying ourselves from its power (cf. 2 Cor. vii. 1; 1 Tim. v. 22; Jas. iv. 8; 1 Pet. i. 22).

ii. Christ's past appearing (iii. 4–10). John now proceeds to the second part of his elaboration of the moral test, and this time he links righteousness with Christ's past appearing. His argument for the indispensable necessity of holy living is drawn now, not from the expectation of the Lord's second coming, when we shall see Him and become like Him, but from the purpose of His first coming which was to remove sins and to destroy the works of the devil. The argument is repeated, each time with a different emphasis.

	Verses 4–7	**Verses 8–10**
The introductory phrase:	*whosoever committeth sin* (4)	*He that committeth sin* (8)
The theme	The nature of sin is lawlessness (4)	The origin of sin is the devil (8)
The purpose of Christ's appearing:	*he was manifested to take away our sins* (5)	*the Son of God was manifested, that he might destroy the works of the devil* (8)
The logical conclusion	'No one who abides in him sins' (6, RSV)	'No one born of God commits sin' (9, RSV).

To continue in sin is thus shown to be completely opposed to the whole purpose of Christ's first appearing, which is twice mentioned (5, 8), just as His second appearing has been mentioned twice in the previous section (ii. 28, iii. 2).

I. THE NATURE OF SIN: LAWLESSNESS (iii. 4–7)

4. *Whosoever committeth sin.* John states a universal truth, from which there is no escape and to which there is no exception. This passage (and indeed the whole Epistle) is full of such generalizations, which are directed against the heretics' arrogant assumption that they constituted an initiated *élite* set apart from the rank and file. John will admit no such distinction. A dual standard of morality is quite foreign to the Christian religion. Thus, six times in this section he uses the expression *pas ho*, translated either 'every one that', 'every man that', or 'whosoever' (ii. 29, iii. 4, 6a and b, 9, 10b), and three times the simple relative *ho* is followed by a verb in the present participle, which phrase is translated 'he that' (7, 8, 10c). The gospel, with its moral implications, concerns all men, not just some.

There follows a definition of sin. *Whosoever committeth sin transgresseth also the law: for sin is the transgression of the law (hē anomia*, 'lawlessness'). There are other definitions of sin in the New Testament (e.g. Rom. xiv. 23; Jas. iv. 17; 1 Jn. v. 17); but this, far from being 'somewhat superficial' (Dodd), is the clearest and most revealing. The statement 'sin is lawlessness' (RV, RSV) so identifies the two as to render them interchangeable terms. Wherever one of them is read, it is possible to substitute the other. It is not just that sin manifests itself in disregard for God's law, but that sin is in its very nature lawlessness. Lawlessness is the essence, not the result, of sin. Thus exposed in its ugly reality, the seriousness of sin emerges. The heretics seem to have taught that to the enlightened Christian questions of morality were a matter of indifference, just as today the truth about sin is concealed by euphemisms, and our sins become mere 'peccadilloes', 'temperamental weaknesses' or 'personality problems'. In contrast to such underestimates of sin, John declares that it is not just a negative failure (*hamartia*, sin, means literally 'missing the mark' and *adikia*, unrighteousness, a departure from what is right or just), but essentially an active rebellion against God's will and a violation of His holy law. It is important to acknowledge this, because the first step towards holy living is to recognize the true nature and wickedness of sin.

5. John appeals many times to the knowledge his readers already possess and urges them to conform their lives to it. In this case the knowledge to which he refers concerns not the nature of sin but the truth about Christ's Person and work. He implies that if they have a right view of these, they will abhor evil. *He (ekeinos*, emphatic, meaning Christ) *was manifested* ('appeared') *to take away our sins; and in him is no sin.* Here Christ's work in the removal of man's sins and the sinlessness of His own Person are wonderfully brought together. He came into the world to take them away (*arē*; the same word occurs in the Baptist's recognition of the Lamb of God, Jn. i. 29; cf. also Heb. ix. 26). Other parts of the New Testament explain that He did this by taking them upon Himself, bearing them in His own body (1 Pet. ii. 24; Heb. ix. 28; cf. Is. liii. 11, 12). And in removing man's sins, He was Himself without sin. The sinlessness of Jesus is commonly mentioned in Scripture almost as an aside, in connection with His work of salvation (e.g. 2 Cor. v. 21; Heb. vii. 26; 1 Pet. i. 19, ii. 22). John stresses it much, stating it both positively, 'he is righteous', 'he is pure' (ii. 29, iii. 3, 7) and negatively, 'in him is no sin'. In each case he uses the verb 'is' (*estin*), for the sinlessness of Christ belongs neither to His pre-existence, nor to the days of His flesh, nor to His present heavenly condition, but to His essential and eternal nature.

6. The logical deduction follows. If the eternal nature of Jesus is sinless and if the purpose of His historical appearing was to remove sin, then *whosoever abideth in him sinneth not*, while, on the other hand, *whosoever sinneth hath not seen him, neither known him*. It is typical of John's method that he should drive the truth home by this double hammerblow about sinning and not sinning. Since there is in Him no sin, it is obvious that if we abide in Him we shall not sin either. If we do sin, it shows not only that we are not abiding in Him (present tense) but that we have *not seen him* (cf. 3 Jn. 11) or *known him*, that is never really come to know or see Him (perfect tenses). Not until He appears in glory shall we 'see him as he is' (verse 2); yet every Christian has seen Him with the eye of faith. And the sight of Christ, both in present experience and in future prospect, is a strong incentive to holiness. These verses teach the utter incongruity of sin in the Christian. To see and to know Christ, the sinless Saviour of sinners, is to outlaw sin; to sin is to deny Christ and to reveal that one is not abiding in Him. Sin and Christ are irreconcilably at enmity with each other. Christ in His sinless Person and saving work is fundamentally opposed to it.

7. The first part of the exposition of this theme ends with a solemn warning to his *little children*. 'The tenderness of the address is called out by the peril of the situation' (Westcott). *Let no man deceive you.* The false teachers, tools of Satan, the arch-deceivers, were seeking to lead them astray, not only theologically (ii. 26) but morally as well. Let them be on their guard. *He that doeth righteousness is righteous, even as he is righteous.* The heretics appear to have indulged in the subtly perverse reasoning that somehow you could 'be' righteous without necessarily bothering to 'practise' righteousness. John roundly denies the possibility. The only person who is righteous in himself is he who does right like Jesus (*he,* the emphatic pronoun *ekeinos* again), who is righteous, as has already been stated several times (ii. 1, 29; cf. iii. 3, 5). 'Doing is the test of Being' (Law).

II. THE ORIGIN OF SIN: THE DEVIL (iii. 8–10)

John follows the same pattern in the second exposition of his argument from Christ's first appearing. He again begins with a reference to the seriousness of sin; continues with the purpose of Christ's mission on earth; and concludes with a deduction about holiness. But this time his emphasis is rather on the origin, than on the nature, of sin, and he insists that for the Christian its practice is not merely incompatible, but impossible (9).

8. *He that committeth sin is of the devil.* This second generalization links sin not with the law of God, which it breaks (5), but with the devil in whom it originates. He *sinneth from the beginning* (cf. Jn. viii. 44), meaning, presumably, from the moment of his proud rebellion against God, from the beginning of his devilish career. Since sin is his characteristic activity (*sinneth, hamartanei,* is in the present continuous tense), everyone who sins exhibits a character which must have been derived, at least ultimately, from him. The existence and malevolence of the devil are everywhere assumed in the Johannine literature.[1]

If the characteristic work of the devil is to sin, the character-

[1] See Additional Note on John's teaching about the devil, p. 136.

istic work of the Son of God is to save. *For this purpose the Son of God was manifested* ('appeared', *ephanerōthē* again, as in verse 5), *that he might destroy the works of the devil.* These are many and evil. They include all those things which he has insinuated into the perfect creation of God, to spoil it. Morally, his work is enticement to sin; physically, the infliction of disease; intellectually, seduction into error. He still assaults man's soul, body and mind in these three ways; and Christ came to destroy his works. The destruction was a 'loosing' (*lusē*), as if these diabolical works were chains which bound us. Of course we know from experience that they are not in an absolute sense 'destroyed' (cf. Rom. vi. 6; 2 Tim. i. 10; Heb. ii. 14 where the verb *katargeō* evidently does not mean to liquidate or to annihilate, but to negative, to deprive of force, to render inoperative, to conquer and to overthrow). The devil is still busy doing his wicked works, but he has been defeated and in Christ we can escape from his tyranny.

If, then, the whole purpose of Christ's first appearing was to remove sins and to undo the works of the devil, Christians must not compromise with either sin or the devil, or they will find themselves fighting against Christ. If the first step to holiness is to recognize the sinfulness of sin, both in its essence as lawlessness and in its diabolical origin, the second step is to see its absolute incompatibility with Christ in His sinless Person and saving work. The more clearly we grasp these facts, the more incongruous will sin appear and the more determined we shall be to be rid of it.

9. John again draws a logical conclusion. He makes two searching statements of fact. The first states that the Christian *doth not* sin, and the second that he *cannot*. These expressions have sometimes been taken as teaching that a true Christian, one who has been *born of God*, is constitutionally incapable of sinning. But such an interpretation cannot be maintained unless we are to suppose that John contradicts himself within this Epistle. In i. 8, 10 he has declared that those who deny that they are sinners by nature and by practice deceive themselves and make God a liar; and in ii. 1, though stating that he is writing 'that ye sin not', he explicitly added that 'if any man sin' (evidently a possibility to be considered), gracious provision has been made for his forgiveness. It is plain, therefore, that John is not denying the possibility of sin in the Christian. But he is not asserting its impossibility either. The first way to reconcile the teaching of John in chapters i and iii is to recognize that in each he is opposing a different error. Gnosticism led its adherents to different conclusions. Some supposed that their possession of *gnōsis* had made them perfect; others maintained that sin did not matter because it could not harm those who had been enlightened. Both positions are morally perverse. The first is blind to sin and denies its existence; the second is indifferent to sin and denies its gravity. To the first John declares the universality of sin, even in the Christian; to deny sin is to be a liar. To the second John declares the incompatibility of sin in the Christian; to commit sin is to be *of the devil*. It is in order to confound these particular views of his opponents that John states the Christian position in such categorical terms.

What, then, does he mean in verse 9 when he writes that a Christian does not and cannot sin? An examination of his expressions will tell us. He uses three. First, he says that the Christian who abides in Christ 'sinneth not' (6a and v. 18, *hamartanei*); this is a present tense, indicating a settled character like that of 'the devil' who 'sinneth from the beginning' (8). Cf. *hamartanōn*, a present participle, in 6b, whereas the verbs in ii. 1 are both aorists. The second statement is that he who has been born of God 'doth not commit sin' (*hamartian ou poiei*, 9a). Again, it is not the isolated act of sin which is envisaged, but the settled habit of it, indicated by the verb *poiein*, to do or to practise, which is used of 'doing' sin in 4a, 8 and 9, of 'doing' lawlessness in 4b, and of 'doing' righteousness in ii. 29, iii. 7 and 10a. The third expression is that the Christian 'cannot sin' (*ou dunatai hamartanein*, 9), 'he is not able to sin', where 'to sin' is a present, not an aorist, infinitive. If the infinitive had been an aorist it would have meant 'he is not able to commit a sin'; the present infinitive, however, signifies 'he is not able to sin habitually'. In this whole section

John is arguing rather the incongruity than the impossibility of sin in the Christian. If even isolated sins are so incongruous, what is utterly impossible is persistence in sin, 'a character, a prevailing habit, and not primarily an act' (Westcott).

Wherein lies this 'impossibility'? John's answer is given in two phrases: *for his seed remaineth in him* and *because he is born of God*. *His seed* could be a collective noun for the children of God (cf. Jn. viii. 33; Gal. iii. 29), and *in him* could mean 'in God'. The whole phrase would then be translated 'the offspring of God abide in him, and they cannot sin because they are born of God' (RSV margin and cf. Moffatt. The sense is parallel to verse 6). It is more probable, however, that *his seed* is accurately rendered in the RSV text 'God's nature', or 'the divine seed' (NEB), and that *in him* refers to the child of God. In this way the two parts of verse 10 become exactly parallel, each part consisting of a statement that the Christian does not or cannot sin, to which is added the reason for such an assertion. The implication will then be this: the new birth involves the acquisition of a new nature through the implanting within us of the very seed or lifegiving power of God. Birth of God is a deep, radical, inward transformation. Moreover, the new nature received at the new birth remains. It exerts a strong internal pressure towards holiness. It is the abiding influence of *his seed* within everyone who is *born of God*, which enables John to affirm without fear of contradiction that *he cannot* go on living in *sin* (cf. 2 Cor. v. 17; 2 Pet. i. 4). Indeed, if he should thus continue in sin, it would indicate that he has never been born again. It was this conviction which enabled John to assert that the heretics, who not only persisted in sin but had seceded from the Christian fellowship altogether, were not true Christians at all (ii. 19).[1]

10. This verse is at the same time a summary and conclusion of what has gone before and a transition to what follows. John has spoken twice of Christ's first appearing (iii. 5, 8) and twice of His second which is yet to come (ii. 28 and iii. 2); but he speaks twice in this passage also of the appearing

[1] See pp. 129 ff. for Additional Notes on 'his seed' and on the whole interpretation of verses 4-9.

or manifestation of men. It does not yet appear what we shall be in our final state, he has said (2), but it already appears what we are, whether we are *children of God* or *of the devil*. The difference is apparent to the discerning, and John's purpose is to supply the test by which the two groups are recognized. And there are only two groups. There are not three. Nor is there only one. This 'very plain black-and-white' is not only true in itself, but, according to C. H. Dodd, also necessary because 'sophistry can as easily prove that evil is an aspect of good as that error is an aspect of truth. But truth and false-hood, good and evil, right and wrong, God and the devil are irreconcilable opposites'. Our parentage is either divine or diabolical. The universal fatherhood of God is not taught in the Bible, except in the vague, physical sense that God is the Creator of all (Acts xvii. 28). But in the intimate, spiritual sense God is not the Father of all men, and all men are not His children. Indeed, John here is only echoing what Jesus once said to certain unbelieving Jews: 'Ye are of your father, the devil' (Jn. viii. 44; cf. Mt. xiii. 38; Acts xiii. 10).

The way to become a child of God is, on the human side, by believing on or receiving Christ, and on the divine side, by new birth (Jn. i. 12, 13). Meanwhile God's children (9) and the devil's (8) may be recognized by their moral behaviour. 'By their fruits ye shall know them' (Mt. vii. 20). He now writes negatively, with the sinful and unloving heretics in his mind: *whosoever doeth not righteousness is not of God, neither he that loveth not his brother.* The lack of righteousness and love proves the lack of a divine birth. Not that righteousness and love are entirely distinct. John adds the second phrase almost as an interpretation of the first. 'Love is righteousness in relation to others' (Plummer). The mention of love introduces the subject of the next paragraph.

We are in a position now to look back over the foregoing twelve verses (ii. 28–iii. 10), in which the moral test has been elaborated, and feel the compulsion of its argument. If Christ appeared first both 'to take away our sins' and to 'destroy the works of the devil', and if, when He appears a second time, 'we shall see him' and, in consequence, 'we shall be like him', how can we go on living in sin? To do so is to deny the purpose of His two appearings. If we would be loyal to His first coming and ready for His second, we must purify ourselves, as He is pure. By so doing we shall give evidence of our birth of God.

Additional Note: The meaning of 'his seed' (iii. 9)

C. H. Dodd (p. 76) gives a series of quotations from Hermetic tractates, Philo and Gnostic writings in which reference is made to the implantation of a divine 'seed' in man. In some of these the divine principle is in all men; in others it is planted into good souls only. In either case salvation was thought to consist of the liberation or redemption of this seed which was already imprisoned within them. It is possible that the heretics of John's day taught a similar doctrine about a divine element immanent in man; that they called it *sperma Theou*, God's seed; and that John deliberately borrowed the expression from their vocabulary (as he may have borrowed *chrisma* in ii. 20, 27, q.v.). If so, it is not necessary to suppose that he endorsed their theology. This should be clear from three questions. First, who is it in whom 'his seed remaineth' (rsv 'abides')? If the heretics were teaching that the divine principle is already resident by nature either in all men or in 'good souls' (Valentinus), John's position is rather that it is implanted into some by grace and that those who receive it are thereby 'born of God'. Secondly, what is the effect of the implantation of the divine principle? John insists in this passage that the reception of the divine *sperma* causes a new birth which asserts itself against sin and manifests itself in righteous conduct. Thirdly, what is the character of this *sperma*? In other New Testament passages the word of God is pictured as 'seed' (1 Pet. i. 23, 25; Jas. i. 18, 23; cf. Lk. viii. 11). Is John's use of 'seed' a reference to the gospel also? Such was the view of Augustine, adopted by Bede, Luther, Alford (who emphasizes Jn. v. 38 as the 'key' to this interpretation) and others, and, more recently, by C. H. Dodd. William Barclay favours it also. C. H. Dodd concludes that 'there is . . . a fairly well established association of the ideas "seed" and "word" ', and that 'when our author speaks of divine "seed" he is thinking of the Word of God, or the Gospel'. Certainly the concept of the seed 'remaining in' Christians is reminiscent of ii. 24, where what remains in them is 'what you heard from the beginning'. Since C. H. Dodd regards ii. 24 as referring to the *chrisma*, he thinks the *sperma* is identical with it, both being the gospel, the former initiating into knowledge, the latter 'producing in men the regenerate nature which does not sin'. Findlay makes the same identification between *chrisma* and *sperma* but regards them both as allusions to the Holy Spirit, who is the author of truth and holiness. That *sperma*, like *chrisma*, refers to the Holy Spirit is not impossible, since the new birth is clearly in the Fourth Gospel a birth 'of the Spirit' (Jn. iii. 6, 8). We shall probably never know for certain precisely what John intended, or his readers understood, by *sperma autou*. But whether the implanted and abiding seed is the word of the gospel, or the Holy Spirit, or the divine nature thus imparted (cf. 2 Pet. i. 4), John's meaning is the same, namely that it is the Christian's supernatural birth from God which keeps him from sinning.

Additional Note: The interpretation of 1 John iii. 4-9

The difficulty which commentators have experienced in interpreting this paragraph is evidenced in the variety of explanations which have been offered. It is important that subjective considerations should not influence us. The criterion of interpretation is what John intended to teach, not whether this coincides with our experience of holiness. We agree with Alford, therefore, that 'the plain words of the Apostle must be held fast' and must not 'be tamed down' to suit our convenience.

If, as we have argued in the commentary on these verses, John is not teaching that the Christian is impeccable, or that the condition of everyone who has been born of God is one of sinless perfection (cf. i. 8, 10, ii. 1, iii. 3), what does he mean when he asserts that the Christian does not and even 'cannot' sin? Seven answers appear to have been given to this question.

1. Some have tried to narrow the definition of 'sin' in this passage and to restrict the sins which the Christian 'cannot' do to notorious crimes, or offences against love (so Augustine, Bede and Luther, interpreting 'righteousness' as 'love' from verse 10), or 'mortal' as opposed to 'venial' sins (Roman Catholic commentators). This is certainly special pleading. No such limitations are in John's mind. On the contrary, he begins by defining sin as 'lawlessness'. The references to 'sin' in this passage are general, not specific.

2. Others have attempted to argue that the Christian 'cannot' sin because what is sin in the life of an unbeliever is not so regarded by God in a believer. It is inconceivable that such a preposterous idea even occurred to John's mind. 'Sin is lawlessness', whoever commits it. Besides, this double standard or view of morality was just the kind of subtle argument which the heretics were using to justify their continuance in sin. John is clear that 'every one who commits sin is guilty of lawlessness' (iii. 4, RSV), whether he be Christian or non-Christian.

3. Others have drawn a distinction not between the believer and the unbeliever, but between the old and the new natures of the believer. The old nature may continue to sin; it is the new nature which 'cannot', they argue. 'It is literally true of the Divine nature imparted to the believer. That does not sin and cannot sin' (Plummer). But, apart from the fact that such an argument would play into the hands of the heretics John is opposing, it is very doubtful if we can find biblical warrant for thus isolating a man's 'natures' from his 'person'. Our two natures can be separated in their desires and promptings, but not in their activities. The 'lust of the flesh' and 'the lust of the Spirit' are contrasted in Galatians v. 17, and it is stated that they are at variance with each other; but when Paul goes on to catalogue the 'works of the flesh' and the 'fruit of the Spirit' what he is envisaging is the activities not of two 'natures' but of a 'person', dominated now by the flesh and now by the Spirit. The practical relevance of this should be clear. We can distinguish between our different desires within ourselves, attributing some to the flesh and some to the Spirit. But we

cannot ascribe an act to one of our two natures *in such a way as to distinguish ourselves from it*. We cannot say of a sin: 'my old nature did it; I did not'. What either of my natures prompts me to do, *I* do, and I cannot relieve myself of the responsibility for it. It is true that in Romans vii. 17 Paul says 'it is no more I that do it, but sin that dwelleth in me'. Nevertheless, his purpose in that context is not to deny that he is himself acting sinfully, but to explain why his behaviour conflicts with his will. So throughout this paragraph it is a person who sins or does not sin, not one of his natures. The subject of the verbs 'to sin' and 'not to sin' is in each case 'he', a person, not 'it', a nature. This is particularly clear in verse 9, where John does not write 'his seed remaineth in him; and *it* cannot sin', but 'his seed remaineth in him: and *he* cannot sin'. There can be no doubt that this is the correct translation, since John goes on 'because *he* is born of God'. It is not the 'seed' which is born of God but the 'person', through the implantation of the seed; and it is, therefore, the 'person' in whom the seed remains who 'cannot sin'.

4. A more popular interpretation of this paragraph has been the suggestion that what John is here describing is not a reality, but the ideal. Alford follows the German commentator Düsterdieck (on whom he depends a great deal in his exposition of this Epistle) in adopting this view. John speaks throughout the Epistle, he asserts, 'of the ideal reality of the life of God and the life of sin as absolutely excluding one another'. So too Westcott, 'the ideas of divine sonship and sin are mutually exclusive'. C. H. Dodd and William Barclay both mention this view as a possibility, and, in support of it, quote the description of life in the new age from Enoch v. 8: 'they will all live and never again sin, either through heedlessness or through pride'. The argument seems to be this: it was anticipated that sinlessness would be a characteristic of the age to come, and since John believed that the age to come had come (ii. 8), he naturally asserted the sinlessness of Christians! I find this very unsatisfying. John was writing in a time of crisis. The situation he was addressing was one of harsh reality; it would be no good if he resorted only to 'ideas' and 'ideals'. The

Gnostics made concrete claims, and John was outspoken in contradicting them and calling them lies. In doing so, he also made counter-claims. Are we to imagine that these were 'ideals' which his opponents could have dismissed as untrue, unpractical and unattainable? Besides, John did not write as an idealist that, ideally speaking, the Christian 'should not' sin. His language was that of the realist. He stated categorically that the Christian 'does not', and indeed 'cannot', sin.

Law, who rejects the idealistic interpretation, nevertheless proposes a somewhat similar solution. He emphasizes that John was not writing with the calm of a theologian, but 'in view of a definite controversial situation and in a vehemently controversial strain'. He was opposing those who turned Christian liberty into licence. So he used absolute assertions, 'suffused with holy passion', 'unqualified contradictions of tenets of unqualified falsity'. In doing so his expressions were coloured by 'apparent exaggeration and over-emphasis' and are only 'theoretically . . . true'. But what is the difference between 'ideal' and 'theoretical' statements? We must insist that John sought to overthrow the false theories of the heretics not with alternative 'theories', however true, but with facts.

5. Those who hold that John was expressing an 'ideal' mostly go on to assert that it was nevertheless a relatively realistic ideal. Thus, Alford quotes Düsterdieck as writing, 'None . . . of all the expositors, who in any way has recognized the ideal character of St. John's view, has overlooked the fact, that even in the actual life of all that are born of God there is something which in full verity answers to the ideal words "they cannot sin" . . . they sin not, and they cannot sin, just in proportion as the new divine life, unconditionally opposed to all sin . . . is present and abides in them'. Commentators who pursue this explanation tend to concentrate on verse 6: ('no one who abides in him sins', RSV) and to interpret this abiding in Christ, not as a description of all Christians, but as a condition which some Christians fulfil. The degree of the Christian's holiness then varies in proportion to his abiding in Christ. 'In quantum in ipso manet, in tantum non peccat' (Augustine, Bede). Hence the command 'abide in him' (ii. 28).

If the command is disobeyed, the Christian sins: if it is obeyed, he does not sin.

This is quite true. It is clearly taught by our Lord in His allegory of the vine and the branches (Jn. xv. 1 ff.). The fruitfulness of the branches depends on their abiding in the vine. But this interpretation cannot be said to exhaust the meaning of this paragraph. It may be a legitimate exposition of verse 6; it is not of verse 9. There are two differences between the verses. In verse 6 it is stated that the Christian 'sinneth not'; in verse 9 it is said that 'he cannot sin'. Secondly, the Christian's conquest of sin is attributed in verse 6 to his present abiding in Christ, but in verse 9 to his past birth of God, as a result of which, God's seed 'abides' in him. And the 'abiding' of God's seed in us is as constant and invariable as our abiding in Christ may be inconstant and variable. In a word, the statement he 'does not' sin (verse 6) may be conditional, depending on 'he who abides in Christ'; the statement he 'cannot sin' (9) is absolute, since it depends on 'because he is born of God'.

6. Ebrard interprets the sin which a regenerate Christian 'cannot' do as wilful and deliberate sin. 'To the truly regenerate man', he writes, 'it is altogether impossible willingly and wilfully to do that which he knows to be forbidden by God.' He concedes that a Christian may be ensnared by sin, but sin 'is contrary to the bent of his will', 'he cannot love, and cherish, and entertain sin' or sin in such a way as 'knowingly and willingly to act contrary to the will of God'. From these quotations it will be seen that Ebrard emphasizes the Christian's knowledge (or conscience) and will, and affirms that the Christian does not and cannot violate either. As in Romans vii. 20 'a Christian does not *do* sin, he suffers it' (Besser, quoted by Law). Calvin writes similarly, 'they are said not to sin because . . . they do not consent to sin, but in fact struggle and groan, so that they can truly testify with Paul that they do the evil they would not'. Candlish is right to ask 'was it true of David?' Indeed, are there not many examples of God's people in the Bible who have sinned knowingly and wilfully? Christian biographies would endorse this. 'I dare not persuade

myself that I never sin voluntarily' (Candlish). More important, can it be shown that this is what John meant? I think not. All sin, he says, is 'lawlessness', a breach of the laws of God. He draws no distinction between voluntary and involuntary, knowing and unknowing, lawlessness.

7. The seventh interpretation is that the sin a Christian 'does not' and 'cannot' do is habitual and persistent sin. He may sin sometimes, even with the consent of the mind and the will, but he is overwhelmed by grief and repentance afterwards (Ps. li). And the whole direction of his life is towards God and holiness. His mind is set on the Spirit (Rom. viii. 6) and on the things above (Col. iii. 2), not on earthly things (Phil. iii. 19). His eyes are ever towards the Lord (Ps. xxv. 15), whom he sets always before him (Ps. xvi. 8). His eyes are fixed upon all God's commandments (Ps. cxix. 6, RSV); his heart is fixed also (Ps. lvii. 7). 'Although the believer sometimes sins, yet not sin, but opposition to sin, is the ruling principle of his life' (Plummer). His whole life is one of 'truceless antagonism to sin' (Law). The 'seed' within the believer's spirit 'fills it with an irreconcilable hate against every sin, and urges it to an unceasing conflict against all unrighteousness' (Alford). It is not that Christians are 'wholly free from all vice' but that they 'heartily strive to form their lives in obedience to God' (Calvin). 'Sin does not reign in them', for the Spirit 'does not let it flourish' (Calvin).

That this is what John meant is evident from his use o tenses, as has been shown in the commentary on verse 9. This is surely not 'a grammatical subtlety' (Dodd, Alexander), but one which his readers will have readily grasped. 'The present tense in the Greek verb implied habit, continuity, unbroken sequence', writes E. M. Blaiklock, who renders John's expression: 'does not continue in sin' (6), 'does not practise sin' and 'cannot continue sinning' (9).

Turning back to John's own words (1 Jn. iii. 4–9), it may be helpful to summarize the sequence of his argument. The paragraph is in two symmetrical sections (verses 4–7 and 8, 9). Each begins with a statement of the gravity of sin (its nature 'lawlessness', verse 4; its origin diabolical, verse 8); continues with a reference to the purpose of Christ's appearing ('to take away sins', verse 5; 'to destroy the works of the devil', verse 8); and concludes with a moral deduction, first concerning the incompatibility of sin ('sinneth not', verse 6) and secondly concerning its impossibility ('cannot sin', verse 9).

The argument concerning the incompatibility of sin with the Christian is theological. It is based on the doctrine of Christ's saving work. Sin is lawlessness, but Christ (in whom is no sin) appeared to remove sins. His nature is without sin and His mission was against sin. 'You know this', John says (5). Therefore, of course everyone who abides in Christ does not sin. The two are incompatible. To continue in sin is to supply clear evidence that we have never seen or known Christ. If we have seen and known Christ, we have seen and known Him as the sinless taker away of sins; how then can we tolerate sin in our lives and still claim to have seen and known Him? In verse 8 the theme begins in the same way. Christ appeared to destroy the works of the devil. He came to undo the devil's work; to sin is to undo the Saviour's work. Again, sin and Christ are shown to be incompatible, and therefore sin and the Christian are incompatible also. 'The whole passage is a keen, concise demonstration of the inadmissibility of sin' (Findlay).

But the Christian has not just 'seen and known' Christ as the sinless Saviour of sinners; he has been born of God. His theology (the doctrine of Christ) makes persistent sin incompatible; his experience (birth of God) makes it impossible. The divine nature within the regenerate believer asserts itself against all evil. It is impossible for him to make a practice of sin. 'We are children of God, and sin is abnormal and unnatural to us' (Dodd). 'The believer may fall into sin, but he will not walk in it' (Smith).

Additional Note: John's teaching about the devil (iii. 8, 10)

1. *His origin.* According to John viii. 44 he 'abode not in the truth'. This seems to indicate a fall from the truth in which he

once 'stood' (RV), in which case the following clause, 'because there is no truth in him', indicates not why he fell, but how we know that he fell. The explanation of his present lack of truth is that he fell from the truth long ago. For a similar use of *hoti* see Luke vii. 47. Twice the expression 'from the beginning' (*ap' archēs*) is used of the devil (Jn. viii. 44; 1 Jn. iii. 8). If we are right to interpret the clause 'abode not in the truth' as referring to his fall from the condition in which he was created, then his murderous and evil activity must be dated from the 'beginning', not of his existence, but of his fallen career. 'He is the aboriginal sinner; and what he became he still is' (Law).

2. *His activity* is constantly malevolent because he is by nature 'the wicked one'. This title was used by our Lord (e.g. Mt. vi. 13) and six times by John (Jn. xvii. 15; 1 Jn. ii. 13, 14, iii. 12, v. 18, 19). The devil's evil work belongs particularly to three spheres, in which are seen his complete lack of righteousness, love and truth, and which correspond to the three tests which John applies in his First Epistle. First, he 'sinneth' (1 Jn. iii. 8) and tempts others into sin (cf. Mt. vi. 13). He is, in fact, so certainly the origin of all sin that it may be said: 'he that committeth sin is of the devil' (1 Jn. iii. 8). Secondly, he is 'a murderer' (Jn. viii. 44). Thus Cain, in killing his brother Abel, gave evidence of his diabolical origin (1 Jn. iii. 12). So did the Jews who sought to kill Jesus (Jn. viii. 40, 41). Foiled in his assault upon Jesus, the devil now persecutes the Church (Rev. xii. 4–6, 13–17). He is called 'the destroyer' (Rev. ix. 11; cf. Heb. ii. 14). Thirdly, the devil is 'a liar, and the father of it' (Jn. viii. 44). This is due to the fact we have already noted that he fell from the truth and 'there is no truth in him'. Consequently, he both accuses the brethren (Rev. xii. 10), being their adversary (the meaning of the Hebrew word *Satan*) and a slanderer (the meaning of the Greek word *diabolos*), and seeks to deceive them into error by the lies of false prophets (cf. 1 Jn. ii. 21, 22, iv. 2).

3. *His power* is considerable, as is plain from his widespread, malicious activity. It is not just that he is able to insinuate evil thoughts and designs into the minds of men (Jn. xiii. 2; cf.

Lk. xxii. 3; Mt. viii. 33) and even enter into them himself personally (Jn. xiii. 27), but that 'he that is in the world' (1 Jn. iv. 4) is 'the prince (lit. "ruler", *archōn*) of this world' (Jn. xii. 31, xiv. 30, xvi. 11; cf. 2 Cor. iv. 4; Eph. vi. 12). He rules from a 'throne' (Rev. ii. 13), and his dominion is so extensive that 'the whole world is in the power of the evil one' (1 Jn. v. 19, RSV). Indeed, men are said to be not only *in*, but *of*, the devil. He is their 'father' and they his 'children' (Jn. viii. 44; 1 Jn. iii. 10). Phrases such as these express the real and terrible influence which the evil one has over men's lives, so that they are motivated by and succumb to his desires (Jn. viii. 44; cf. 2 Tim. ii. 26). Their will is to do his will.

4. *His overthrow* began with the arrival of the Son of God in whom the devil had 'nothing' (Jn. xiv. 30, AV), that is over whom he had no power (RSV). The express purpose of His appearing was to 'destroy the works of the devil' (1 Jn. iii. 8). This He accomplished supremely by His death and resurrection. The emphatic repetition of 'now' in relation to the judgment of this world and the casting out of its ruler (Jn. xii. 31) refers in the context to the hour of the Son of man's glorification (verses 23, 27). In anticipation of this hour Jesus could say both that the ruler of this world 'has been judged' (Jn. xvi. 11, translating *kekritai*, perfect tense) and that as a result He would draw all men to Himself (Jn. xii. 32). It may be to this preliminary downfall that the binding of Satan refers (Rev. xx. 1 ff.; cf. Mk. iii. 27). So far, however, his overthrow has been a dethronement rather than a decisive destruction. His final defeat will not take place until the last day (Rev. xx. 10). Meanwhile, it is possible for the Father to 'keep' from the evil one those whom He has taken out of the world. So Jesus prayed (Jn. xvii. 15), and John affirms that, because those who are born of God are 'kept' (the verb is *tērein* again) by the only begotten of God, the evil one does not even 'touch' them (1 Jn. v. 18). It is, of course, by this power of Christ and by the Word of God that the young men can be said to 'have overcome the wicked one' (1 Jn. ii. 13, 14; cf. iv. 4).

b. An elaboration of the social test: love (iii. 11–18)
The last phrase of the previous section has prepared us for the change of subject from righteousness to love. In ii. 7–11 John has briefly outlined his social test of the true Christian, namely that to love is the new commandment (which is yet old) and belongs to the new age in which the true light is already shining. As he now fills in his preliminary sketch, he uses no colours but black and white. He continues the stark contrast he has already pointed in verse 10 between the children of God and the children of the devil, and writes of hatred and love, life and death, murder and self-sacrifice. After reminding his readers that the duty of reciprocal love is the original message they had heard (11), the first part of this paragraph concerns the hatred of Cain, the prototype of the world (12, 13), while the second describes the love of Christ, which should also be seen in the Church (14–18).

11. The heretics were boasting about their new teaching; John's appeal here, as in i. 5, is to a primitive authority which was also public knowledge in contrast to the private and secret enlightenment which the false teachers claimed. His readers will be safe if they hold fast to the message which they *heard*, and that publicly and openly, *from the beginning*. This was exactly John's concern when treating the theological error of the followers of Cerinthus. 'Let that . . . abide in you', he wrote, 'which ye have heard from the beginning' (ii. 24). Now that he is expounding ethical rather than doctrinal truth, his appeal is the same. See also ii. 7. The gospel does not change. The truth about the Person of Christ and about Christian conduct is unalterable. In both doctrine and ethics we must go right back to *the beginning* and enquire what the apostles originally taught and their first converts both *had* (ii. 7, *eichete*, aorist) and *heard* (ii. 24 and iii. 11, *ēkousate*, another aorist). The *message* was *that we should love one another* (cf. iii. 23, iv. 7, 11, 12; 2 Jn. 5; Jn. xiii. 34, xv. 12, 17).

i. The hatred of Cain, and of the world (iii. 12, 13). With this mutual love which is commanded us, John immediately contrasts the behaviour of *Cain*. His hatred originated in the devil, *that wicked one,* and issued in murder, indeed in an act of brutal slaughter *(esphaxen, slew,* would mean literally 'cut his throat' and is rendered by Law 'butchered'). It is not only sin in general which is 'of the devil' (8), but hatred and murder in particular, for as Jesus had said, 'the devil . . . was a murderer from the beginning' (Jn. viii. 44). And what was the cause of Cain's murder of Abel? John asks. It was not because Abel was wicked, but the reverse: *because his own works were evil, and his brother's righteous.* Jealousy lay behind his hatred, not the jealousy which covets another's superior gifts but that which resents another's superior righteousness, the 'envy' which made the Jewish priests demand the death of Jesus. Jealousy-hatred-murder is a natural and terrible sequence.[1]

13. Cain was the prototype of *the world,* which manifests today the ugly qualities he first displayed. The 'world' is Cain's posterity; so we are not to *marvel* if the world hates us.[2] It is only to be expected that the wicked should continue to regard and treat the righteous as Cain regarded and treated his righteous brother Abel. Jesus warned us that it would be so (e.g. Jn. xv. 18, 19, 25, xvi. 1ff., xvii. 14), and by its hatred the world is simply giving evidence of its true spiritual condition, which is 'death' (14). A similar instruction not to be surprised by the opposition and persecution of the world is given in 1 Peter iv. 12 ff.

ii. The love of Christ, and of the Church (iii. 14–18). It is a relief to turn from John's exposition of the world's hatred

---

[1] The Genesis story of Cain and Abel (Gn. iv. 1–8) does not tell us explicitly why Abel's sacrifice of the firstlings of his flock was acceptable to God, while Cain's offering of the fruit of the ground was not. It is, however, implied that Cain had no ground for complaint (verse 6); if he had done 'well', his sacrifice also would have been accepted (verse 7). According to Heb. xi. 4 it was 'by faith' that 'Abel offered unto God a more excellent sacrifice than Cain', and since faith is always a response to God's word of promise and command, we may assume that God had revealed His will to the two brothers. By faith Abel obeyed; indeed, his 'righteousness' consisted of his believing obedience. Cain, on the other hand, was wilfully disobedient, as is indicated in Jude 11. His murder of Abel exemplified the violent antipathy which righteousness always provokes in the unrighteous (cf. Jn. iii. 19, 20).

[2] See Additional Note on the meaning of 'the world', p. 101.

to his teaching about the love which should be manifest in the
Church. He writes first of the evidence of love, what it proves,
namely life (14, 15), and then of the essence of love, what it is,
namely self-sacrifice, whether in Christ or in His people
(16–18).

14. This verse begins dramatically in the Greek with the
pronoun *we* (*hēmeis*). Let the world hate; *we* do not hate, but
love. Moreover, the fact that *we love the brethren* gives us a good
ground for certainty that we possess eternal life. John associates
himself with his readers in this glorious affirmation. *We know*
(*oidamen*, 'we know as a fact') *that we have passed* (NEB 'crossed
over') *from death unto life*. Becoming a Christian is nothing less
than a resurrection or quickening 'out of' (*ek*) spiritual death
'into' (*eis*) eternal life (cf. Jn. v. 24). Great stress is laid in the
New Testament on love as the pre-eminent Christian virtue,
the first-fruit of the Spirit (Gal. v. 22), the sign of the reality of
faith (Gal. v. 6) and the greatest of the three abiding Christian
graces, which never ends and without which we are 'nothing'
(1 Cor. xiii. 2, 8, 13). Love is the surest test of having life, as
it has already been shown to be the test of being in the light
(ii. 10). The contrary is also true: *he that loveth not his brother
abideth in death*, just as he is 'in darkness' (ii. 9, 11). In the
vocabulary of John love, light and life belong together, as do
hatred, darkness and death. It is noteworthy, however, that
the precise proof of life which he gives is that *we love the
brethren*, just as the people the world hates is 'you . . . my
brethren' (13).

It is appropriate that John should depart from his normal
custom of calling his readers 'beloved' or 'children' and should
here, uniquely, address them as 'brethren' (ii. 7 should read
'beloved'). It is not just hatred, but hatred of Christian people,
which reveals the world in its true colours, for in their persecution of the Church their antagonism to Christ is concealed.
'Why persecutest thou me?' Similarly, eternal life is evidenced
not only in a general love for all mankind (although it is thus
evidenced; see verse 14b in RV, RSV, which omit the words *his
brother*), but in a particular love for the brethren. True

Christians, who have 'passed from death unto life', will hunger for Christian fellowship. They will not forsake the assembling of themselves together (Heb. x. 25), but will delight to meet together, to worship and pray together, and to talk together on spiritual topics, while their personal relationship with each other will be marked by unselfish and caring love.

15. John now proves his point, that lack of love is evidence of spiritual death. He is not necessarily denying the possibility of repentance and of forgiveness to a murderer (Jesus prayed that His murderers might be forgiven). He is rather stating as a general principle that to take life is to forfeit life and that no murderer has *eternal life abiding in him* as a present and permanent possession. If this is so, and John accepts it as axiomatic, then clearly he who *hateth his brother* does not possess eternal life either, because to hate is to be *a murderer*. This is a faithful echo of the teaching of Jesus in the Sermon on the Mount (see Mt. v. 21 f., and cf. Mt. v. 27 f.). In equating the hater with the murderer, John is not exaggerating, 'for we wish him to perish whom we hate' (Calvin). So hatred is murder, and it is true to say that *whosoever hateth his brother is a murderer.*

16. Having shown that love is the evidence of life, he explains that the essence of love is self-sacrifice, which has been perfectly manifested in Christ and should characterize the lives of Christian people also. Hate is negative, seeks the other person's harm, and leads to activity against him, even to the point of murder ('Cain rose up *against* his brother Abel, and killed him', Gn. iv. 8). Love is positive, seeks the other person's good, and leads to activity *for* him, even to the point of self-sacrifice ('he laid down his life *for* us', verse 16). The RSV 'By this we know love' is to be preferred to the AV reading. John is discussing love in general, not God's love in particular. He is about to explain just how Christians have come to know (*egnōkamen*, perfect) the true meaning of love. It is in this way: *he* (again the emphatic *ekeinos*, referring of course to Christ) *laid down his life for us*. The expression is peculiar to John (Jn. x. 11, 15, 17, 18, xiii. 37, 38, xv. 13). It seems to imply not so much the laying down as the laying aside of something like clothes, the 'divesting oneself of a thing' (Westcott). It is, in fact, used in John xiii. 4 of Christ laying aside His garments. As Cain has been given as the supreme example of hate, Christ is presented as the supreme example of love. A person's life is his most precious possession. To rob him of it is consequently the greatest sin we can commit against him, which is presumably why the prohibition of murder is the first commandment of the second table of the law. For the same reason, to give one's own life on another's behalf is the greatest possible expression of love for him (cf. Jn. xv. 13; Rom. v. 6-10). This, then, is the ultimate contrast: Cain's hatred issued in murder, Christ's love in self-sacrifice. Indeed, true love, *agapē*, is self-sacrifice. 'Love is the giving impulse' (Law).

But His self-sacrifice is not just a revelation of love to be admired; it is an example to copy. *We ought* (i.e. should be willing) *to lay down our lives for the brethren*, or our profession to love them is an empty boast. We 'ought' to do this, as a definite Christian obligation, because we belong to Christ, just as we 'ought' to follow His example in all things and walk even as he walked (ii. 6), and just as, if God's love for us is so great, we 'ought' also to love one another (iv. 11). For the cross as an example of humility and forbearance see Philippians ii. 5-8 and 1 Peter ii. 19-23 respectively.

17. But true love is not only revealed in the supreme sacrifice; it is expressed in all lesser givings. Not many of us are called to lay down our lives in some deed of heroism, but we constantly have the much more prosaic opportunity to share our possessions with those in need (cf. Jas. ii. 15, 16). Love is 'the willingness to surrender that which has value for our own life, to enrich the life of another' (Dodd). The transition from the plural (*the brethren*, verse 16) to the singular (*his brother*, verse 17) is deliberate and significant. 'It is easier to be enthusiastic about Humanity with a capital "H" than it is to love individual men and women, especially those who are uninteresting, exasperating, depraved, or otherwise unattractive. Loving everybody in general may be an excuse for loving nobody in particular' (Lewis). So John writes that if anybody *hath this world's good* (RSV 'goods', Gk. *bion*) *and seeth his brother have need,* he is in debt to him. Two factors place him, as they placed the Good Samaritan, in a position of inescapable responsibility. First, he must see a brother's need, 'not merely cast a passing glance, but see, long enough to appreciate and understand the circumstances of the case' (Brooke). Secondly, he must himself be better off. If he sees his brother's necessity and has the wherewithal to supply it, he cannot stand idly by.

If nevertheless he 'closes his heart against him' (RSV; the term *bowels* being used then in much the same way as 'heart' is used today), one thing is certain, *the love of God* is not in him. As life does not dwell in the murderer (15), love does not dwell in the miser (17). The genitive may be objective, 'love for God' (cf. ii. 5, 15, iv. 20); or it may be definitive and qualitative, describing a 'love like God's love', 'the divine love' (NEB). But it is probably subjective and should be translated simply 'God's love' (RSV). God's love was revealed historically in the death of Christ (16; cf. iv. 9, 10); but it 'dwells', or should do, in us. It is not to be understood merely as displayed once in Christ, but as continuously active in His followers. And the essence of such divine love, whether in Christ or in us, is costly self-giving, the giving of our *bios* (17, which is translated *life* in ii. 16 in the phrase 'pride of life'), if not of our physical *psuchē* (verse 16), i.e. life itself.

18. John's final plea in this section, addressed to himself as well as to his readers, whom he again fondly calls *my little children,* is a reminder that protestations of love are not enough. Actions speak louder than words. Love is essentially neither sentiment nor talk, but deeds. Indeed, if our love is to be genuine (*in truth*), it will inevitably be positive and active (*in deed*).

It may be helpful to summarize the teaching in this passage about hatred and love. Hatred characterizes the world, whose prototype is Cain. It originates in the devil, issues in murder and is evidence of spiritual death. Love characterizes the Church, whose prototype is Christ. It originates in God, issues in self-sacrifice, and is evidence of eternal life.

c. A digression about assurance and the condemning heart (iii. 19–24)

The link between this new paragraph and what has gone before seems to be the word 'truth'. John has urged upon his readers the necessity of loving 'in truth' (18) and immediately goes on to indicate that this is how we may 'know that we are of the truth' (19). Truth can only characterize the behaviour of those whose very character originates in the truth, so that it is by our loving others 'in truth', that we know that we are 'of the truth'. For the expression to 'be of the truth' cf. John xviii. 37.

This paragraph begins (19) and ends (24) with a sentence introduced by the words 'hereby we know' (although in verse 19 the verb is future, *gnōsometha*, while in verse 24 it is present, *ginōskomen*), and is concerned, as is the whole Epistle, with the doctrine of assurance.

i. The condemning heart, and how to reassure it (iii. 19, 20).[1]
It is within the general context of the Epistle's teaching on assurance that this remarkable paragraph about the condemning heart must be read. However firmly grounded the Christian's assurance is, his heart may sometimes need reassurance. Indeed, if the RSV is correct in translating the first phrase of verse 20 'whenever our hearts condemn us', the suggestion seems to be that it may not be either an unusual or an infrequent experience for the Christian's serene assurance to be disturbed. Sometimes the accusations of our 'conscience' (as the NEB legitimately renders *heart*) will be true accusations, and sometimes they will be false, inspired by 'the accuser of our brethren' (Rev. xii. 10). In either case, the inner voice is not to overcome us. We are rather to *assure our hearts before him*, that is, we must be able to do so in the sight of God (the words *before him* are emphatic).

It is implied that we shall be able to do this only if *we know that we are of the truth*. It is the mind's knowledge by which the heart's doubts may be silenced. But how can we know this? What is the meaning of the *hereby* with which the verse begins?

[1] See Additional Note, p. 147, for linguistic and grammatical points.

Usually in the Epistle this phrase looks on to what follows, but here (as in iv. 6) it seems to refer back to the preceding paragraph about love. It is 'every one that loveth' who 'is born of God and knoweth God' (iv. 7). Love is the final objective test of our Christian profession, for true love, in the sense of self-sacrifice, is not natural to man in his fallen state. Its existence in any man is evidence of new birth and of the indwelling Spirit (iii. 24, iv. 12, 13), and it shows itself 'in deed'. 'There are actual things we can point to—not things we have professed or felt or imagined or intended, but things that we have done' (Law). If we thus love 'in truth' (18), we may indeed have full assurance in our hearts. 'The fruit of love is confidence' (Westcott).

20. It is not easy to determine the grammatical construction of this verse. See Additional Note, p. 147. The RSV is probably correct that we can reassure our hearts 'whenever our hearts condemn us; for God is greater than our hearts'. There are then three actors in this spiritual drama, three speakers in this inward debate. It is a kind of trial, with our heart as the accuser, ourselves as the defendant and God as the Judge (Law). *If our heart condemn us, we,* who are distinct from our heart and stand, as it were, outside it, must *assure,* or reassure and pacify, our heart's misgivings. But how? Partly, as we have already seen, by the fact that 'we know that we are of the truth' (19), and partly by the fact that *God is greater than our heart,* and Himself *knoweth all things.* Our conscience is by no means infallible; its condemnation may often be unjust. We can, therefore, appeal from our conscience to God who is greater and more knowledgeable. Indeed, He knows all things, including our secret motives and deepest resolves, and, it is implied, will be more merciful towards us than our own heart. His omniscience should relieve, not terrify, us (cf. Ps. ciii. 14; Jn. xxi. 17). So it is knowledge which alone can quieten the condemning heart, our own knowledge of our sincere love for others and supremely God's knowledge of our thoughts and motives. Stronger than any chemical tranquillizer is trust in our all-knowing God.

Additional Note: The meaning of 1 John iii. 19, 20

This passage is a *locus vexatissimus* (Law). Its general sense is clear, but it is grammatically confused, and the variant readings betray the difficulty which even in the earliest days was found in interpreting them. The three chief problems concern the meaning first of the verb *assure* (*peisomen*), secondly of the two clauses in verse 20 beginning with *hoti*, and thirdly of God being *greater than our heart*.

1. *Peithein* usually means to 'convince' or 'persuade' (RV mg.) and is followed by a clause defining the truth of which the person is to be convinced or persuaded. If this is the meaning here, some have suggested either supplying a clause, e.g. 'that we are of the truth' (so Plummer), which is forced, or using the second *hoti* clause, 'we shall convince our hearts before him . . . that God is greater than our hearts'. But this yields no satisfactory sense, although the NEB appears to adopt it. 'The consciousness of a sincere love of the brethren does not furnish the basis of the conviction of the sovereign greatness of God' (Westcott).

The second meaning of *peithein* is to 'pacify', although it is rare, occurring in the New Testament only in Matthew xxviii. 14. Compare 2 Maccabees iv. 45. The RV ('assure') and the RSV ('reassure') take the verb in this sense. 'We shall still and tranquillize the fears and misgivings of our heart' (Westcott).

2. How are we to render the two *hoti* clauses? The second *hoti* must be translated 'because' rather than 'that'. God's greatness thus becomes not the truth of which we convince our hearts but the truth by which we pacify them.

The first *hoti* could also mean 'because'. In this case the words 'if our heart condemn us' are a subordinate clause almost in parenthesis and the second *hoti* merely resumes the first. But this is clumsy, and the parenthetic clause is not long enough to warrant a resumptive *hoti*. The AV recognizes this and does not translate the second *hoti*, which is indeed omitted in a few minor MSS. The alternative is to separate *ho* and *ti*, which words with *ean* added become a construction meaning 'whenever' (RSV), 'whereinsoever' (RV, Westcott, Law) or

(NEB mg.) 'in matters where'. This is the solution adopted by most modern commentators. It is satisfactory because it preserves the antithesis between verse 20 ('if our heart condemn us') and verse 21 ('if our heart condemn us not'), and such opposites are not uncommon in the Epistle (e.g. i. 9, 10, ii. 10, 11, iii. 7, 8, iv. 2, 3).

3. The third question concerns the description of God as 'greater than our heart'. Is He so called 'because He is more merciful than our heart,' or because He is more rigorous in His judgment upon us' (Ebrard)? Alford's interpretation may be taken as an example of the latter view, which was adopted by the early Greek commentators and the Reformers. He translates the second *hoti* 'because', but regards the clause as elliptical and supplies a verb before it: 'if our heart condemn us (it is) because God is greater than our heart . . .' The greatness of God is thus viewed as a challenge not a comfort. It explains not why we can pacify our hearts but why they condemn us and we therefore need to pacify them. 'Our conscience is but the faint echo of His voice who knoweth all things: if it condemn us, how much more He?' (Alford). Cf. 1 Corinthians iv. 3, 4. The main objection to this interpretation is that the emphatic purpose of this paragraph is to heal the wounded conscience not to open its wound wider, 'to give assurance, and not to strike terror into their hearts' (Brooke).

ii. The uncondemning heart, and its blessings (iii. 21–24). John turns from the curse of a condemning heart, and how to reassure it, to the blessing of a heart which has been made tranquil or which does not condemn. This blessing is not only in itself, in the peace of an untroubled conscience, but in its result, namely a communion with God which is free and unrestricted (*parrēsian*) on the one hand, and actively sought and experienced (*pros ton Theon, toward God*) on the other. For *parrēsia* see note on ii. 28. 'The thought here is of the boldness with which the Son appears before the Father, and not of that with which the accused appears before the Judge' (Westcott).

22. The second blessing of an uncondemning heart is now

stated. We have confidence not only to have access to Him in prayer (*pros ton Theon*), but to receive answers from Him (*ap' autou*). The same combination of confidence and granted petitions is found in v. 14, 15. But John does not mean to imply that God hears and answers our prayers merely for the subjective reason that we have a clear conscience and an uncondemning heart. There is an objective, moral reason, namely *because we keep his commandments, and,* more generally, *do those things that are pleasing in his sight.* Obedience is the indispensable condition, not the meritorious cause, of answered prayer. *Whatsoever we ask, we receive* describes the Christian's habitual experience (the verbs are in the present tense), and Candlish is right to point to the incarnate Son as the supreme example of pleasing God and so being heard by God (Jn. viii. 29, xi. 41, 42). The statement echoes our Lord's promise, where the same two verbs occur: 'Ask, and it shall be given you . . . for every one that asketh receiveth' (Mt. vii. 7, 8).

This simple and unqualified promise must, of course, be interpreted in the light of the conditions upon which, in other parts of Scripture, God promises to grant His people's requests. If a prayer is to be answered it must be 'according to his will' (v. 14; cf. Ps. xxxvii. 4; Jn. xv. 7). Law is probably right that to 'keep his commandments' is the condition of being heard simply because such obedience is the evidence that 'our will is in inward harmony with God's'. We must also pray in Christ's name (Jn. xvi. 23, 24), and for God's glory (Jas. iv. 2, 3), while the petitioner must be cleansed from his sins (Ps. lxvi. 18; Pr. xv. 29; Is. lix. 1, 2; Jas. v. 16), forgiven and himself forgiving others (Mk. xi. 25), believing God's promises (Mt. xxi. 22; Mk. xi. 24; cf. Jas. i. 5–7) and obeying His commandments. For the concept of pleasing God cf. Jn. viii. 29; 2 Cor. v. 9; Eph. v. 10; Col. i. 10, iii. 20; 1 Thes. iv. 1; Heb. xiii. 21.

23. And what are the commandments of God which we must obey if we are to receive our petitions? Fundamentally, there is only one *commandment* (the word is singular), embracing faith in Christ and love for one another. The faith that is commanded is variously expressed in these Epistles. It is

simply to 'confess Jesus' (iv. 3, RSV), to believe and acknowledge 'that Jesus is the Christ' (ii. 22, v. 1; cf. 2 Jn. 9) or 'the
Son' (ii. 23); or, more elaborately, to believe 'that Jesus is
the Son of God' (iv. 15, v. 5), and 'Christ come in the flesh'
(iv. 2; 2 Jn. 7). But here the credal confession is given in full,
namely, to *believe on* (although there is no preposition in the
Greek as there is in v. 13; the simple dative is used) *the name*,
the revealed Person, *of his Son Jesus Christ*. That is, Jesus of
Nazareth, the historic Person, is to be identified with the Christ,
the Son of God. He is given His complete title also in i. 3 and
v. 20.

The second part of the commandment is that we should
love one another, as he gave us commandment, he meaning perhaps
'Christ', and the commandment He gave, that of John xiii. 34
and xv. 12, 17. Reciprocal love has already been mentioned as
a commandment in ii. 7, 8 (cf. 2 Jn. 6) but here for the first
time faith and love are brought together (cf. Gal. v. 6). Both
are the will of God, and both are commanded by Him. There
is a significant difference in the tense of the two verbs, *believe*
and *love*, faith in Christ being here regarded as a decisive act
(assuming that *pisteusōmen* is the correct reading), and love for
the brethren as a continuous attitude. Both are tests of a true
Christian. In iii. 10 John linked the practice of righteousness
with brotherly love. Here he links love with belief in Christ,
and in the next verse completes the trio by adding a general
obedience to the commandments of God, of which he has also
written in verse 22.

24. The concept of a mutual abiding, mentioned here in
this Epistle for the first time, we in Him and He in us, is
derived ultimately from our Lord's allegory of the vine and the
branches (Jn. xv. 1 ff.). There it is Christ who dwells in His
own, and they in Him. Here, if we may judge from the use of
him, his and *he* in verses 22, 23, it is 'God' who dwells in us, as
in iv. 12, and we in Him. The difference would have been
unimportant to John, however, for in John xvii. 21 Jesus prays
that 'they . . . may be in *us*' (RSV; cf. Jn. xiv. 23, '*we* will come
unto him, and make our abode with him'). Both here and in

John xv (verse 10) the condition of continuous abiding is obedience; although obedience is the issue and evidence of abiding also. Cf. ii. 3–6 for an exposition of the same truth.

With this verse John unites the various strands which he has been unfolding separately in these first three chapters of his Epistle. No-one may dare to claim that he abides in Christ and Christ in him unless he is obedient to the three fundamental commandments which John has been expounding, which are belief in Christ, love for the brethren and moral righteousness. 'Abiding in Christ' is not a mystical experience which any man may claim; its indispensable accompaniments are the confession of Jesus as the Son of God come in the flesh, and a consistent life of holiness and love. It is *hereby*, he concludes, that *we know that he abideth in us, by the Spirit which he hath given us*, or rather 'gave us' (*edōken*) at the beginning of our Christian life. It may at first sight seem that this reference to the Holy Spirit within us introduces a subjective criterion of assurance (like Rom. viii. 15, 16) which is inconsistent with what has gone before. But this is not so. The Spirit whose presence is the test of Christ's abiding in us, manifests Himself objectively in our life and conduct. It is He who inspires us to confess Jesus as the Christ come in the flesh, as John immediately proceeds to show (iv. 1ff.; cf. ii. 20, 27). It is also He who empowers us to live righteously and to love the brethren (cf. iv. 13; Gal. v. 16, 22). So if we would assure our hearts, when they accuse and condemn us, we must look for evidence of the Spirit's working, and particularly whether He is enabling us to believe in Christ, to obey God's commandments and to love the brethren; for the condition of abiding is this comprehensive obedience (24a), and the evidence of abiding is the gift of the Spirit (24b).

d. An elaboration of the doctrinal test: belief (iv. 1–6)

The background of these verses, as of 1 Corinthians xii and xiv, is a situation in which supernatural phenomena such as 'prophecy' and 'tongues' were prevalent. Simple souls were (and still are) so impressed by such manifestations as to be dazzled by them. The present tense of 'believe not every spirit' (1) indicates that John's readers were tending to accept uncritically all teaching which seemed to be given under inspiration. They needed to be shown that 'to identify the supernatural and the Divine is a perilous mistake' (Findlay). John's concern was that they should test not so much the *character* of inspired utterance, whether it was genuine or spurious, as its *origin*, whether it was diabolical or divine. This need for the critical assessment of religious teachers has always been felt. The test given by our Lord was moral: 'by their fruits ye shall know them'. John also applied moral tests, both righteousness (iii. 10) and love (iv. 8); but there are theological tests as well (as in Dt. xiii. 1–5 and Je. xxiii. 9 ff.). In iii. 23 John linked under a single divine commandment the duty to love one another, which had been his main theme during the latter part of that chapter, with the duty to believe on the name of God's Son Jesus Christ. Now he takes up and further develops this central Christian belief as a searching test of the true Christian and the true prophet. The test is applied in two ways, first with reference to the teachers and, secondly, with reference to the hearers. 'Hereby know ye' (2), he says, and indicates that the content of the teaching is a decisive test. 'Hereby know we' (6b), he says again at the end of the paragraph, showing that the character of the audience is an almost equally revealing test.

i. The content of the teaching (iv. 1–3). God has given us His Spirit (iii. 24), but there are other spirits active in the world. It is important to observe that the command to believe on the name of God's Son Jesus Christ (iii. 23) is followed by a prohibition, *believe not every spirit*, much as the commandment to love (ii. 7, 8) was followed by the prohibition, 'love not the world, neither the things that are in the world' (ii. 15). Neither Christian faith nor Christian love is indiscriminate. In particular, Christian faith is not to be mistaken for credulity. True faith examines its object before reposing confidence in it. So John tells his readers to *try*, that is, 'test' (RSV, NEB), *the spirits whether they are of God*. He is urging them to apply a test to all human teachers who claim to speak under spiritual inspiration. Properly understood, a prophet is the mouthpiece of some spirit. True prophets are the mouthpiece of 'the Spirit of God' (2), who in verse 6 is called 'the Spirit of truth'; *false prophets* are the mouthpiece of 'the spirit of error' (6b) or 'the spirit of antichrist' (3) and thus 'prophets falsely inspired' (NEB). So behind every prophet is a spirit, and behind each spirit either God or the devil. Before we can trust any spirits, we must test them, *whether they are of God*. It is their origin that matters. We may note the similar command given by Paul in I Thessalonians v. 19–22. The apostles Paul and John assumed that even the humblest Christian possessed 'the right of private judgment', as the Reformers properly insisted, and both could and should apply the objective test John is about to give in the next verse.

The reason for this need to try the spirits is now given. The reference may be general, to false teachers setting forth on a missionary expedition, or, more particularly, to the 'many antichrists' described in ii. 18, 19 who had formerly been church members but had now gone out. Westcott thinks the allusion is to 'the great outbreak of the Gentile pseudo-Christianity which is vaguely spoken of as Gnosticism'. Jesus warned His disciples of false prophets (Mt. vii. 15; Mk. xiii. 22, 23). So did Paul (Acts xx. 28–30) and Peter (2 Pet. ii. 1). Still today there are many voices clamouring for our attention, and many cults gaining widespread popular support. Some of them claim some special revelation or inspiration to authenticate their particular doctrine. There is an urgent need for discernment among Christians. We are often too gullible, and exhibit a naïve readiness to credit messages and teachings which purport to come from the spirit-world. There is such a thing, however, as a misguided charity and tolerance towards false doctrine. Unbelief (*believe not every spirit*) can be as much a mark of spiritual maturity as belief. We need to preserve the biblical balance, avoiding on the one hand the extreme superstition which believes everything and on the other the extreme suspicion which believes nothing.

2. From the command to test and the need to test, John

passes to the way to test. *Hereby know ye the Spirit of God.*[1] The origin of the inspiring spirit, he says, may be discerned by the teaching of the prophet through whom it speaks. *Every spirit that confesseth that Jesus Christ is come in the flesh is of God.* By this confession is meant not merely a recognition of His identity, but a profession of faith in Him 'openly and boldly' (Westcott) as the incarnate Lord. Even evil or unclean spirits recognized the deity of Jesus during His ministry (e.g. Mk. i. 24, iii. 11, v. 7, 8; cf. Acts xix. 15). But though they knew Him, they did not acknowledge or 'confess' Him. The Spirit of God, on the other hand, always honours the Son of God. Jesus taught that it is the Holy Spirit's particular ministry both to testify to, and to glorify, Him (Jn. xv. 26, xvi. 13–15; cf. also 1 Cor. xii. 3). Here His testimony is to the incarnation. It is understandable that the same Spirit, through whom the miraculous conception took place (Mt. i. 20; Lk. i. 35), should bear faithful witness to it. The precise words which John uses as the test formula must be carefully noted. It is probable that the phrase should read, 'confesseth that Jesus is the Christ come in the flesh'.[2] The confession is that the man Jesus of Nazareth is Himself none other than the incarnate Christ or Son, which is the doctrine Cerinthus and his disciples denied. The perfect tense, *come (elēluthota)* compared with the present tense in 2 John 7 *(erchomenon)*, seems to emphasize that the flesh assumed by the Son of God in the incarnation has become His permanent possession. Far from coming upon Jesus at the baptism and leaving Him before the cross, the Christ actually came in the flesh and has never laid it aside. Such a confession of faith is sufficient to show that the *spirit* inspiring it *is of God.* The fundamental Christian doctrine which can never be compromised is the eternal divine-human Person of Jesus Christ, the Son of God.

---

[1] The verb *know ye (ginōskete)* could be an imperative or an indicative. In favour of the imperative some commentators have argued that John is adding to the two commands of verse 1 not to believe every spirit but to test the spirits, the further instruction to recognize the Spirit of God. Since, however, every other occurrence in the Epistle of the phrase *hereby know we* (although in the first person, while here it is in the second) is followed by an indicative verb, the indicative seems preferable here also. John is making a statement, not issuing a command.

[2] See Additional Note on the meaning of this verse, p. 155.

3. The contrary is also true: 'and every spirit which does not confess Jesus is not of God' (RSV). The better MSS omit the other words *Christ is come in the flesh*. They are not necessary. To confess Jesus, in the mind of John, can mean only one thing, namely to confess Him as the Christ come in the flesh. To deny this, whatever claim to inspiration may accompany the denial, is to reveal not only the absence of a divine origin but the working of *that spirit of antichrist*, of which John's readers had *heard* (no doubt from himself in his previous teaching) *that it should come* (*erchetai* as in ii. 18). As the true Christ had come in the flesh, so the false Christ, the *antichrist*, aping the true Christ, had also come, *and even now already is it in the world.* John has said the same thing in ii. 18, 22, although what he here calls *the spirit of antichrist* is there yet more explicitly said to be embodied in *many antichrists*, i.e. false prophets, who are abroad. Cf. 2 Thessalonians ii. 3–8 where, although 'the man of lawlessness' is still to be revealed, 'the mystery of lawlessness' is already at work, albeit under restraint.

Comparing the two passages, ii. 18–23 and iv. 1–3, it is instructive to observe the difference of emphasis. In chapter ii John teaches that on our confession or denial of the Son depends whether we possess the Father or not, while in chapter iv he says that on our confession or denial of the Son depends whether we are inspired by the Spirit or not. The Person of Christ is central. No system can be tolerated, however loud its claims or learned its adherents, if it denies that Jesus is the Christ come in the flesh, that is, if it denies either His eternal deity or His historical humanity. Its teachers are false prophets and its origin is the spirit of antichrist. Those who deny the Son have neither the Father nor the Spirit.

Additional Note: The interpretation of 1 John iv. 2

Brooke points out that when the verb *homologein*, to confess, is followed by an accusative, the latter may be single or double. The single accusative occurs in ii. 23 and iv. 3, to confess 'the Son' and to confess 'Jesus', and the double in John ix. 22, to confess 'Him' (i.e. Jesus) as 'Christ'. Which is it here (and in

2 Jn. 7)? Brooke prefers to regard 'Jesus Christ come in the flesh' as a single, comprehensive accusative and thinks this 'the simplest construction'. Other commentators, surely correctly, have looked for a double accusative, either 'Jesus Christ' as 'come in the flesh', or 'Jesus' as 'Christ come in the flesh'. The former is unlikely. John does employ the combined name 'Jesus Christ' (i. 3, ii. 1, iii. 23, v. 20) but to speak of 'Jesus Christ' as having 'come in the flesh' would be a strange 'theological anachronism' (Findlay), since it was not until *after* the incarnation that He was called 'Jesus'. It is better, therefore, to adopt the alternative double accusative, to confess 'Jesus' as 'Christ come in the flesh', 'the Christ incarnate' (Moffatt). This accords both with the use of the name 'Jesus' alone in the best MSS of verse 3 (as RSV), and with what is known of the heretics' views. They taught that the Christ, a divine aeon, descended upon the man Jesus at his baptism, withdrawing from him before his death. John repudiates this doctrine. It was not that the Christ came 'into' the flesh of Jesus, but that Jesus was the Christ come 'in' the flesh. The two are to be identified. 'The statement, simple as it is, is of exquisite precision' (Law).

This interpretation is consistent also with the interesting variant reading of verse 3, which instead of *mē homologei* (*confesseth not*) has the verb *luei*. This could be translated 'destroys' (as in iii. 8) or 'looses'. Its attestation, which is slight, is summarized in full by Brooke (pp. 111–114). It is found in the Vulgate as 'solvit', in other Latin versions, in Latin translations of Irenaeus and Origen, and in Tertullian and Augustine. It is preserved in the RV margin as 'annulleth'. Doubtless it was an early scribal gloss, and is not authentic; but it is significant as showing that 'not to confess Jesus' was regarded as to 'loose' Him, that is, to 'divide' Jesus from the Christ, instead of identifying them. Later the verb *luein* came to be used almost technically for the Gnostic heresy which 'separated' Jesus from the Christ; and this variant reading was used in argument against the Nestorian heresy.

ii. The character of the audience (iv. 4–6). John now

turns from a consideration of the teachers and their message to an examination of the audience which listens to them. In the Greek text, each of these three verses (4, 5 and 6) begins with an emphatic personal pronoun—*ye* (4, *humeis*), referring to his Christian readers in general, *they* (5, *autoi*), referring to the false teachers, and *we* (6, *hēmeis*), referring to himself as representative of the authoritative apostles. See Introduction, p. 29.

4. *Ye are of God*, he says (as is 'every spirit that confesseth Jesus Christ come in the flesh', verse 2), *and have overcome them*, i.e. 'these false prophets' (NEB). This 'overcoming' is not so much moral (as in ii. 13, 14, where the same word occurs) as intellectual. The false teachers have not succeeded in deceiving you. Not only have you tested them and found them wanting, but you have conquered them. You have not succumbed to their blandishments or believed their lies. Hence, no doubt, they 'had found themselves obliged to depart' (Ebrard), as ii. 19 declares. And the cause of your victory is not hard to find. *He that is in you* is likely to be the 'Spirit of truth' (6), 'the anointing' which 'abideth in you' (ii. 20, 27), while *he that is in the world* is the devil, the spirit of error (6). We may thank God that, although (it is implied) the evil spirit is indeed 'great', the Holy Spirit is *greater*, and that by His illumination we too may be sure to overcome all false teaching. Here, as in ii. 18–27, protection against error or victory over it is ascribed both to an objective standard of doctrine and to the indwelling Spirit who illumines our minds to grasp and apply it, for 'unless the Spirit of wisdom is present, there is little or no profit in having God's Word in our hands' (Calvin).

5, 6. These two verses are complementary. In them John contrasts in striking fashion not only the false prophets and the true apostles (*they* and *we*), but the different audiences who listen to them, namely *the world* and *he that knoweth God*. The world recognizes its own people and listens to a message which originates in its own circle. This explains their popularity. But *we are of God*. This is not the same as 'ye are of God' in verse 4. There he declares the divine origin of his Christian readers; here he is particularizing. The *we* of this verse is in direct antithesis to the *they* of the previous verse, and if the *they* means the false teachers, the *we* must be the true teachers, namely the apostles. But how can it be known that *we are of God* and are teaching the truth? John answers, in effect, that you can tell that our message is God's message because God's people listen to it and receive it. These statements sound the height of arrogance. So they would be if uttered by an individual Christian. No private believer could presume to say: 'whoever knows God agrees with me; only those who are not of God disagree with me.' But this is what John says. The fact is that he is not speaking in his own name, nor even in the name of the Church, but as one of the apostles, who were conscious of the special authority bestowed upon them by Jesus Christ. He is carrying a stage further the argument of the first three verses. There the test of doctrine was whether it acknowledged the divine-human Person of Jesus Christ; here the test is whether it is accepted by Christians and rejected by non-Christians. There is a certain affinity between God's Word and God's people. Jesus had taught that His sheep hear His voice (Jn. x. 4, 5, 8, 16, 26, 27), that everyone who is of the truth listens to His witness to the truth (Jn. xviii. 37), and that 'he who is of God hears the words of God' (Jn. viii. 47, RSV). In the same way John asserts that since *we are of God* (6) and *ye are of God* (4), you listen to us. There is a correspondence between message and hearers. The Spirit who is in you (4) enables you to discern His own voice speaking through us (2). So you can recognize God's Word because God's people listen to it, just as you can recognize God's people because they listen to God's Word. Those who do not listen to apostolic teaching, but prefer to absorb the teaching of the world, not only pass judgment on themselves but thereby also on the message to which they do give attention.

All this is consistent with John's repeated emphasis that safety from error is to be found in loyalty to that which his readers 'had' or 'heard' 'from the beginning' (ii. 7, 24, iii. 11; 2 Jn. 5; cf. 2 Jn. 9). The phrase *he . . . heareth us* cannot be referred to the traditions of the Church (or of the Papacy) without doing violence to John's insistence in this Epistle upon primitive apostolic doctrine, quite apart from the historical question whether the consensus of Christian opinion has been a reliable criterion of truth. C. H. Dodd is right to say that prophets, representing spontaneity and freedom, were (and are) always 'subordinate to apostles' and their authority (pp. 103–106).

Hereby know we the spirit of truth, and the spirit of error, John concludes. We can test the spirits, and 'get to know' which is which (*ginōskomen*, present tense), by examining not only the message they proclaim through their human instruments but the character of the audience which listens to them. For the title *the spirit of truth* as applied to the Holy Spirit, see John xiv. 17, xv. 26, xvi. 13.

V. THIRD APPLICATION OF THE TESTS
(iv. 7–v. 5)

a. A further elaboration of the social test: love (iv. 7–12)
In iii. 23 John summarized God's commandment as being 'to believe in Christ and to love one another'. He has unfolded in iv. 1–6 some of the implications of belief in Christ; he now turns abruptly to the subject of mutual love. This is the third time in the Epistle that he takes up and applies the supreme test of love. (See also ii. 7–11 and iii. 11–18.) Each time the test is more searching. In this third treatment the author is concerned to relate the love which should be in us not to the true light which is already shining (ii. 8, 10), nor to the eternal life of which it is the evidence (iii. 14, 15) but to God's very nature of love and with His loving activity in Christ and in us. 'Here the epistle rises to the summit of all revelation' (Law).

The refrain of this paragraph is the reflexive *love one another.* It occurs three times—as an exhortation (7, 'let us love one another'), as a statement of duty (11, 'we ought . . . to love one another'; cf. ii. 6, iii. 16), and as a hypothesis (12, 'if we love one another . . .'). What John is at pains to demonstrate is the ground of this imperative obligation. Why is reciprocal love the plain duty of Christians? He does not rest content with his former declarations either that love is part of the commandment, new and old (ii. 7–11), or that love is evidence that they are 'in the light' and possess 'eternal life' (iii. 11–18). He now elaborates what he had already begun to say in iii. 16, that God has revealed Himself to us in Jesus Christ as self-sacrificial love. It is because God is love in Himself (8, 16), has loved us in Christ (10, 11), and continues to love in and through us (12, 13), that we must love each other.

7, 8. The first part of the argument for brotherly love is taken from God's eternal nature. Verse 7 opens with a striking assonance, *Beloved, let us love* . . . , which is more forceful in the Greek words *agapētoi, agapōmen*. . . . Here and in verse 11 (cf. ii. 7) the author practises what he preaches. In urging them to love each other, he first assures them of his own love for them. The first reason why Christians should love each other is now stated twice, first, *for love is of God* (7) and secondly, *for God is love* (8). Because God is the source and origin (*ek*) of love and all true love derives from Him, it stands to reason that *every one that loveth*, that is, loves either God or man with that selfless devotion which alone is true love according to John's teaching, *is* (literally, has been) *born of God, and knoweth God* (7). But not only is God the source of all true love; God is love in His inmost being. There are three other statements in the New Testament concerning what God is in substance and nature: He is 'spirit' (Jn. iv. 24), 'light' (1 Jn. i. 5) and 'a consuming fire' (Heb. xii. 29 from Dt. iv. 24). The Gnostics believed and taught that God was immaterial spirit and light, but to the truth that God is love they did not attain. It is the most comprehensive and sublime of all biblical affirmations about God's being, and is repeated twice (8, 16). Nevertheless, it is important to hold these assertions about God together. It is true that the words *God is love* mean not that loving is 'only one of God's many activities' (Alexander) but rather that '*all* His activity is loving activity' and that, therefore, 'if He judges, He judges in love' (Dodd). Yet, if His judging is in love, His loving is also in justice. He who is love is light and fire as well.

Far from condoning sin, His love has found a way to expose it (because He is light) and to consume it (because He is fire) without destroying the sinner, but rather saving him.

From the truth that *God is love* John draws a further deduction, not now positive and inclusive like that of verse 7, but negative and exclusive: *he that loveth not knoweth not God.* The argument is plain and compelling. For the loveless Christian to profess to know God and to have been born of God is like claiming to be intimate with a foreigner whose language we cannot speak, or to have been born of parents whom we do not in any way resemble. It is to fail to manifest the nature of Him whom we claim as our Father (*born of God*) and our Friend (*knoweth God*). Love is as much a sign of new birth as is righteousness (ii. 29).

John bases his second argument (verses 9–11) for mutual love not on God's eternal nature, but on His historical gift. The God who is love (8) 'loved us' (10) and expressed His love by sending His Son to earth. While the origin of love is in the being of God, the manifestation of love is in the coming of Christ. And, John writes, 'if God so loved us, we ought also to love one another' (11). This time the duty of reciprocal love is enforced not merely by the abstract truth that God is love, but by the concrete fact that He so loved us as to send 'his only begotten Son into the world' for us (9). It should be added that the concept of God 'sending' His Son (9, 10, 14) 'involves the doctrine of Christ's pre-existence and divinity' (Ebrard) as well as the doctrine of the love of God. John is already hinting at the organic relation between his doctrinal and social tests which he elaborates later.

9, 10. There have been and are many manifestations of the love of God. It is no doubt constantly manifest in heaven (though not to men's eyes) in the mysterious relations between the Persons of the Godhead. 'Among us' (RSV; Gk. *en hēmin*), however, God's love, which had already been displayed in His choice, redemption and protection of Israel, has been pre-eminently made known in the gift of His Son. This is stated with emphasis twice in this paragraph (cf. also verses 14, 16). The sending of God's Son was both the revelation of His love (*In this was manifested* . . . , 9) and, indeed, the very essence of love itself (*Herein is* . . . , 10). It is not our love that is primary, but God's (10), free, uncaused and spontaneous, and all our love is but a reflection of His and a response to it.

The coming of Christ is, therefore, a concrete, historical revelation of God's love, for love (*agapē*) is self-sacrifice, the seeking of another's positive good at one's own cost, and a greater self-giving than God's gift of His Son there has never been, nor could be. The way in which John sees this emerges from the similar pattern in which the three statements of verses 9, 10 and 14 are made.

1. Each says that God sent His Son, called now *the Son* (14), *his Son* (10) and *his only begotten Son* (9). 'Only begotten' (*monogenēs*) occurs only here in the Epistles of John, but four times in the Gospel (i. 14, 18, iii. 16, 18). In the LXX it sometimes translates the Hebrew word 'well beloved' (cf. Mk. i. 11, ix. 7, xii. 6). Applied to Jesus Christ, it indicates His uniqueness; He is 'the Son' in an absolute sense. No greater gift of God is conceivable because no greater gift was possible. This was God's 'unspeakable gift' (2 Cor. ix. 15). Cf. John iii. 16; Romans viii. 32.

2. It is further implied that the Father sent His Son to die for us. Not the incarnation but the atonement is the pre-eminent manifestation of love (cf. iii. 16). It is true that no explicit reference is made in these verses to the Son's death, but that it was in John's mind is certain from his theology of salvation. To be *the Saviour of the world* (14), the Lamb of God bore away the sin of the world (Jn. i. 29; cf. 1 Jn. iii. 5). *That we might live through him* (9), He died (Jn. iii. 14, 15, xi. 49–52, xii. 24). In order *to be the propitiation for our sins* (10), He shed His blood (i. 7, ii. 2, where see notes; cf. Rom. iii. 25).

3. The greatness of God's love, manifest in the nature of His gift and its purpose, is seen also in its beneficiaries, for God gave His Son to die for us undeserving sinners. The degraded condition to which our sins had brought us is clearly implied. If we need a *Saviour* (14), it is because we are sinners.

Christ came *that we might live through him* (9) and *to be the propitiation for our sins* (10) because otherwise we are 'dead in trespasses and sins' (Eph. ii. 1; cf. iii. 14) and under the holy wrath and judgment of God. He loved us and sent His Son to rescue us, not because we are in any sense lovable, but because He is love. So the greatness of His love is seen in the costliness of His self-sacrifice for the wholly undeserving (cf. Rom. v. 7, 8). A clearer manifestation of God's love could not be imagined.

11. The deduction which John draws from the historical manifestation of God's love in Christ is different. The gift of God's Son not only assures us of God's love for us, but lays upon us an obligation. No-one who has been to the cross and seen God's immeasurable and unmerited love displayed there can go back to a life of selfishness. Indeed, the implication seems to be that *if God so loved us, we ought also*—'so', in like manner and to a like degree of self-sacrifice—*to love one another.* Cf. iii. 16, where the duty of Christian self-sacrifice is deduced from the self-sacrifice of Christ.

12. The author's third argument to enforce the duty of reciprocal love takes his readers a stage further. We are not to think of love only as constituting God's eternal being and as historically manifested in the sending of His Son into the world. God who is love still loves, and today His love is seen in our love. So John's third argument is based on God's present and continuous activity of love. His opening statement is indisputable. God is spirit (Jn. iv. 24) and in Himself invisible (1 Tim. i. 17, vi. 16). Even if He were visible, no man could see Him and live (Ex. xxxiii. 20). In fact, no man has seen Him (cf. verse 20). The Old Testament theophanies were revelations of God in human disguise; they were not visions of God as He is in Himself (*Theon* without the article). The vision of God lies still in the future when Christ appears (iii. 2).

It is significant that this is not the only occurrence in the Johannine literature of the phrase: *No man hath seen God at any time.* It comes also (in almost identical words) at the end of the Prologue to the Gospel (i. 18). How then can He be known?

In the Gospel Prologue John continues: 'the only begotten Son, which is in the bosom of the Father, he hath declared him' (cf. Col. i. 15). But here, to our astonishment and confusion, he goes on: *If we love one another, God dwelleth in us, and his love is perfected in us.* That is, the unseen God, who was once revealed in His Son, is now revealed in His people if and when they love one another. God's love is seen in their love because their love is His love imparted to them by His Spirit (cf. verse 13). The words do not mean that when we begin to love, God comes to dwell in us, but the reverse. Our love for one another is evidence of God's indwelling presence. See iii. 17 for another reference to God's love dwelling in us.

John goes further still. Reciprocal Christian love means not only that God dwells in us but also that *his love is perfected in us.* It would be hard to exaggerate the greatness of this conception. It is so daring that many commentators have been reluctant to accept it and have suggested that the genitive in *his love* is not subjective ('God's love') but objective ('our love for God; cf. ii. 5) or definitive ('godlike love'). But the whole paragraph is concerned with God's love, and we must not stagger at the majesty of this conclusion. God's love which originates in Himself (7, 8) and was manifested in His Son (9, 10) is perfected in His people (12). It is 'brought to perfection within us' (NEB). God's love for us is perfected only when it is reproduced in us or (as it may mean) 'among us' in the Christian fellowship. It is these three truths about the love of God which John uses as inducements to brotherly love. We are to love each other, first because God is love (8, 9), secondly because God loved us (10, 11), and thirdly because, if we do love one another, God dwells in us and His love is perfected in us (12).

b. A combination of the doctrinal and social tests (iv. 13-21)

The two phrases with which the previous paragraph concluded, 'God dwelleth in us' and 'his love is perfected in us', are now taken up and elaborated—God's indwelling in verses 13 to 16 and perfect love in verses 17 to 21.

i. God's indwelling (iv. 13–16). The new paragraph is introduced by the familiar formula, *Hereby know we* (NEB, 'Here is the proof that . . .'). The previous two sections have been exhortations—a warning not to believe every spirit (1–6) and an appeal to love one another (7–12). These two tests of belief and love are now applied more personally, no longer in exhortation but in affirmation. The belief and love, which John has been urging upon his readers, are now assumed, and deductions are drawn from them. Moreover, their relation to each other is for the first time indicated. This passage 'is the high-watermark of the thought of the epistle' (Dodd). That 'the Father sent the Son' is not only the chief test of doctrinal orthodoxy but also the supreme evidence of God's love and inspiration of ours. The deity of Christ, God's love for us and our love for God and man cannot be separated. The theology which robs Christ of His Godhead, robs God of the glory of His love, and robs man of the one belief that generates a perfect love within him. 'To weaken faith is to deaden love' (Findlay). Further, the ability to believe and the ability to love are alike attributable to the Holy Spirit. Thus belief and love are seen to be related in the mission of the Son and the indwelling of the Spirit.

God's indwelling is mentioned three times in this paragraph, and what in verse 12 was single ('God dwelleth in us') is now each time reciprocal (verse 13, *we dwell in him, and he in us*; verse 15, 'God dwelleth in him, and he in God'; verse 16, 'he . . . dwelleth in God, and God in him'). Moreover, each time the reciprocal indwelling is described, evidence of it is supplied as follows: verse 13, *because he hath given us of his Spirit*; verse 15, 'whosoever shall confess that Jesus is the Son of God'; verse 16, 'he that dwelleth in love'.

Of these three tests of the indwelling of God, the last two are developments of the first. It is by the Spirit that we come to confess the deity of Jesus (cf. iv. 1–3 and 1 Cor. xii. 3), and by the same Spirit that we are enabled to love (verses 12, 13; cf. iii. 23, 24). The natural man can neither believe nor love. In his fallen and unredeemed state he is both blind and selfish. It is only by the grace of the Holy Spirit, who is the

Spirit of truth and whose first-fruit is love (Gal. v. 22), that man ever comes to believe in Christ and to love others. Emphasis on the Holy Spirit is, in fact, 'the *predominant idea* of this section' (Ebrard). This, then, is the sequence of thought in this passage: we know that we abide in God and God in us 'because he hath given us of his Spirit' (13), and we know He has given us of His Spirit because we have come to 'confess that Jesus is the Son of God' (15), and to dwell 'in love' (16).

Some commentators make the mistake of seeing in this paragraph the conditions of our dwelling in God and of His dwelling in us. Belief and love are not the conditions of the indwelling, but the tests and evidences of it. John writes 'by this we know that we abide in him' not 'by this we abide in Him'. The theme of this section, as of the whole Epistle, is 'the grounds of assurance' (Dodd).

14. The subjective experience of the Spirit's power is not to be considered in isolation; it confirms the objective fact of the Son's coming to earth. This, John says, *we have seen*. He uses the same word as in verse 12. God in Himself no man has seen, but we have seen the Son whom He has sent. 'The word must here refer to the actual eyewitnesses of the life of Jesus on earth' (Brooke). See Introduction, pp. 26 ff. It is because we have seen that we can and do testify. The unity of these two witnesses to the truth is in the Father, for there is reference in these verses to the three Persons of the Trinity. It has been the Father's gracious purpose both to send His Son into the world as Saviour and to send His Spirit into our hearts as witness (cf. Gal. iv. 4–6). Christian certainty rests both on the objective historical fact of the Son's mission and on the subjective inward experience of the Spirit's witness. Another way of putting it is that there are two witnesses—the apostles (14) and the Holy Spirit (13). Cf. John xv. 26, 27 and Acts v. 32. We must not divorce what God has purposed to unite.

Much Christian truth is contained in the straightforward affirmation of this verse. Here is the essence of the gospel. *The world* means sinful society, estranged from God and under the dominion of the evil one (cf. v. 19). Its urgent need was to be rescued from sin and Satan. And *the Father* 'so loved the world' (Jn. iii. 16) that He *sent the Son*, His dear and only Son, to be its *Saviour*. The perfect tense of the verb (*apestalken*, lit. 'has sent') points not just to the historical event of the sending, but to the purpose and result of it, namely the salvation of the world. Further, within this statement of the gospel all three of the apostle's tests are implicitly contained, doctrinal (it was *the Son* Himself whom the Father sent), social (God's love is clearly seen in the sending of His Son, 9, 10, 16, thus obliging us to love each other) and ethical (if Christ came to be our *Saviour*, we must forsake the sins from which He came to save us). It is clear, then, that John's tests are not arbitrary. He has not made a random selection. They arise inexorably from the central Christian revelation. The mission of Christ manifests both His divine Person, God's great love and our moral duty. Once grasp the truth of verse 14, and we shall confess Christ, love one another and keep the commandments.

15. Of these three tests it is the doctrinal one on which John now lays emphasis (cf. ii. 23, iv. 2). The aorist tense (*homologēsē*) cannot be rendered precisely in English. John is referring neither to a future confession (AV, RV *shall confess*), nor to a present and continuing confession ('confesses', RSV; 'acknowledges', NEB) but to a single and decisive public confession, the time of which is unspecified. But how do men come thus to acknowledge the deity of Jesus? The apostolic testimony is necessary (14) but it does not compel assent. It is by the Spirit of God that men confess that Jesus is the Christ come in the flesh (iv. 2). Or, as he puts the same truth here, *whosoever shall confess that Jesus is the Son of God* thereby gives evidence of the fact that *God dwelleth in him, and he in God*. As we have pointed out above, the witness of the apostles must be supplemented by the witness of the Spirit (cf. v. 7).

16. The historical mission of Jesus is evidence as much of the Father's love as of the Son's deity. It tells us not only that God loved, but that *God is love*. However, it is one thing to know and believe *the love that God hath to us* and that *God is love*; it is another to learn to love and to abide *in love* ourselves. Yet this we must do, for (as John has unfolded at great length in verses 7–12) the love that is eternally in God and was historically manifested in Christ is to come to fruition in us. The only way to love, as the only way to believe (15), is by dwelling in God and God in us. The apostle does not mean that the way to come to dwell in God and He in us is to confess Christ's divine Sonship (15) and to abide in love (16), but the reverse. It is the divine indwelling which alone makes possible both belief and love. They are its fruit, and therefore its evidence: 'he who dwells in love is (i.e. is thereby seen to be) dwelling in God' (NEB).

There is, then, in these verses a double interweaving of themes, first of believing and loving (the doctrinal and social tests), and secondly of the mission of the Son and the witness of the Spirit through which both are possible. There is objective historical evidence in the sending of the Son both of His deity (which *we have seen*, 14) and of the Father's love (which *we have known and believed*, 16). But even this is insufficient. Without the Holy Spirit our minds are dark and our hearts cold. Only the Holy Spirit can enlighten our minds to believe in Jesus and warm our hearts to love God and each other. So believing and loving are evidence that His Spirit is at work within us.

ii. Perfect love (iv. 17–21). In verse 12 John declared that if we love each other, God dwells in us and His love has been perfected in us. In verses 13–16 he has enlarged on the divine indwelling; in verses 17–21 he reverts to the theme of perfect love, although now he is concerned with the perfection not of God's love in us but of our love for God. John is not suggesting that any Christian's love could in this life be flawlessly perfect, but rather developed and mature, set fixedly upon God. 'Herein is our love made perfect' should literally read 'in this is love perfected with us' (RSV), but that the AV certainly gives the correct sense is clear from the two marks of love for God which are now described, namely confidence before God and love of the brethren.

17. *Parrēsia, boldness* or confidence, is a characteristic word

of this Epistle. The author has already written of the un-
shrinking confidence which we shall have at Christ's coming
if we abide in Him now (ii. 28 and note), and of our present
confidence before God in prayer (iii. 21, 22), which, as he says
later, is an assurance not only of access but of being heard and
answered (v. 14, 15). Here, however, he reverts to the future,
to *the day of judgment* which will follow the Lord's return. There
is no evidence that John has jettisoned belief either in the
Parousia or in the Judgment Day. That day will be one of
shame and terror for the wicked, but not for the redeemed
people of God. Our confidence (like obedience in ii. 5) is a
sign that our love is *made perfect*. It is grounded upon the fact
that *as he is* (i.e. Christ), *so are we in this world*. Jesus is God's
beloved Son, in whom He is well pleased; we too are God's
children (cf. iii. 1) and the objects of His favour. If He called
and calls God 'Father', so may we. We are 'accepted in the
beloved' (Eph. i. 6); we can share His confidence towards
God.

18. The same truth is now stated negatively. The love that
spells confidence banishes fear. *There is no fear* (i.e. no servile
fear) *in love*, that is, 'there is no room for fear in love' (NEB).
The two are as incompatible as oil and water. We can love
and reverence God simultaneously (cf. Heb. v. 7), but we
cannot approach Him in love and hide from Him in fear at
the same time (cf. Rom. viii. 14, 15; 2 Tim. i. 7). Indeed, it is
by love for God that a false cringing fear of God is overcome.
It 'flings it out of doors' (Law). The reason why perfect love
cannot coexist with fear is now given. *Torment* should be
'punishment' (RV, RSV, the word being *kolasis* which occurs
elsewhere in the New Testament only in Mt. xxv. 46). *Hath*
(*echei*) may mean 'has to do with punishment' (RSV). That is,
fear introduces the category of punishment, which is quite
alien to God's forgiven children who love Him. Or it may
signify rather 'includes, brings with it' (Westcott, cf. NEB) the
punishment it fears. In other words, 'fear has in itself something of the nature of punishment' (Brooke, Law); to fear is to
begin to suffer punishment already. Once assured that we are

'as he is' (17), God's beloved children, we cease to be afraid of Him. It is evident, therefore, that *he that feareth is not made perfect in love.*

19. So we are not afraid of God. Instead, *we love him*, or, following the better reading, simply and absolutely without any expressed object, *we love* (*agapōmen*, which is here surely an indicative statement and not an exhortation in the subjunctive as it is in verse 7). Our great characteristic if we are Christians, he says, is not that we fear, but that we love. God's love was primary; all true love is a response to His initiative. John repeats the truth he has asserted in verse 10. Fear dwells within us by nature and needs to be cast out (18). *Agapē*, godlike love, on the other hand, does not reside in our fallen nature; 'our very capacity to love, whether the object of our love be God or our neighbour' (Dodd) is due entirely to His prior love for us and in us.

20. Love for God does not only express itself in a confident attitude towards Him, devoid of fear, but in a loving concern for our fellow Christians (cf. iii. 14). The perfect love that casts out fear, casts out hatred also. If God's love for us is made perfect when we love one another (12), so is our love for God. John does not mince his words. If what a man is contradicts what he says, *he is a liar.* To claim to know God and have fellowship with God while we walk in the darkness of dis-obedience is to lie (i. 6, ii. 4). To claim to possess the Father while denying the deity of the Son is to lie (ii. 22, 23). To claim to love God while hating the brethren is to lie also. These are the three black lies of the Epistle, moral, doctrinal and social. However loudly we may affirm ourselves to be Christian, our habitual sin, denial of Christ and selfish hatred expose us as the liars we are. Only holiness, faith and love can prove the truth of our claim to know, possess and love God.

That it is ludicrous for a man to say he loves God while he hates his brother should be clear from the fact that he can see his brother but cannot see God. Indeed, the verb indicates not only that he 'can' see his brother, but that he *hath seen* him (*heōraken*); he has him 'continually before his eyes' (Plummer), with ample opportunity to serve him in love. It is obviously easier to love and serve a visible man than an invisible God, and if we fail in the easier task, it is absurd to claim success in the harder. 'It is a false boast when anyone says that he loves God but neglects His image which is before his eyes' (Calvin). According to a reading followed by RV, RSV, NEB, the sentence is in the form not of a question (*pōs dunatai*; *how can he?*), but of an assertion (*ou dunatai*; 'he cannot'). As C. H. Dodd points out, this 'cannot' expresses not so much the man's incapacity to love God, as the proof that he does not. It is easy to deceive oneself. The truth, however, is plain. Every claim to love God is a delusion if it is not accompanied by unselfish and practical love for our brethren (iii. 17–18).

21. The folly of the liar's position is seen not only in its inherent inconsistency, but in the fact that love for God and for our brother form one single commandment (cf. iii. 23). *From him* seems to refer to Christ, as NEB makes explicit. Jesus Himself taught this twofold commandment. It was He who united Deuteronomy vi. 4 and Leviticus xix. 18 and declared that all the law and the prophets depended upon them (Mt. xxii. 37–40). Man may not separate what Jesus has joined. Besides, if we love God we shall keep His commandments (ii. 5, v. 3), and His commandment is to love our neighbour as ourselves.

c. A combination of the three tests (v. 1–5)

We have by now become familiar with the three tests which John applies, with repeated but varied emphasis, to the professing Christian. In chapter ii he describes all three tests in order, obedience (3–6), love (7–11) and belief (18–27). In chapter iii he treats only obedience (ii. 28–iii. 10) and love (11–18), while in chapter iv only belief (1–6) and love (7–12). In iv. 13–21 he has combined the doctrinal and social tests. Now, however, in the brief opening paragraph of chapter v, we meet the three together again. The words 'believe' and 'faith' occur in verses 1, 4 and 5, 'love' in verses 1, 2 and 3, and 'obey' or 'keep his commandments' in verses 2 and 3.

What he is at pains to show is the essential unity of his three-fold thesis. He has not chosen three tests arbitrarily or at random and stuck them together artificially. On the contrary, he shows that they are so closely woven together into a single, coherent fabric that it is difficult to unpick and disentangle the threads.

The previous paragraph, at the end of chapter iv, ended with a statement of our duty, if we love God, to love our brother also. The author now elaborates the essential connection between these two loves and between them and both belief and obedience. This compressed paragraph begins and ends with belief, but between these two termini he writes about love and obedience. The real link between the three tests is seen to be the new birth. Faith, love and obedience are the natural growth which follows a birth from above, just as in iv. 13–16 faith and love were shown to be evidences of the mutual indwelling of God and His people.

1. Neither AV *is born of God* nor RSV, NEB 'is a child of God' is a very satisfactory translation of *ek tou theou gegennētai*, whose perfect tense means literally 'has been born (RV "begotten") of God'. The combination of present tense (*ho pisteuōn*, *believeth*) and perfect is important. It shows clearly that believing is the consequence, not the cause, of the new birth. Our present, continuing activity of believing is the result, and therefore the evidence, of our past experience of new birth by which we became and remain God's children. Moreover, belief in Christ is congruous with birth of God just because Christ is Son of God (cf. verses 1 and 5). Clearly the sons of God will manifest the fact that they have been begotten of God by recognizing and believing in God's eternal, only begotten Son.

This new birth, which brings us into believing recognition of the eternal Son, also involves us in a loving relationship with the Father and His other children. He who has been begotten of God naturally loves Him who begat him (this is to be understood in the sentence), and 'every one who loves the parent loves the child' (RSV). Here is a universal, self-evident principle. And John implies that 'what is true of the human family is also true of the Divine Society' (Brooke). But the clumsier AV sentence retains more obviously the truth that it is the 'begetting' and the experience of being 'begotten' which establish an affinity and therefore an affection not only between parent and child but between children and children. The expression *him . . . that is begotten of him* can hardly in this context be made to refer to the only begotten Son (as Augustine thought), but rather to every child of God.

2, 3. Indeed, so surely and unavoidably does love for the heavenly Parent carry with it love for His children on earth that we can say, *by this we know that we love the children of God, when we love God.* It is as impossible to love the children of God (as such) without loving God as it is to love God without loving His children (iv. 20, 21). A family relationship unites the two loves. Love for God has a second inescapable consequence, namely obedience. If we truly love God, we not only love His children, but also *keep his commandments*. In verse 3 John goes further. So inexorable is the connection between the two that love for God, which in one sense issues in obedience, in another sense may be identified with it. Love for God is not an emotional experience so much as moral obedience. Indeed, whether shown to God or man, *agapē* is practical and active. Love for the brethren expresses itself 'in deed and in truth', in sacrificial service (iii. 17, 18); love for God in keeping His commandments. Jesus said the same thing about the meaning of love for Himself (Jn. xiv. 15, 21).

Nor should we find it difficult to express our love by our obedience, *for his commandments are not grievous*, 'irksome' (Moffatt), or 'burdensome' (RSV, NEB). The pernickety regulations of the scribes and Pharisees were 'heavy burdens, hard to bear' (Mt. xxiii. 4, RSV; cf. Lk. xi. 46), but the yoke of Jesus is easy and His burden light (Mt. xi. 30). God's will is 'good, acceptable and perfect' (Rom. xii. 2). It is the will of an all-wise, all-loving Father who seeks our highest welfare.

4a. The reason why we do not find the commandments of God burdensome lies not, however, only in their character. It lies also in ourselves, namely that we have been given the possibility of keeping them. The commandments of God today, whether found in the Old Testament or the New, appear intolerably burdensome to the world. But to the children of God they are not 'grievous', because *whatsoever is born of God overcometh the world*. By the use of the neuter *whatsoever* John states the principle in its most general and abstract form. He does so to emphasize not 'the victorious *person*' but 'the victorious *power*' (Plummer). 'It is not the man, but his birth from God, which conquers' (*ibid.*). The new birth is a super-natural event which takes us out of the sphere of the world, where Satan rules, into the family of God. We have been delivered from the dominion of darkness and transferred into the kingdom of God's dear Son (Col. i. 13). The spell of the old life has been broken. The fascination of the world has lost its appeal.

4b, 5. Three times in three successive sentences, as if to rub the truth home irresistibly, John repeats the phrase *overcometh the world*. First, he declares that *whatsoever is born of God overcometh the world*. He goes on to ascribe the Christian's conquest not to his birth but to his *faith*. He then proceeds to enlarge on this fact in the form of a question: *Who is he that overcometh the world, but he that believeth that Jesus is the Son of God?*

It is noteworthy that in the second of these three references to overcoming the verb is an aorist participle (*hē nikēsasa*). It 'naturally points to a definite act, or fact' (Brooke), not to the victory which Christ claimed to have won in John xvi. 33 (Westcott), but either to the conversion of the readers, or, more probably, to their decisive rejection of the false teaching and the withdrawal of the false teachers from the Church. This was the victory mentioned in iv. 4 (*nenikēkate*, perfect). However, the other two occurrences of the verb here are in the present tense (*nika*, verse 4, and *ho nikōn*, verse 5) and describe the continuous victory which the Christian should enjoy. What is this victory? It is won over *the world*, by which word John 'gathers up the sum of all the limited, transitory powers opposed to God which make obedience difficult' (Westcott).

Sometimes these are moral pressures—the outlook, standards and preoccupations of a godless, secular society, 'the lust of the flesh, and the lust of the eyes, and the pride of life' (ii. 16). Sometimes they are intellectual (heresy) and sometimes physical (persecution). But, whatever form the world's assault upon the Church may take, the victory is ours. The unshakable conviction that the Jesus of history is 'the Christ' (v. 1), in the sense in which the false teachers denied it (ii. 22), the pre-existent 'Son of God' (v. 5), who came to bring us salvation and life (iv. 14, 9), enables us to triumph over the world. Confidence in the deity of Jesus is the one weapon against which neither the error, nor the evil, nor the force of the world can prevail. E. M. Blaiklock, who entitles his devotional studies in this Epistle, *Faith is the Victory*, rightly points out the daring of this first-century claim that the victory belongs not to Rome, then reigning supreme, but to Christ and the humble believer in Christ.

With this final sentence, affirming belief in Jesus, we are back where we started, and the argument has come full circle. Let us summarize it: Christian believers are God's children, born from above. God's children are loved by all who love God. Those who love God also keep His commandments. They keep His commandments because they overcome the world, and they overcome the world because they are Christian believers, born from above.

One way of unravelling this argument is to regard it not as a circle but as a long line and to make obedience the centre of it. The two extremities are identical, namely birth of God leading to belief in Christ. Moving forwards from the beginning, the believing child of God reaches obedience by way of love for God and for the children of God. Moving backwards from the end, the road from belief to obedience is by way of the conquest of the world. In both cases belief and obedience are coupled, whether the link is loving God or overcoming the world. The new birth has the double result of detaching us from the world and attaching us to God. The result in each case is keeping the commandments.

Another way is to regard the centre of the sentence as *this is the love of God* (3). Certainly the word *love* occurs five times in this paragraph and is strongly emphasized. Certainly, too, faith and love are as indissoluble as faith and obedience. Indeed, 'faith . . . worketh by love' (Gal. v. 6). Thus, if we love God, on the one hand we love the children of God because we are born of God and believe in Christ, and on the other hand we keep the commandments of God and overcome the world because we are born of God and believe in Christ. Here love for God and faith in Jesus are chained to each other by the links of brotherly love and obedience.

Whichever is the best way of seeking to follow John's closely-knit argument, what is plain is that his three tests belong together and cannot be separated. The true Christian, born from above, believes in the Son of God, loves God and the children of God, and keeps the commandments of God. Each involves the others. Belief, love and obedience are marks of the new birth. The new birth brings us willynilly into a certain relation to Christ, to God, to the Church and to the world which we cannot repudiate and which marks us out as Christians.

VI. THE THREE WITNESSES AND OUR CONSEQUENT ASSURANCE (v. 6–17)

We have already noted that the previous paragraph begins and ends with a reference to faith, viz. believing that the human Jesus is (i.e. is the same Person as) the Christ (1), or the Son of God (5). John's full formula of Christian faith is that Jesus is 'the Christ come in the flesh' (iv. 2; 2 Jn. 7).

But how can we come to faith in the divine-human Person of Jesus? John's answer here, as in the Gospel, is that faith depends on testimony, and that the reasonableness of believing in Jesus is grounded upon the validity of the testimony which is borne to Him. Verses 6–9 describe the nature of the testimony (by the 'three witnesses' 8, RSV) and verses 10–12 its results; while in verses 13–17 the Christian's consequent assurance is unfolded.

a. The three witnesses (v. 6–12)

6. Jesus, who has been called 'the Christ' (v. 1) and 'the Son of God' (v. 5), is now further and more fully described, particularly with regard to His mission on earth. *This is he that came by water and blood, even Jesus Christ; not by water only, but by water and blood.* Various interpretations have been given to these phrases, which Plummer calls the 'most perplexing' in the Epistle. There can be little doubt that John was using an expression which was already familiar to his readers, either through his own teaching or through that of the false teachers, and which is not so readily understood by us. There have been three principal suggestions about the meaning of *water and blood*.

First, some commentators (including Luther and Calvin) have seen in them a reference to the two sacraments of the gospel. This is extremely doubtful, at least as the primary thought. If *water* stands for baptism, *blood* would be an unprecedented symbol for the Lord's Supper. It would also be an unnatural symbol, both because blood is one of the things signified, not one of the signs, and because no reference is made to the body of Christ. Further, although it might be possible to describe Jesus as 'coming' through the sacraments, it is difficult to see how it could be said that He came (aorist, *ho elthōn*) through them. The verb clearly indicates not some present activity of Jesus but His past historical coming.

The second interpretation (adopted by Augustine and other ancient commentators) links the passage with the spear thrust and the issue of blood and water from the side of Jesus recorded in John xix. 34, 35. Certainly, both passages are Johannine, and both are associated with testimony, and the flow of blood and water was a past, historical event. Even so, it would be forced to say that in this incident Jesus *came by* (that is, 'through') *water and blood*, when in fact they came out of Him. Moreover, the link between blood and water and testimony, which we have observed in both passages, is not identical. In the Gospel it is the Evangelist who bears witness to them; here it is they which bear witness to Christ. Again, if in the Gospel they are taken as bearing any witness it must be to the reality of Christ's death, and perhaps to the saving efficacy of it; but here in the Epistle they bear witness to Christ's divine-human Person.

We need therefore to find an interpretation of the phrase which makes *water and blood* both historical experiences 'through' which He passed and witnesses in some sense to His divine-human Person. The third and most satisfactory interpretation, first given by Tertullian, does this. It takes *water* as referring to the baptism of Jesus, at which He was declared the Son and commissioned and empowered for His work, and *blood* to His death, in which His work was finished. True, 'water' and 'blood' remain strange and surprising word symbols, and we can only guess that they were thus used in the theological controversy which had engulfed the Ephesian church. At least this meaning of the expression tallies with what Irenaeus disclosed of the heretical teaching of the Cerinthian Gnostics. They distinguished between 'Jesus' and 'the Christ'. They held that Jesus was a mere man, born of Joseph and Mary in natural wedlock, upon whom the Christ descended at the baptism and from whom the Christ departed before the cross. According to this theory of the false teachers, Jesus was united with the Christ at the baptism, but became separated again before the cross. It was to refute this fundamental error that John, knowing that Jesus was the Christ before and during the baptism and during and after the cross, described Him as 'he who came through water and blood'. Neither word has the definite article. The author is stressing the unity of the earthly career of Jesus Christ. He who came (from heaven, that is) is the same as He who passed 'through' water and blood. For further emphasis he adds (using the definite article this time before each noun, and changing the preposition from *dia*, 'through', to *en*, 'in'), 'not with the water only', since the heretics agreed that at least He was the Christ at His baptism, 'but with the water and (with) the blood' (RV, RSV). 'The statement is as precise as grammar can make it' (Brooke), and it is disappointing that the NEB does not express this precision. For full measure, in opposition to the heretics' differentiation between Jesus and the Christ, John adds that the One who so came was *even Jesus Christ*, one Person who was simultaneously from His birth to His death and for evermore (*this is he*, present tense) both the man Jesus and the Christ of God. See notes on iv. 3.

Cerinthus and his followers are dead, and their particular creed has no adherents today. Yet all who deny the incarnation, whether or not they believe that the Person of Jesus underwent a change at the baptism to fit Him for His public ministry, deny that He *came by water and blood*. This is no trivial error. It undermines the foundations of the Christian faith and robs us of the salvation of Christ. If the Son of God did not take to Himself our nature in His birth and our sins in His death, He cannot reconcile us to God. So John emphasizes not just that He *came*, but especially that He came by water and *blood*, since it is His blood which cleanses from sin (i. 7).

Having accepted that the primary reference of this verse is to the historical events of the baptism and crucifixion of Jesus, it is not impossible that it also contains secondary allusions, since the past events remain present witnesses (8). 'Water and blood', which occur together in some of the Levitical rituals, are intelligible symbols of 'purification and redemption' (Plummer). Candlish, who insists much on this interpretation, draws the distinction between 'precious blood to atone for all guilt' and 'pure water to cleanse from all pollution', and refers the symbols to the blessings of justification and sanctification available through the gospel. To these aspects of salvation Jesus Himself had referred in the discourses which John recorded in chapters iii, iv and vii ('water') and vi ('blood') of his Gospel. Perhaps John also saw them set forth once in the issue of blood and water from the side of the Crucified, and even regularly in the two sacraments.

And it is the Spirit that beareth witness. This is undoubtedly a reference to the Holy Spirit. The form of the Greek construction indicates that it is characteristic of the Spirit that He 'bear witness' as it is of Christ that He 'came' (at the beginning of the verse). The fact that He is said to bear witness gives evidence, 'the more striking because involuntary' (Smith), of His personality, since testifying is an activity of persons. Of what His witness consists is not explicitly stated, but both the

context and the teaching of Epistle and Gospel suggest that
He testifies to Christ (e.g. iv. 2). He is competent to do so,
Jesus said, because He is 'the Spirit of truth' (Jn. xv. 26, xvi.
13; cf. 1 Jn. iv. 6). John goes further and writes *because the
Spirit is truth*, or, more accurately, 'is the truth' (RV, RSV;
contrast Jn. xiv. 6)—conveying either that He is 'essentially
fitted' to bear witness, or that He is 'constrained' to do so
(Westcott). The truth cannot be hid. But how does the Spirit
bear witness? John appears to be referring to the inward
witness of the Holy Spirit, who opens our eyes to see the truth
as it is in Jesus (cf. 1 Cor. xii. 3, etc.). Certainly he has written
twice already of how the Spirit has been 'given to us' as an
indwelling possession (iii. 24, iv. 13) and has twice ascribed
our confession of Christ as the divine-human Lord to the
'anointing' or enlightenment of the Spirit (ii. 20, 27 and iv.
1–6). We have then here, as in iv. 13, 14, two kinds of corro-
borative testimony, objective and subjective, historical and
experimental, *water and blood* on the one hand and *the Spirit*
on the other. 'He it is who seals in our hearts the testimony of
the water and the blood' (Calvin).

7. The whole of this verse must be regarded as a gloss, as
must the words *in earth* in verse 8. Plummer calls the reading
'quite indefensible' and gives a very thorough survey of the
evidence in an Appendix (pp. 163–172), and so does Brooke
(pp. 154–165). The words do not occur in any Greek MS,
version or quotation before the fifteenth century. They first
appear in an obscure fourth-century Latin MS and found their
way into the AV because Erasmus reluctantly included them in
the third edition of his text. They are rightly absent even from
the margin of RV and RSV. Some tidy-minded scribe, impressed
by the threefold witness of verse 8, must have been made to
think of the Trinity and so suggested that there was a threefold
witness in heaven also. Actually, his gloss is not a very happy
one, as the threefold testimony of verse 8 is to Christ; and the
biblical teaching about testimony is not that Father, Son and
Holy Spirit bear witness together to the Son, but that the
Father bears witness to the Son through the Spirit.

8. Having written independently of 'the water and the blood' (6, RSV), and of the Spirit, without stating that the former were in any sense a 'witness', John now brings the three together and declares that they all *bear witness*. Moreover, *these three agree in one*, or better, simply 'agree' (RSV) or 'are in agreement' (NEB). The false witnesses at the trial of Jesus, seeking to discredit Him, did not agree (Mk. xiv. 56, 59); the true witnesses, however, the Spirit, the water and the blood, seeking to accredit Him, are in perfect agreement. The importance of the 'three witnesses' (RSV, NEB) is that according to the law no charge could be preferred against a man in court unless it could be confirmed by the evidence of two or three witnesses (Dt. xix. 15; cf. Jn. viii. 17, 18). In contrast to verse 6, the Spirit is here placed as the first witness, partly because 'the Spirit is, of the three, the only living and active witness', and partly because 'the water and the blood are no witnesses without Him; whereas He is independent of them, testifying both in them and out of them' (Alford).

9. The importance of this verse is that it declares explicitly what has so far only been hinted, namely both the subject (God) and the object (Christ) of the witness. The Spirit, the water and the blood all bear witness to Christ, and the reason why they agree is that God Himself is behind them. The three witnesses form, in fact, a single divine testimony to Jesus Christ, which God *hath testified*. The perfect tense indicates the abiding validity (in itself and through the Spirit) of God's historical witness to Christ. It is God who bore witness to His Son in history, in the water and the blood, and it is God who bears witness to Him today through His Spirit in our hearts. Moreover, it is because (*for, hoti*) the witness is divine, that we ought humbly to receive it, for *if we receive the witness of men*, when it consists of the evidence of two or three, we should certainly receive *the witness of God* which is itself threefold and which, because it is God's, *is greater* than any man's. The word *if* expresses not a doubt, but a fact: 'we accept human testimony, but surely divine testimony is stronger' (NEB).

10. Having described the nature of the testimony (the threefold divine witness to the Son through the Spirit, the water and the blood), John proceeds to unfold its results (10–12). The purpose of testimony to Christ is to evoke faith in Christ (e.g. Jn. i. 7, xx. 31). Receiving the testimony leads naturally to believing in the One to whom the testimony is borne. Indeed, to 'receive the witness . . . of God' (9) and to 'believe on the Son of God' (10) are virtually synonymous expressions. Further, so identical in meaning are the two phrases, that at the end of the verse John can use the preposition *eis* with *the record that God gave of his Son*, making the object of our personal confidence not the Son but God's witness to Him. The results of belief and disbelief are starkly contrasted. The believer *hath the witness in himself*, or 'in his own heart' (NEB). That is, he is given a yet deeper assurance by the inward witness of the Spirit that he was right to trust in Christ, a striking example of the spiritual principle that 'to everyone who has will more be given' (Mt. xxv. 29; Lk. xix. 26, RSV; cf. Mk. iv. 25). Testimony is thus both the cause and the consequence of belief, and belief is a stepping-stone between God's first and further testimony. The unbeliever, on the other hand, who 'has not believed' (RSV, the perfect tense indicating a past 'crisis of choice'—Westcott), forfeits the possibility of receiving any further testimony from God because he has rejected the first and in so doing *hath made him a liar*. Unbelief is not a misfortune to be pitied; it is a sin to be deplored. Its sinfulness lies in the fact that it contradicts the word of the one true God and thus attributes falsehood to Him. Another example of 'making God a liar' is to be found in i. 10.

11, 12. John now forgets the unbeliever and summarizes the blessing granted to the believer who receives and responds to the testimony of God. *This is the record* is the same expression as that in verse 9, 'this is the witness'. There it looks back to what I have called the 'first' testimony, that of the water, the blood and the Spirit. Here it seems to include also the 'further' testimony which, according to verse 10, the believer receives 'in himself'. This becomes more plain when we consider how the record is here described, namely *that God hath given* (RSV, rightly, 'gave') *to us eternal life, and this life is in his Son.* To what event does it refer? Some commentators refer it to the historical career of Jesus (cf. i. 2 and Jn. x. 10, 28, xvii. 2) and some to our conversion, at which we personally appropriated, or were given, the life that is in Christ (cf. iii. 14). Perhaps both are true, and both are part of the 'record', historical and experimental, which God has given concerning His Son. Historically, God's witness concerning (*peri*, verses 9, 10) Jesus is not only that He is the divine-human Christ but that He is the Life-giver, 'the Saviour of the world' (iv. 14), not only that He is the Son, but that in Him is life. *Eternal life* is emphatic in the sentence; i.e. the record is that it is eternal life which God gave us in giving His Son. But the witness is not only objective to Christ as the Life-giver but subjective in the gift of life itself. Eternal life is a free gift which God gives to those who believe in His Son, and the gift of life, the experience of fellowship with God through Christ which is eternal life (cf. Jn. xvii. 3), is God's final testimony to His Son (cf. verse 20). John has previously written: 'he that believeth on the Son of God hath the witness in himself' (10). He now puts the same truth in these words: *He that hath the Son* (cf. ii. 23 for another use of the verb *echein* to describe our personal possession of the Father through confessing the Son) *hath life; and he that hath not the Son of God hath not life* (literally, both times, 'the life', RV). The alternative is clear and uncompromising. We cannot escape its logic. Eternal life is in His Son and may be found nowhere else. It is as impossible to have life without having Christ as it is to have Christ without thereby having life also. This is because the Son is the life (i. 2; Jn. xi. 25, xiv. 6).

Three important truths are taught in these verses about eternal life. First, it is not a prize which we have earned, but an undeserved gift. Secondly, it is found in Christ, so that, in order to give us life, God both gave and gives us His Son. Thirdly, this gift of life in Christ is a present possession. True, it is further described as *eternal, aiōnios*, which means literally 'belonging to the age', i.e. the age to come. But since the age to come has broken into this present age, the life of the age to come, namely 'eternal life', can be received and enjoyed here and now.

In this paragraph (6–12) John has been elaborating what he has stated briefly in one verse of the Gospel: 'But these are written, that ye might believe that Jesus is the Christ, the Son of God; and that believing ye might have life through his name' (Jn. xx. 31). The Gospel, recording the words and works of Jesus, was John's testimony to Jesus as 'the Christ, the Son of God'. The purpose of this testimony was 'that you may believe', and the result of faith is 'that believing you may have life in his name'. The way to life is faith, and the way to faith is testimony. The sequence of thought is the same here. God has borne witness to His Son that men may believe in Him and so 'have' Him, and having Him may have life.

b. Our consequent assurance (v. 13–17)

13. Although the RV, RSV and NEB begin a new paragraph with this verse, it belongs essentially to the previous section and forms a fitting conclusion to what the author has there written both about the three witnesses and about having eternal life in the Son. Here he tells his readers the ostensible purpose of his Epistle, now drawing to a close—and it is natural to contrast it with the purpose of his Gospel in xx. 31 to which we have just referred. The Epistle was *written . . . that ye may know that ye have eternal life*, the last sentence of the verse in the AV being rightly omitted in the RV, RSV and NEB. It does not occur in the best manuscripts and is clearly a gloss, whose intrusion destroys the evident meaning of the verse. The Gospel was written for unbelievers, that they might read the testimony of God to His Son, believe in the Son to whom the testimony pointed, and thus receive life through faith. The Epistle, on the other hand, was written for believers. John's desire for them is not that they may believe and receive, but that having believed, they may know that they have received, and therefore continue to *have* (present), *eternal life. That ye may know (eidēte)* means, both in word and tense, not that they may gradually grow in assurance, but that they may possess here and now a present certainty of the life they have received in Christ. They had been unsettled by the false teachers and become unsure of their spiritual state. Throughout the Epistle

John has been giving them criteria (doctrinal, moral, social) by which to test themselves and others. His purpose is to establish their assurance. 'This letter is to assure you that you have eternal life' (NEB).

Putting together the purposes of Gospel and Epistle, John's purpose is in four stages, that his readers should hear, hearing should believe, believing should live, and living should know. His emphasis is important because it is common today to decry any claim to assurance of salvation, to dismiss it as presumptuous, and to affirm that no certainty is possible on this side of death. But certainty and humility do not exclude one another. If God's revealed purpose is not only that we should hear, believe and live, but also that we should know, presumptuousness lies in doubting His word, not in trusting it.

14, 15. In verses 14–17 John moves to a second assurance enjoyed by the believing Christian, not now of eternal life, but of answered prayer. This assurance is not so much a 'knowledge' (as in verse 13, although it results in one, 15) as a *confidence*, a 'freedom of speech' as *parrēsia* means literally, or 'boldness . . . toward' God (RV; Gk. *pros*). See note on ii. 28. The preposition points to that active approach to God and fellowship with Him which are the expression of the eternal life of which John has been writing (11–13). This Christian confidence belongs not just to the future, to the Parousia (ii. 28) and the Judgment Day (iv. 17), but to the here and now. It is a confidence both in the manner of our approach to God, free and bold (iii. 21), and in its outcome, namely *that . . . he heareth us*. The qualification, however, is *if we ask any thing according to his will*. In iii. 22 the condition of answered prayer is whether our behaviour accords with God's commandments; here whether our requests accord with His will. Prayer is not a convenient device for imposing our will upon God, or bending His will to ours, but the prescribed way of subordinating our will to His. It is by prayer that we seek God's will, embrace it and align ourselves with it. Every true prayer is a variation on the theme 'Thy will be done'. Our Master taught us to say this in the pattern prayer He gave us, and added the supreme example of it in

Gethsemane. In such prayers, and only in such, *he heareth us*, that is, not just that our petitions register and He takes note of them, but He listens favourably to us, He gives ear to our cry (as in Jn. ix. 31, xi. 41, 42). The Christian confidence is tantamount to a double certainty (*oidamen . . . oidamen*), which is in reality one. To say *we know that he heareth us* is the same as saying *we know that we have the petitions that we desired of him*. The present tense *we have, echomen* (RSV, 'we have obtained') is striking, and reminiscent of Mark xi. 24 where we are told to believe we did receive (*elabete*) what we request, and so it shall be (*estai*). 'Our petitions are granted at once: the results of the granting are perceived in the future' (Plummer).

16. Having written generally of answered prayer (14, 15), John now gives a specific illustration and a limitation (16, 17). It is not now a case of petition, but of intercession. The assurance of eternal life which the Christian should enjoy (13) ought not to lead him into a preoccupation with himself to the neglect of others. On the contrary, he will recognize his duty in love to care for his brother in need, whether the need which he 'sees' be material (as in iii. 17, 18) or, as here, spiritual: *if any man see his brother sin*. He cannot say 'am I my brother's keeper?' and do nothing. The future tense *he shall ask* expresses not the writer's command but the Christian's inevitable and spontaneous reaction. This is the way to deal with sin in the congregation. And God hears such prayer. *He shall ask, and he shall give him life*. Since God is the giver of life (cf. verses 11, 20), and since usually 'asking is man's part and giving God's' (Plummer), some have suggested a change of subject in the middle of this sentence, so that the second *he* refers to God and not to the intercessor. So RV, RSV. But the verbs are so simply and closely coupled in the Greek (*aitēsei kai dōsei*), that a different subject would be very forced. It is better to accept the ascription of real efficacy to prayer (as in verse 15), so that, under God, he who asks life for a man may be said not just to gain it for him but to give it to him. In either case the *him* to whom life is given is the sinner, not the intercessor. Cf. James v. 15, 20 where the prayer of faith for a sick man and the one who brings back a sinner are both said to 'save' him.

Not every sinner can be given life in answer to prayer, however. John draws a distinction between *a sin which is not unto death* and *a sin unto death.* For those who commit the former the Christian will pray, and by prayer will give them life. For the latter John does not enjoin prayer; *I do not say that he shall pray for it,* that is, for one who is recognized as committing it. True, he does not explicitly forbid prayer, as God forbade Jeremiah to pray for the people of Judah (Je. vii. 16, xi. 14, xiv. 11; cf. 1 Sa. ii. 25); but he does not advise it, for he clearly doubts its efficacy in this case.

What, then, is the *sin unto death*? John's readers were no doubt familiar with the expression, but commentators since the subapostolic Fathers have debated its meaning. It cannot refer to a sin punishable by physical death, as in Acts v. 1–11 and 1 Corinthians v. 5, xi. 30, since the life with which it is contrasted is clearly spiritual or eternal life. In one sense all sin is 'unto death' spiritually, for death is the penalty for sin (Rom. v. 12, vi. 23; Jas. i. 15); but here John distinguishes between sin which is unto death and sin which is not. We may divide the possible interpretations into three.

1. *A specific sin.* In the Mosaic law certain sins were listed as capital offences, punishable by death (e.g. Lv. xx. 1–27; Nu. xviii. 22; cf. Rom. i. 32). Further, in the Old Testament generally a distinction was drawn between sins of ignorance, committed unwittingly, which could be cleansed through sacrifice, and wanton or 'presumptuous' sins (Ps. xix. 13), committed 'with a high hand', for which there was no forgiveness. The same distinction was 'common among Rabbinic writers' (Westcott), and certain early Christian Fathers carried it over into the gospel age. Clement of Alexandria and Origen both accepted that a line could be drawn between forgivable and unforgivable sins, but declined to classify them. Tertullian went a stage further and listed the grosser sins (including murder, adultery, blasphemy and idolatry) as beyond pardon, while minor offences could be forgiven. This developed into the familiar, casuistical differentiation between 'mortal' and

'venial' sins and the specification of the 'seven deadly sins'. But there is no New Testament warrant for such an arbitrary classification of sins, and certainly 'it would be an anachronism to try to apply it here' (Dodd). Indeed, although the rendering is 'a mortal sin' in RSV and 'a deadly sin' in NEB, it is doubtful whether John is referring to specific 'sins' at all, as opposed to 'sin' (as in i. 8), that is, 'a state or habit of sin wilfully chosen and persisted in' (Plummer).

2. *Apostasy*. The second suggestion, favoured among modern commentators by Brooke, Law and C. H. Dodd, is that the 'sin unto death' is neither a specific sin, nor even a 'back-sliding', but a total apostasy, the denial of Christ and the renunciation of the faith. Those who hold this view usually link these verses with such passages as Hebrews vi. 4–6, x. 26 ff. and xii. 16, 17, and apply them to the false teachers who had, in fact, so clearly repudiated the truth as to withdraw from the Church (ii. 19).

But can a Christian, who has been born of God, apostatize? Surely John has taught clearly in the Epistle that the true Christian cannot sin, that is, persist in sin (iii. 9), let alone fall away altogether. He is about to repeat it: 'we know that anyone born of God does not sin, but He who was born of God keeps him, and the evil one does not touch him' (18, RSV). Can he who does not sin, 'sin unto death'? Moreover, John has just written of having life (12) and knowing it (13). Can someone who has received a life which is eternal lose it and 'sin unto death'? It seems clear, unless John's theology is divided against itself, that he who sins unto death is not a Christian. If so, the sin cannot be apostasy. We are left with the third alternative.

3. *The blasphemy against the Holy Spirit*. This sin, committed by the Pharisees, was a deliberate, open-eyed rejection of known truth. They ascribed the mighty works of Jesus, evidently done 'by the Spirit of God' (Mt. xii. 28), to the agency of Beelzebub. Such sin, Jesus said, would never be forgiven either in this age or in the age to come. He who commits it 'is guilty of an eternal sin' (Mk. iii. 29, RSV; cf. Mt. xii. 22–32). It leads him inexorably into a state of in-

corrigible moral and spiritual obtuseness, because he has wilfully sinned against his own conscience. In John's own language he has 'loved darkness rather than light' (Jn. iii. 18–21), and in consequence he will 'die in his sins' (Jn. viii. 24). His sin is, in fact, *unto death*. That is, the outcome of his sin will be spiritual ruin, the final separation of the soul from God, which is 'the second death', reserved for those whose names are not 'written in the book of life' (Rev. xx. 15, xxi. 8).

But, it may be objected, if the sin unto death is the blasphemy against the Holy Spirit committed by a hardened unbeliever, how can John call him a *brother*? To be exact, he does not. It is the one whose sin is 'not unto death' who is termed a brother; he whose sin is 'unto death' is neither named nor described. Nevertheless, supposing John thinks of each as a brother, we must still assert that neither can be regarded as a child of God. The reasons for denying that he who sins 'unto death' is a Christian have already been given; what can be said about him whose sin is 'not unto death'? An important point, to which commentators surprisingly give no attention, is that he is given *life* in answer to prayer. This means that, although his sin is 'not unto death', he is in fact dead and needs to be given life. How can you give life to one who is already alive? This man is not a Christian, for Christians do not fall into death when they fall into sin. True, 'life' to John means communion with God, and the sinning Christian cannot enjoy fellowship with God (i. 5, 6), but John would certainly not have said that when the Christian sins he dies and needs to receive eternal life again. The Christian has 'passed out of death into life' (iii. 14, RSV; cf. Jn. v. 24). Death and judgment are behind him; he 'has life' (12) as a present and abiding possession. When he stumbles into sin, which he may (ii. 1), he has a heavenly Advocate (ii. 2). He needs to be forgiven and cleansed (i. 10), but John never says he needs to be 'quickened', 'made alive', or 'given life' all over again.

If this is so, neither he whose sin is 'unto death' nor he whose sin is 'not unto death' is a Christian, possessing eternal life. Both are 'dead in trespasses and sins' (Eph. ii. 1). Each 'abideth in death' (iii. 14). The difference between them is that one may receive life through a Christian's intercession, while the other will die the second death. Spiritually dead already, he will die eternally. Only such a serious state as this would lead John to say that he will not advise his readers to pray for such.

The question remains: How can someone who (if the above interpretation be correct) is not a Christian be termed a *brother*? The only answer is that John must here be using the word in the broader sense of a 'neighbour' or of a nominal Christian, a church member who professes to be a 'brother'. Certainly in ii. 9, 11 the word 'brother' is not used strictly, for he who hates him is not a Christian at all but 'in the darkness'. In iii. 16, 17 also the word seems to have this wider connotation, where we are bidden to lay down our lives 'for the brethren' and to supply the material necessities of a 'brother in need'. Since Christ died for the ungodly and for His enemies, we can scarcely suppose that we are to limit our self-sacrifice and service exclusively to our Christian brethren, and to have compassion only upon them. Such a wider connotation of the word *brother*, implied also in the teaching of Jesus (Mt. v. 22–24, vii. 3–5), 'arises not so much out of the character and standing of him whom you call your brother, as out of the nature of the affection with which you regard him' (Candlish). This suggestion is supported by the somewhat similar passage in the Epistle of James (v. 19, 20).

We have a further confirmation of the interpretation argued above if under the description of the 'sin unto death' John is alluding, as many commentators believe, to the false teachers. In John's view they were not apostates; they were counterfeits. They were not true 'brothers' who had received eternal life and subsequently forfeited it. They were 'antichrists'. Denying the Son, they did not possess the Father (ii. 22, 23; 2 Jn. 9). They were children of the devil, not children of God (iii. 10). True, they had once been members of the visible congregation and had then no doubt passed as 'brothers'. But they went out, and by their withdrawal it was made evident that they had never been truly 'of us' (ii. 19). Since they rejected the Son, they forfeited life (v. 12). Their sin was indeed *unto death*.

17. *All unrighteousness is sin.* Sin is injustice, *adikia* (cf. i. 9), or 'wrongdoing' (RSV), as previously John had defined it as 'lawlessness', *anomia* (iii.4). Both words imply that there is an objective moral standard, the will of God, whether expressed in 'law' or in 'justice', and that sin is to be understood as a violation of both. John adds these words because he does not want to be misunderstood. In distinguishing between 'sin unto death' and 'sin not unto death', he is not meaning to minimize the gravity of sin. Nor does he mean to discourage his readers from praying, for although he cannot advise them to pray for those who sin unto death, *there is a sin* (better, RSV, 'there is sin') *not unto death*, and such sinners may receive life in answer to believing prayer.

VII. THREE AFFIRMATIONS AND A CONCLUDING EXHORTATION (v. 18–21)

The Epistle ends characteristically. It has been concerned throughout with the proper grounds, moral, doctrinal and social, of Christian assurance. So the author takes up the theme of what we should know (13) and do know (15) and concludes with the statement of three clear and candid certainties, each introduced by *oidamen, we know*. Here are no tentative, hesitant suggestions, but bold, dogmatic, Christian affirmations which are beyond all dispute and which neatly summarize truths already introduced in earlier parts of the Epistle.

18. The first assertion concerns every child of God. It is expressed as a generalization, which admits of no exception. *Whosoever is born of God sinneth not.* The Christian is again described as one who, literally, 'has been begotten (*gegennēmenos;* cf. v. 1, 4) of God'. The perfect participle indicates that the new birth, far from being a transient phase of religious experience, has an abiding result. He who has been begotten of God remains God's child with permanent privileges and obligations. One of these obligations is expressed in the phrase that he *sinneth not*. The previous two verses (16, 17) concerning the sin unto death applied to unbelievers. Very different is the case of him who has been born of God. As in iii. 4–10 (where see notes) the tense of the verb is present and 'implies continuity, habit, permanence' (Blaiklock). It expresses the truth, not that he cannot ever slip into acts of sin, but rather that he does not persist in it habitually or 'live in sin' (Dodd). The new birth results in new behaviour. Sin and the child of God are incompatible. They may occasionally meet; they cannot live together in harmony.

The apostle now proceeds to give the reason for his assurance that the Christian does not sin, and introduces it with a strong adversative, *but*. The AV, following the Codex Sinaiticus and most of the Greek manuscripts, reads *he that is begotten of God keepeth himself* (*heauton*). For the concept of 'keeping oneself' see 1 Timothy v. 22; James i. 27; Jude 21, and also iii. 3. The Alexandrine and Vatican Codices, however, which are followed by the Vulgate, have not *himself* (*heauton*) but *him* (*auton*). So RV. If, as seems probable, the latter is the correct reading, then the subject of the verb (viz. *he that is begotten of God*) is Christ, not the Christian, and the truth here taught is not that the Christian keeps himself but that Christ keeps him. The RSV adopts this interpretation and eliminates ambiguity by printing 'He' with a capital letter: 'but He who was born of God keeps him'. So too the NEB: 'it is the Son of God who keeps him safe'. It is the high privilege of the Christian to be like Christ, 'as he is' (iv. 17), begotten of God and therefore son of God. True, our begetting and our sonship are different from His, which are unique and eternal; yet they are sufficiently similar to make it possible for John to use almost identical expressions to cover both, *born of God* and *begotten of God*. Indeed, we may suppose that he uses this language deliberately, in order to show the appropriateness of his statement that 'He who was born of God' keeps 'any one born of God' (RSV). Note that power for deliverance from sin, which is here attributed to the Son, is in iii. 9 attributed to God's 'seed' which remains in the Christian.

The Christian can only hope to 'keep' the commandments of God (iii. 24, v. 3) if the Son of God 'keeps' him. Cf. Jude 24;

1 Peter i. 5. But why does he need to be 'kept'? If he has been begotten of God, is he not immune to temptation? No. The devil, *that wicked one*, is maliciously active. Strong and subtle, he is more than a match for him. But the Son of God came to destroy the works of the devil (iii. 8), and if He 'holds' (*tērei*) the Christian, the devil will not be able to 'lay hold of' him. 'Touch' is too weak a rendering of *haptetai* as may be seen from John xx. 17, the only other occurrence of the verb in the Johannine writings. It is here perhaps an echo of Psalm cv. 15 (LXX) 'Touch not mine anointed'. Observe that the three verbs are all in the present tense. They indicate abiding truths. The devil does not touch the Christian because the Son keeps him, and so, because the Son keeps him, the Christian does not sin. This is that 'deliverance from the evil one' for which we pray at the end of the Lord's Prayer. For Christ's promise and power to keep, cf. John x. 28, xvii. 12, 15.

19. The second affirmation is couched not in the third person singular, but in the first person plural and thus supplies a personal and particular application of the generalization of verse 18. *We know that we* (the apostle associates himself with his readers and thus with all Christian people) *are of God.* Having been 'born of God' (18), God remains the source of our spiritual life and being. But, in dreadful contrast, *the whole world lieth in wickedness*, or better 'in the evil one' (RV), taking *en tō ponērō* as masculine not neuter, just as in the previous verse and in ii. 13, 14 and iii. 12. John does not say that the world is 'of' the evil one as we are *of God* (although he has already declared this in iii. 8, 10, 12; cf. Jn. viii. 44, 47), but *in* him, since he is thinking now not so much of the godless world's origin as of its present sad and perilous condition. It is 'in the evil one', in his grip and under his dominion. Moreover, it *lies* there. It is not represented as struggling actively to be free but as quietly lying, perhaps even unconsciously asleep, in the arms of Satan. The evil one does not 'touch' the Christian, but the world is helplessly in his grasp. The RSV and NEB translate the phrase 'in the power of the evil one'. 'On the child of God the Evil One does not so much as lay his hand;

the world lies in his arms' (David Smith). For the devil's sway over the world, see his title 'the ruler of this world' (rsv) in John xii. 31, xiv. 30, xvi. 11 and Paul's teaching in Ephesians ii. 2 and vi. 12.

John wastes no words and blurs no issue. The uncompromising alternative is stated baldly. Everyone belongs either to 'us' or to 'the world'. Everyone is therefore either 'of God' or 'in the evil one'. There is no third category. Nowadays, when the line of demarcation between Church and world is confused, it is important to learn again that all but those who have had a heavenly birth are under the authority and power of 'the world rulers of this present darkness' (Eph. vi. 12, rsv) and of their chief, the god and prince of this world. We need to remember, however, that although the whole world lies in the power of the evil one, it is for the sins of the whole world (the only other occurrence of the expression in the Epistle) that Jesus Christ is the propitiation (ii. 2).

20. The third affirmation is the most fundamental of the three. It undermines the whole structure of the heretics' theology. It concerns the Son of God through whom alone we can be rescued from the evil one and delivered from the world. Both revelation and redemption are His gracious work. Without Him we could neither know God nor overcome sin. These are possible to us today only because *the Son of God is come*, and, having come, *hath given us an understanding.* . . . The verbs must be viewed together. The Christian gospel is not concerned merely with the truth that Christ 'has given us' certain things, but that He 'has come'. This is another example in the Epistle of John's emphasis that the Christian religion is both historical and experimental, and not one without the other. Moreover, both verbs are in the perfect tense. The benefit of His coming abides. His gift He will not take away (cf. Rom. xi. 29).

What He has given us is *an understanding, dianoia*, 'the power or capacity of knowing' (Ebrard), *that we may know him that is true*. God is here described not as 'true', *alēthēs*, but as 'real' (neb), *alēthinos*. This is a favourite Johannine adjective. Just as Jesus called Himself the 'true' or 'real' Bread and Vine (Jn. vi. 32, xv. 1), as opposed to the baker's bread and the farmer's vine which are the shadows of which He is the substance (and not vice versa), so God is the ultimate reality ('the only true God', Jn. xvii. 3) as opposed to idols (21). This real God Christ has given us understanding to *know* (*ginōskomen* in contrast to *oidamen* at the beginning of the verse). We might paraphrase 'we know as a fact that the Son of God has . . . given us understanding to come to perceive and know in experience Him who is Real . . .'. The present tense of *ginōskomen* implies 'a continuous and progressive apprehension' (Westcott).

Not only do we know Him; we are also *in him*. Unlike the world who are 'in the evil one', we are in God, sharing His very life, as well as 'of God' (19), having derived our spiritual being from Him. Moreover, we are *in his Son Jesus Christ*. The AV and RV, by inserting the word *even* before this phrase, place it in apposition to the preceding phrase, as if to say that being 'in Him who is Real' and 'in His Son Jesus Christ' were equivalent expressions. But the possessive *his* would make this very awkward. It is more probable that the words of the second phrase 'supply a needed explanation' (Brooke) of the first. It is by being *in his Son Jesus Christ* that we are *in him that is true*. In this way the first two sentences of verse 20 teach the necessity of the mediation of Jesus for both the knowledge of God and communion with God. We know Him that is true only because the Son of God is come and has given us understanding; we are in Him that is true only because (NEB 'since') we are in His Son Jesus Christ. We cannot be in the Father without being in the Son, nor in the Son without being in the Father (cf. ii. 22, 23 and e.g. 1 Thes. i. 1). Our Lord is here at the end of the Epistle significantly given His full title as He was at the beginning (i. 3). He is *Jesus* the man, *Christ* the Messiah, God's eternal *Son*.

The final sentence of verse 20 runs: *This is the true God, and eternal life.* To whom does *this* refer? Grammatically speaking, it would normally refer to the nearest preceding subject, namely *his Son Jesus Christ*. If so, this would be the most unequivocal statement of the deity of Jesus Christ in the New Testament, which the champions of orthodoxy were quick to exploit against the heresy of Arius. Luther and Calvin adopted this view. Certainly it is by no means an impossible interpretation. Nevertheless, 'the most natural reference' (Westcott) is to *him that is true*. In this way the three references to 'the true' are to the same Person, the Father, and the additional points made in the apparent final repetition are that it is *this* One, namely the God made known by Jesus Christ, who is *the true God*, and that, besides this, He is *eternal life*. As He is both light and love (i. 5, iv. 8), so He is also life, Himself the only source of life (Jn. v. 26) and the giver of life in Jesus Christ (11). The whole verse is strongly reminiscent of John xvii. 3, for there as here eternal life is defined in terms of knowing God, both Father and Son.

21. In his last sentence, in place of any formal farewell, John uses again his tender and affectionate address, *little children*, which has not occurred since iii. 8. His final exhortation is based on the three great assurances he has just uttered. The charge, *keep yourselves from idols*, arises naturally from the condition and character of the true Christian which he has been expounding. The Son of God will keep him (18), but this does not relieve him of the responsibility to keep himself. For these two keepings, His and ours, see Jude 21, 24. Actually, the verb here is not *tērein* (as in verse 18) but *phulassein*. It means properly to 'guard' (so RV), and David Smith points out that it is used of guarding 'a flock (Lk. ii. 8), a deposit or trust (1 Tim. vi. 20; 2 Tim. i. 12, 14), a prisoner (Acts xii. 4)'.

What the *idols* were to which John is referring we can only guess. He may have been uttering only a general warning that knowledge of, and communion with, *the true God* is inconsistent with the worship of idols. Or he may have been using the word 'idols', as Plato did, of the illusions of sense in opposition to ultimate reality. In this case John is saying: 'Do not abandon the real for the illusory' (Blaiklock). But the addition of the definite article (*apo tōn eidōlōn*, 'from the idols' or 'from your idols') suggests that he had some particular danger in mind.

Perhaps he was thinking of the pagan idolatries with which Ephesus at that time was filled. (So Barclay.) It is more likely, however, that the allusion is to 'the untrue mental images fashioned by the false teachers' (Brooke), which, because of their false view of the Son and therefore of the Father, constituted a monstrous idolatry. This may explain the 'peremptory aorist imperative' (Brooke, *phulaxate*). John was writing in a time of crisis. 'The Cerinthian heresy was a desperate assault demanding a decisive repulse' (Smith). What is certain is that all 'God-substitutes' (Dodd) are properly 'idols', and that from them the Christian must vigilantly guard himself.

The worship of idols, unreal and dead, is inconsistent and incompatible with that knowledge of the true God, which is eternal life, just as sin and selfishness are incompatible with the knowledge of God who is light and love. It is this incompatibility, this incongruity, of sin, lovelessness and error with the true Christian, which is the underlying theme of the Epistle. Let the Christian once recognize who he is, what he has become, 'born of God', 'of God', 'knowing God', 'in God', the possessor of 'eternal life' in Christ (all these characteristic expressions occur in these final verses), and he will surely live a life which is consistent with, and worthy of, his Christian status.

II JOHN: COMMENTARY

The Second and Third Epistles of John are the shortest documents of the New Testament—shorter even than the Epistle to Philemon and the Epistle of Jude, which are the only other New Testament Epistles consisting of but one chapter. Each of John's Second and Third Epistles contains less than 300 Greek words and was no doubt written on a single sheet of papyrus. The same themes which the author has elaborated in the First Epistle recur in brief in the Second and Third, but the form of what he writes is now less a treatise, than a letter, and the particular subject treated is hospitality to travelling missionaries.

The establishment and consolidation of the Roman Empire made travel throughout the inhabited world much easier and safer than it had ever been before. It was facilitated by the great roads which the Romans built and the *pax Romana* which their legions maintained, as well as by a commonly understood language. The rapid spread of the gospel in the first century AD owed much to these advantages.

But where should travelling Christians stay when they came to some city on a business journey or, more important still, on a missionary journey? 'The comforts of the modern hotel, or even of the village inn, were then unknown' (Findlay). Besides, according to W. M. Ramsay[1] 'the ancient inns . . . were little removed from houses of ill-fame. . . . The profession of inn-keeper was dishonourable, and their infamous character is often noted in Roman laws'. 'Inns were notoriously dirty and flea-infested', while 'innkeepers were notoriously rapacious' (Barclay). As a result, it was natural that Christian people on their travels should be given hospitality by members of local churches. There are many traces in the New Testament of this custom. For example, Paul was entertained by Lydia in

[1] Article 'Roads and Travel (New Testament)' in Hastings' *Dictionary of the Bible.*

198

Philippi, Jason in Thessalonica, Gaius in Corinth, Philip the evangelist in Caesarea and the Cypriot Mnason in Jerusalem (Acts xvi. 15, xvii. 7; Rom. xvi. 23; Acts xxi. 8, 16).

Such hospitality was open to easy abuse, however. There was the false teacher, on the one hand, who yet posed as a Christian: should hospitality be extended to him? And there was the more obvious mountebank, the false prophet with false credentials, who was dominated less by the creed he had to offer than by the material profit and free board and lodging he hoped to gain. It is against this background that we must read the Second and Third Epistles of John, for in them the Elder issues instructions concerning whom to welcome and whom to refuse, and why. Genuine Christian missionaries, he writes, may be recognized both by the message they bring and by the motive which inspires them. If they faithfully proclaim the doctrine of Christ (cf. 2 Jn. 7), and if they have set out not for filthy lucre but for the sake of His Name (3 Jn. 7), then they should be both received and helped forward on their journey 'as befits God's service' (3 Jn. 6, RSV).

Rather similar instructions may be found in *The Didachē*, a Manual of Church order which is thought to date from the end of the first century AD and to offer guidance to the rural churches of Syria.[1] It is assumed that travelling Christians will visit the churches. Each must be examined, so that the genuine may be discerned from the false (xi. 7, 11, xii. 1). The tests given concern his doctrine (xi. 1, 2), his motives, and especially his attitude to money, board and lodging (xi. 5, 6, 9, 12, xii. 2–5) and his moral conduct (xi. 8, 10).

We may divide 2 John into three sections—the Introduction (1–3), the Message (4–11) and the Conclusion (12, 13).

I. THE INTRODUCTION (1–3)

1. The Introduction consists of both an address (1, 2) and a greeting (3). In accordance with Greek epistolary custom, the

---

[1] So Cyril C. Richardson, from whose translation of *The Didachē* the extracts quoted here are taken (*Early Christian Fathers*, Vol. I of *The Library of Christian Classics*, S.C.M. Press, 1953, pp. 161–179).

author begins his letter by announcing himself. He uses, however, not his personal name (as, e.g., in the Pauline Epistles) but his title, *the elder* (cf. 3 Jn. 1). 'It described not age simply, but official position' (Westcott). It is evident that he was thus known to his readers. He had no doubt that they would immediately identify him by this title, which bears witness to his recognized authority. See Introduction, pp. 35ff.

His letter is addressed to *the elect lady (eklektē kuria)*. Commentators differ as to whether these words describe an individual person or are the personification of a church. Those who believe her to have been a person, have vied with one another in ingenious guesses about her identity. Some (beginning with Clement of Alexandria) have thought that her name was 'Electa'. J. Rendel Harris in *The Expositor* (March 1901) argued from papyri parallels that *kuria* was a term of endearment, and that 2 John was virtually a love-letter, written to a certain Electa who was far from being what he called 'a prehistoric Countess of Huntingdon'! But, if the lady's name was Electa, we should have to believe, according to verse 13, that she had a sister called Electa also! Others think, more reasonably, that she was called 'Kyria', a name vouched for in the papyri, and that John addresses her as 'chosen' (NEB, 'chosen by God') or 'elect'; but in this case the adjective would probably have been preceded by the definite article, as in 3 John 1 ('the beloved', RSV), verse 13 and Romans xvi. 13. A third group have even hazarded that both words are proper names and that she was called 'Electa Kyria'. These suggestions are all improbable. If the recipient was an individual, she was no doubt an anonymous 'elect lady'. The absence of the definite article confirms this, and 'the combination of terms is a natural expression of Christian courtesy' (Brooke). All attempts to identify her as Mary, the mother of our Lord (because of John xix. 27 and her traditional residence in Asia), or Martha (which is Aramaic for 'lady' or 'mistress') are pure conjecture.

The phrase is, however, more likely to be a personification than a person—not the Church at large but some local church over which the elder's jurisdiction was recognized, *her children*

(1, cf. 4, 13) being the church's individual members. John's language is not appropriate to a real person, either in his statement of love (1, 2) or in his exhortation to love (5). The elder could hardly refer to his personal love for a lady and her children as a 'commandment . . . which we had from the beginning' (see 5). The situation envisaged is no more suggestive of an individual than is the language, unless we are to imagine that she was a widow with a large family of children, only some of whom (4) were following the truth, while others had fallen into error, although none is named. The message of verses 7–11 about the treatment of itinerant false teachers may be applicable to every Christian home, but is more likely to have been addressed to a Christian community than to a single home in it. There are no obviously personal references in the Epistle, as there are in the Third Epistle, viz. to Gaius, Diotrephes and Demetrius (verses 1, 9, 12). Moreover, the unconscious transition from the second person singular to the second person plural ('thy' and 'thee' in verses 4 and 5 to 'ye', 'yourselves' and 'you' in verses 6, 8 and 10 and from 'you' in verse 12 back to 'thy' and 'thee' in verse 13) seems to betray the fact that the author is thinking of a community rather than an individual. In the Third Epistle, which is addressed to an individual called Gaius, the second person singular is employed consistently throughout. The contrast between the conclusions to the two letters is particularly striking.

Apart from these internal considerations of language and message, 'the personification of cities, countries and provinces in female form was a well-established convention' (Dodd), like our 'Britannia', and there is good biblical precedent for the use of a female personification to indicate the Church, whether universal (Eph. v. 22–33; Rev. xxi. 9) or local. In the Old Testament Israel was now a virgin, 'the daughter of Zion' (Is. lii. 2; cf. Is. xlvii. 1 ff.; Ezk. xvi. 7), now married (Is. lxii. 4, 5; Je. ii. 2) and a mother (Is. liv. 1 ff.; cf. Gal. iv. 26), now a widow (Is. liv. 4; La. i. 1). The Corinthian church had been betrothed to Christ as a bride to her husband (2 Cor. xi. 2), and another church is described by Peter as 'she who is at Babylon, who is likewise chosen' (1 Pet. v. 13,

RSV, *suneklektē*). This 'Babylon' is probably Rome. If the church there could be likened to a lady, 'elect' like the churches to whom Peter was writing (1 Pet. i. 1, 2), *the elect lady* must have been one of the churches of Asia, *her children* its individual members, her 'elect sister' (13) the neighbouring church where John now is, and her sister's 'children' (13) its members. Indeed, John's letter to this church may be the one mentioned in 3 John 9, since both letters are concerned with the question of hospitality.

If it be asked why the apostle should have written thus to a local church, using the expression *elect lady* as 'a disguise for a community', we can only guess the reason. It may have been for 'prudential reasons' in days when the world's persecuting hatred of the Church was overt; or his device may have been 'little more than a "conceit", conforming to the taste of the period' (Dodd).

John describes his relationship to the church in the words *whom* (plural) *I love in the truth*. 'I' is emphatic (*egō*). Perhaps he is casting a side glance at the heretics. Not only had they compromised the truth, but they were a proud and loveless lot. John's declaration is in complete contrast. The Greek phrase translated *in the truth* (as in verse 3 and in 3 Jn. 1) lacks the article. It could therefore be an adverbial expression rendered 'whom I love in truth' (RV, NEB; cf. 1 Jn. iii. 18), or 'truly', that is, 'in all Christian sincerity' (Plummer). But the context, with two subsequent references to *the truth*, with the article (1, 2), surely justifies the AV and RSV translation *whom I love in the truth*. It was *the truth* which bound John in love to this church, especially the truth about Christ in opposition to the 'lie' of the heretics (1 Jn. ii. 21–23). Nor was he alone in his love for them, for *also all they that have known the truth* (literally 'have come to know' it, perfect, *egnōkotes*) shared his love. 'The communion of love is as wide as the communion of faith' (Alford).

2. Why did John and all other Christians love the members of this church? Not *for the truth's sake* (AV, RV) but 'because of the truth' (RSV) *which dwelleth in us, and shall be with us for ever.*

If we are Christians, we are to love our neighbours and even our enemies; but we are bound to our fellow-Christians by the special bond of truth. Truth is the ground of reciprocal Christian love. John stresses the fact by his four references to *the truth* in these three opening verses. We do not love each other because we are temperamentally compatible, or because we are naturally drawn to one another, but because of the truth which we share. Not only have we come to know it objectively (1); but it abides within us (2) as a present indwelling force, and *with us* (emphatic) it will remain *for ever*. Heretics may leave us and go out into the world (7; cf. 1 Jn. ii. 19), but in the Christian society the truth shall remain secure. So long as the truth endures, in us and with us, so long shall our reciprocal love also endure. If this is so, and Christian love is founded upon Christian truth, we shall never increase the love which exists between us by diminishing the truth which we hold in common. In the contemporary movement towards Church unity we must beware of compromising the very truth on which alone true love and unity depend.

3. It is well known that letters written by friends to each other in the Greek language in the first century AD conformed to an accepted pattern with a stylized beginning and end. Usually the letter opened with the writer's name and the identity of the recipients, followed by the single word *chairein*, 'greeting'. This form may be found at the beginning of the Epistle of James and in Acts xv. 23. Other authors of New Testament Epistles, while retaining the announcement of writer and readers, Christianized the greeting, replacing *chairein* by *charis*, 'grace'. Paul's customary formula, though he departed from it sometimes, was: 'Grace to you and peace from God our Father, and the Lord Jesus Christ.' In 2 John 3 four deviations from it may be noted. First, the salutation is neither a prayer, nor a wish, but a confident affirmation. None of Paul's greetings contains a main verb. We have to understand a word like *eiē*, 'be', or Peter's *plēthuntheiē*, 'be multiplied' (1 Pet. i. 2; 2 Pet. i. 2; cf. Jude 2). John, on the other hand, places first in the sentence an emphatic *estai*, which should be translated not as a prayer, *be with you*, but as a declaration (RV, RSV, NEB 'shall/will be with us' or 'you'). In the second place, *mercy* is added between *grace* and *peace*, as in the three Pastoral Epistles. Grace and mercy are both expressions of God's love, grace to the guilty and undeserving, mercy to the needy and helpless. Peace is that restoration of harmony with God, others and self which we call 'salvation'. Put together, peace indicates the character of salvation, mercy our need of it and grace God's free provision of it in Christ. Third, the words *from God the Father, and from the Lord Jesus Christ* are almost identical with Paul's usage, although the better manuscripts omit *the Lord* (RV, RSV). John, however, adds a further designation of Christ as *the Son of the Father*. This is his familiar theological emphasis. The man *Jesus* is not only the Messiah *Christ*, but 'the Father's Son' (RSV). Also John repeats the preposition *from* (*para*), which Paul never does with *apo* in his salutations, as if to emphasize the equality of the Son with the Father as the fount of all blessing.

The fourth Johannine deviation from Paul's normal epistolary greeting is the addition of *in truth and love*. This may mean either that we shall experience grace, mercy and peace from Father and Son only if we abide in truth and love, or that grace, mercy and peace from Father and Son will express themselves, work themselves out, in truth and love. Whether truth and love are the conditions or the consequences, or merely the accompaniments, of our receiving grace, mercy and peace, they are clearly essential marks of the Christian life. They have already occurred in combination in verse 1, 'whom I love in the truth'. Contrast Ephesians iv. 15. The fellowship of the local Church is created by truth and exhibited in love. Each qualifies the other. Our love is not to be so blind as to ignore the views and conduct of others. Truth should make our love discriminating. John sees nothing inconsistent in adding to his command to love one another (5) a clear instruction about the refusal of fellowship to false teachers, who are deceivers and antichrists (7–11). Our love for others is not to undermine our loyalty to the truth. On the other hand, we must never champion the truth in a harsh or bitter spirit. Those who are 'walking in truth' (4) need to be exhorted to 'love one another' (5). So the Christian fellowship should be marked equally by love and truth, and we are to avoid the dangerous tendency to extremism, pursuing either at the expense of the other. Our love grows soft if it is not strengthened by truth, and our truth grows hard if it is not softened by love. We need to live according to Scripture which commands us both to love each other in the truth and to hold the truth in love.

II. THE MESSAGE (4-11)

The practical purpose of the Epistle now emerges. This concerns both the inner life of the local fellowship (4–6) and the doctrinal danger which threatens it from without (7–11). The two are related. John commends the faithful inner nucleus ('some of your children', RSV) who are 'walking in truth' and begs them to keep God's other commandments, especially that of mutual love. His reason for wanting to see the church thus strengthened in truth and love is that many deceivers have gone out into the world to spread their wicked lies (7). He rejoices greatly over the loyal church members (4), but warns them to look to themselves (8) lest they should either succumb to the false teachers or give them any encouragement in the dissemination of their errors. Here then, in this central section of the Epistle, is a succinct summary of those contrasts between truth and lies, the Church and the world, Christ and antichrist, the commandments of God and the deceptions of the devil, with which we have become familiar in the First Epistle.

4. John begins his message, much as Paul began eight of his thirteen Epistles, with an expression of thanksgiving. There is much in the local fellowship to give him cause for rejoicing. Yet he knew that not all the church members were living consistently. He could say no more than: *I rejoiced greatly that I found* (either on a recent visit to them or, as in 3 Jn. 3, from news which had reached him) some *of thy children walking in truth*. The parallel verse in the Third Epistle (4), which has the definite article, suggests that here, too, John is referring to walking in the truth. To 'walk in the truth' (RSV 'follow the truth'; NEB 'living by the truth') includes both believing it, especially the central truth of the incarnation, and obeying it, seeking to conform our lives to it. It dwells in us (2); we walk in it. The truth seems here to be likened to a path along which we walk, by which we keep course, and from which we should not deviate. Indeed, to go astray from revealed truth (whether in doctrine or in morals) is not just an unfortunate error, but an active disobedience, for *we have received a commandment from the Father* to walk in the truth. God has not revealed His truth in such a way as to leave us free at our pleasure to believe or disbelieve it, to obey or disobey it. Revelation carries with it responsibility, and the clearer the revelation, the greater the responsibility to believe and obey it (cf. Am. iii. 2).

5. The commandment to walk in the truth is not the Father's only commandment; the word occurs three times more in verses 5 and 6. To the commandment to believe is added the commandment to love. To be a Christian is to believe in Christ and to love one another (1 Jn. iii. 23; cf. Col. i. 4; 2 Thes. i. 3). If we deny the Son and do not love, we neither have nor know God (1 Jn. ii. 23, iv. 8). Faith and love are signs of new birth (1 Jn. v. 1, iv. 7). They are also commandments. Some people object that faith and love are not amenable to discipline and are beyond the reach of commandments. How can you tell me, they ask, to believe what I do not believe or love whom I do not love? The answer to this question lies in the nature of Christian faith and love. It is when faith is regarded as an intuition and love as an emotion that they appear to lie beyond the sphere of duty. But Christian faith is an obedient response to God's self-revelation in Christ. This revelation has a moral content. If men hate the light, it is because their deeds are evil (Jn. iii. 19–21). They do not 'believe' in the Son because they are resolved not to 'obey' Him (the significant contrast in Jn. iii. 36). This is why unbelief is sin and the unbeliever condemned already (Jn. xvi. 8, 9, iii. 18). Similarly, Christian love belongs rather to the sphere of action than of emotion. It is not an involuntary, uncontrollable passion, but unselfish service undertaken by deliberate choice. So faith and love are both commanded (here and in 1 Jn. iii. 23). Moreover, observe the pronouns: *I beseech thee . . . that we love one another.* John does not issue to the church a commandment from which he is himself exempt. Indeed, he gives no command at all. Brooke well says: 'The Elder who has the right to command merely grounds a personal request, as between equals, on the old command laid on both alike by the Master.' It is *not as though* John *wrote a new commandment* to them, but rather *that which we had from the beginning.* It was not new when John was writing; it was as old as the gospel. It was not even new to his readers; they had known it from the first days of their Christian life (cf. 1 Jn. ii. 7, 8, iii. 11, 23b, iv. 21, with notes *ad loc.*, and verse 6 'as ye have heard from the beginning').

6. The mention of the commandment to love leads John to state in epigrammatic form the reciprocal relation between love and obedience. He interprets each in terms of the other. First, *this is love, that we walk after his commandments*, and secondly *this is the commandment, that . . . ye should walk in it (en autē)*. Since the Greek words for both *commandment* and *love* are feminine, *autē* may refer to either, but more probably to love. So RSV: 'that you follow love'; cf. Ephesians v. 2. It is plain that love is expressed in obedience. If we love God or Christ, we shall show it by keeping His commandments (Jn. xiv. 15, 21, xv. 10; 1 Jn. v. 2, 3). If we love our neighbour, we shall do the same, for 'he who loves his neighbour has fulfilled the law' (Rom. xiii. 8, RSV). But what is the law? It is to love God with all our heart, mind, soul and strength, and to love our neighbour as ourselves. 'On these two commandments hang all the law and the prophets' (Mt. xxii. 40). So law and love are not incompatible; they involve each other.

The Christian life is here viewed from the standpoint of commandments. It is the word *commandment* which, occurring four times in three verses, gives cohesion to the paragraph. We are to *walk after his commandments* (6a) and therefore to walk in truth (4) and to walk in love (6b), because these are His commandments. This is the threefold Christian 'walk'. Christian liberty is not inconsistent with law any more than love is. True, the Christian is not 'under law', in that his salvation does not depend on obedience to the law. Yet this does not relieve him of the obligation to keep the law (Mt. v. 17–20; Rom. viii. 4, xiii. 10). The freedom with which Christ has made us free is not freedom to break the law, but freedom to keep it. 'I shall walk at liberty, for I have sought thy precepts' (Ps. cxix. 45, RSV).

7–11. John now comes to the second part of his message. He turns from the true believers to the false teachers, from the wheat to the tares. Although he is thankful that 'some' (RSV, 4) are walking in truth, he is deeply disturbed that 'many' deceivers have entered into the world (7). Indeed, his entreaty to the church, contained in verses 4–6, is founded upon the dangerous activity of these false teachers. Their error is to deny the incarnation; their character is to be both a deceiver and an antichrist. On this factual situation John bases a double warning to his readers, first not to be deceived themselves lest they lose their full reward (8, 9), and secondly, not to give any encouragement to the deceivers (10, 11).

7. Jesus Himself warned the apostles of the rise of 'false Christs and false prophets' who would attempt to deceive even the elect, and of whom they were to take heed (Mk. xiii. 22, 23). The Lord's prophecy was fulfilled. John wrote in his First Epistle of the 'many false prophets' who were abroad (iv. 1) and here he calls them *many deceivers*. In both passages, although there the tense is perfect and here aorist, he describes them as having *entered into the world*. The verb is *exēlthan* (RSV, 'have gone out'). It may refer to their having left the church, for the same verb occurs in the same tense in 1 John ii. 19. But it seems more likely that the language is deliberately reminiscent of the mission of Christ and of His apostles. Christ was being aped by antichrist. The Son had 'gone out' from the Father into the world (Jn. vii. 29, viii. 42, xiii. 3), and had sent forth the apostles into the world (Jn. xvii. 18, xx. 21; cf. Mt.

xxviii. 19; Mk. xvi. 15 and 3 Jn. 7 which also has *exēlthan*). Perhaps the implication is that as the apostles were sent forth into the world to preach the truth, so these false teachers had gone forth to teach lies, as emissaries of the devil, the father of lies. At all events, we are to think of them as itinerant false prophets, travelling along the great Roman roads of Asia Minor, seeking to insinuate their error into the churches they visited. 'From their own point of view, they were Christian missionaries. From the standpoint of the Presbyter they were impostors' (Dodd).

The heresy of these teachers was that they *confess not that Jesus Christ is come in the flesh*. We are not told that they categorically denied the incarnation, but that they did not 'acknowledge' it (RSV, NEB). Perhaps they were subtle enough to counterfeit rather than contradict it. Nevertheless, their teaching was tantamount to a contradiction. The central Christian affirmation about Jesus is variously phrased in the Johannine Epistles. Sometimes it is simply 'that Jesus is the Christ' (1 Jn. ii. 22, v. 1), which is equivalent to an acknowledgment of Him as the Son (1 Jn. ii. 23, v. 5). The full confession, however, is that He 'has come in the flesh' (1 Jn. iv. 2, RSV) where the perfect participle, *elēluthota*, is used. Compare the use of the aorist participle in 1 John v. 6, *ho elthōn*, 'he that came'. But here the participle is present, *erchomenon*, 'cometh in the flesh' (RV). In strict grammar this should refer to a future coming, and some have wondered if a reference to the Parousia, mentioned twice specifically in the First Epistle (ii. 28, iii. 2), is intended. However, since we know of no early controversy as to whether Jesus Christ would come again in the flesh, whereas these Epistles are concerned to assert that His first coming was in the flesh, the latter is almost certainly in mind here. In this case the present tense is 'altogether timeless' (Alford). 'The Incarnation is not only an event in history. It is an abiding truth' (Brooke). Jesus did not become the Christ or the Son at His baptism, or cease to be the Christ or the Son before His death; Jesus was 'the Christ come in the flesh'. The two natures, manhood and Godhead, were united already at His birth, never to be divided. The use of the perfect and present tenses (in 1 Jn. iv. 2 and here) emphasizes this permanent union of natures in the One Person.

He who denies the incarnation is not just *a deceiver and an antichrist* but 'the deceiver and the antichrist' (RV, RSV) *par excellence*, 'the arch-deceiver' (NEB). There is in this heresy a double affront: it opposes Christ and deceives men. The false teachers were referred to in the First Epistle both as purposing to 'deceive' (ii. 26, RSV) and as 'antichrists' (ii. 18, 22); now the two ideas are brought together.

8. Having described the fact and indicated the danger of the itinerant false teachers, John now issues his first warning: *Look to yourselves*. The verb is the same as in Mark xiii. 23, where the warning of Jesus is recorded. This error was subtle and insidious. They could not afford to relax their vigilance. The importance of such watchfulness is given both negatively (*that we lose not those things which we have wrought*) and positively (*but that we receive a full reward*). In each of the three verbs in this double sentence the MSS vary between the first and second person plural, 'we' and 'you'. The RV, RSV and NEB are almost certainly right to depart from the AV in the first and last, i.e. 'that you may not lose . . . but may win . . .' The middle verb may be either. Westcott and Brooke think the AV *which we have wrought* is 'almost certainly the true text'. On the other hand the RSV gives the better sense, 'what you have worked for'. In this case John is not so much concerned lest his work for them should prove vain (though cf. Gal. iv. 11; Phil. ii. 16), as that they should win and not lose the full reward of their Christian labour. The thought is not of their winning or losing their salvation (which is a free gift), but their reward for faithful service. The metaphor seems to be taken from the payment of labour, since *reward* (*misthos*) is a workman's wage (as in Mt. xx. 8; Jn. iv. 36; Jas. v. 4). John may be thinking of himself and them as 'fellow labourers in the Lord's vineyard', in which case he is anxious that they should not slack and so receive 'less than a full day's pay' (Smith).

9. John's warning to his readers about the false teaching is not exaggerated. Its extreme gravity is now shown. *Whosoever*

transgresseth, and abideth not in the doctrine of Christ, hath not God.
Transgresseth translates *parabainōn*. The true reading, however,
is *proagōn*, which RV renders 'goeth onward', RSV 'goes ahead'
and NEB 'runs ahead too far'. The author is almost certainly
borrowing from the vocabulary of the heretics. They claimed
to have 'go-ahead' views, a superior *gnōsis*, which had enabled
them to advance beyond the rudiments of the faith in which
the common herd were content to 'abide'. John refers sarcastic-
ally to their claim. They had indeed 'gone ahead'. They had
advanced so far that they had left God behind them! He who
denies Christ thereby forfeits God. He cannot 'have' God, that
is, enjoy fellowship with Him. On the other hand, *he that*
abideth in the doctrine of Christ, he hath both the Father and the Son.
This is a repetition of 1 John ii. 22, 23. In both passages 'the
Christ' and 'the Son' are equivalent expressions. No man can
have the Father without confessing the Son. The Son is the
revelation of the Father (e.g. Jn. i. 18, xiv. 7, 9; 1 Jn. v. 20;
cf. Mt. xi. 27) and the way to the Father (Jn. xiv. 6; cf. 1 Tim.
ii. 5), combining the functions of prophet and priest. Therefore
to confess the Son is to possess the Father; to deny the Son is
to forfeit the Father.

This is as true today of all non-Christian religions as it was
of Cerinthian Gnosticism in the first century. Many today
want God without Jesus Christ. They say they believe in God,
but see no necessity for Jesus. Or they want to bring non-
Christian religions on to a level with Christianity, as alternative roads to God. Such errors must be strenuously resisted. In
this the Christian is conservative, not progressive, seeking to
'abide' in the doctrine of Christ, not to 'advance' beyond it.
C. H. Dodd thinks John incautious and adds that he might
appear 'to condemn Christian theology to lasting sterility'.
This is exaggerated. Brooke rightly draws attention to 'the
non-repetition of the article before *mē menōn*', and adds: 'all
"progress" is not condemned, but only such progress as does
not fulfil the added condition of "abiding in the teaching".'
Christian faith is rooted in the historical events of the incarnation and the atonement, the revelation and redemption which
were finished in Christ. To advance beyond Christ is 'not

progress but apostasy' (Plummer), not enlightenment, but darkness. More than that. The Christian seeks to abide not only in Christ but *in the doctrine of Christ*. At first sight this phrase, literally 'the doctrine of the Christ' (NEB), might be taken as meaning 'the teaching which recognizes Jesus as the Christ' (Smith), and this would suit the context well. But the 'usage of the N.T.' (Westcott, Brooke) requires that the genitive be interpreted not as objective, 'the teaching about Christ', but as subjective, 'Christ's teaching'. This no doubt includes what Christ continued to teach through the apostles (cf. Acts i. 1; Col. iii. 16; Heb. ii. 3). Such authoritative apostolic doctrine is equivalent to what in his First Epistle John called 'what you heard from the beginning' (ii. 24, RSV; cf. ii. 7, iii. 11; Jn. viii. 31; 2 Tim. iii. 14 and 2 Jn. 5, 6). The Christian's development is not progress beyond Christ's teaching, whether direct or through the apostles as recorded in the New Testament, but a progressive understanding of it.

10. John now introduces his second warning. So serious is the consequence of the deceivers' error (causing its adherents to lose the Father as well as the Son) that he not only exhorts them to take heed to themselves but instructs them how to treat a false prophet who having 'gone out into the world' (7, RSV) now 'comes to you' (10, RSV). Their duty is clear and definite: *receive him not into your house, neither bid him God speed*. That is, neither welcome him when he comes, nor 'give him any greeting' (RSV) when he goes. This uncompromising order to Christians who are normally to be 'given to hospitality' (e.g. Rom. xii. 13; 1 Tim. iii. 2, v. 3–10; Tit. i. 8; Heb. xiii. 2; 1 Pet. iv. 8–10), and who are generously to entertain true missionaries (3 Jn. 5–8), has proved unacceptable to many. C. H. Dodd suggests that these are 'emergency regulations' relating to 'a situation of extreme danger to the Church', but that 'this fierce intolerance' was neither necessary nor right. He therefore declines 'to accept the Presbyter's ruling here as a sufficient guide to Christian conduct' and declares it 'incompatible with the general purport of the teaching of the New Testament and not really consistent with the teaching of these epistles themselves'. But are we to suppose that John was divided against himself? This instruction is given by the apostle of love immediately following an exhortation to love (6). Did John first insist on the commandment of love and then immediately break it himself? Besides, we are not 'at liberty to set aside direct ethical injunctions of the Lord's Apostles in this manner' (Alford).

This verse is relevant both to compromisers who refuse to withdraw from anyone and to separatists who like to withdraw from almost everybody. For a balanced interpretation of it, the following three facts need to be borne in mind.

First, John is referring to teachers of false doctrine, not merely to believers in it. The person who is not to be received is one who 'comes to you', not as a casual visitor but as an official teacher, and who is said not just to believe, but to *bring*, teaching other than *this doctrine* (of Christ), as a merchant 'brings' with him wares for sale. Christians may surely welcome and entertain someone who holds false views, and will seek to bring him to a better mind. It is those who are engaged in the systematic dissemination of lies, dedicated missionaries of error, to whom we may give no encouragement. C. H. Dodd does not seem to appreciate this difference. Although he writes of 'missionaries', he seems to be thinking of individual heretics. We must 'find a way', he writes, 'of living with those whose convictions differ from our own upon the most fundamental matters'. But of course! In the case of a private individual who denies Jesus Christ, it is enough to look to ourselves (8) lest we embrace his error, and to seek to win him to the truth; but in the case of someone officially commissioned to teach his error to others, we must reject not only it but him.

Second, John's instruction may well relate not only to an 'official' visit of false teachers but to the extending to them of an 'official' welcome, rather than merely private hospitality. Two details suggest this. First, this letter was addressed, as we have seen, to a church, not to an individual, and the phrase *if there come any unto you* (plural, *humas*) describes the anticipated visit of a false teacher (or a group of them, verse 7) to the church in question. They had left the church where John was (cf. verse 7 *exēlthon* with 1 Jn. ii. 19 *exēlthan*), but they had evidently not yet arrived where the recipients of the Second Epistle were. 'A widespread movement of heretical propaganda is afoot, and may at any time reach their city' (Dodd). The second detail is John's order not to *receive him . . . into your house*, which is literally 'into the house' (RSV). Which house? Of course he may mean that every Christian house was to be closed to the false prophets. But may it not be that John was primarily referring to 'the house' (in days before church buildings existed) in which the church met for worship (cf. Rom. xvi. 5; 1 Cor. xvi. 19; Col. iv. 15; Phm. 2)? Perhaps, therefore, it is not private hospitality which John is forbidding so much as an official welcome into the congregation, with the opportunity this would afford to the false teacher to propagate his errors. 'He is to be treated as excommunicate' (Dodd).

In the third place, John is referring to teachers of false doctrine about the incarnation, and not to every false teacher. This verse gives us no warrant to refuse fellowship to those, even teachers, who do not agree with our interpretation of apostolic doctrine in every particular. It is inaccurate to write about ostracizing 'people whose opinions we dislike' (Dodd). It is the entertainment of antichrist which is forbidden us, the arch-deceiver who in his teaching denies the essential deity and humanity of Jesus. If John's instruction still seems harsh, it is perhaps because his concern for the glory of the Son and the good of men's souls is greater than ours, and because 'the tolerance on which we pride ourselves' is in reality an 'indifference to truth' (Alexander). The false teacher whom John will not have entertained by the church, is 'the deceiver' and 'the antichrist' (7). His teaching is derogatory to Christ and dangerous to men. How then can we make him welcome in our home or church or wish him well on his journey? If we do so in the name of love, are we sure we are acting in the best interests of the false teachers, and of those they would pervert? 'Charity has its limits: it must not be shewn to one man in such a way as to do grievous harm to others' (Plummer).

11. The reason for John's instruction is now given. False teaching which denies Christ and so robs men of the Father is not just an unfortunate error; it is a 'wicked work' (RSV; *ponērois, evil,* 'wicked', comes last in the sentence for emphasis). It may send souls to eternal ruin. If, then, we do not wish to further such wicked work (to become 'an accomplice in his wicked deeds', NEB), we must give no encouragement to the worker.

III. THE CONCLUSION (12, 13)

12. The conclusions of the Second and Third Epistles are strikingly similar. With this verse compare 3 John 13, 14. The Elder has come to the end of his sheet of papyrus. The ink, 'commonly made of soot and water thickened with gum' (Alford), was still wet. He has yet *many things* to say (cf. Jn. xvi. 12), but he prefers to speak than to write them. Talking *face to face* (literally 'mouth to mouth' as in Nu. xii. 8; Je. xxxii. 4) is a more satisfactory method of communication between persons than writing. Spoken words are less easily misunderstood than written words, because it is not only by language that the speaker conveys his meaning, but by the tone of his voice and the expression on his face. So John tells them of his hope that he will come to them. And the coming to them of their true teacher will be very different from the coming of the false teachers. He assumes that they will welcome him. Speaking to them will make possible a personal communion with them, which the writer and readers of an Epistle can scarcely enjoy. The purpose of this fellowship is *that our joy may be full* (RSV, NEB, 'complete'). Fulfilled joy is the result of fellowship. The New Testament knows nothing of perfect joy outside fellowship with each other through fellowship with the Father and the Son (cf. 1 Jn. i. 3, 4 and notes *ad loc.*).

13. The Epistle concludes with a message of greeting from *the children of thy elect sister,* namely 'the members of your sister-congregation' (Alexander), the church from which John is writing. See notes on verse 1.

III JOHN: COMMENTARY

Like the Second Epistle, the Third is brief enough to have been written on a single sheet of papyrus. A similar problem lies behind both letters, namely the visits of itinerant teachers and what treatment is to be given to them. Both letters are therefore concerned with Christian truth and love and with their relation to hospitality. There are differences, however. In the second letter the Elder writes to a local church, personified as 'the elect lady and her children', whereas in the third letter he addresses by name one of the leading members of a local church, and refers to two others. This mention of Gaius (1), Diotrephes (9) and Demetrius (12), makes the Third Epistle more vivid than the Second and gives us a clearer glimpse into the inner life of a first-century church. The message differs also. In the Second the church is warned not to extend hospitality to false teachers who deny the doctrine of the incarnation, while in the Third the Elder commends Gaius for the hospitality he has shown to teachers of the truth, urges him to continue it, and sharply rebukes Diotrephes for his refusal to welcome them and for his opposition to those who wished to. In this way the positive instruction of the Third Epistle is complementary to the more negative instruction of the Second. The two letters must be read together if we are to gain a balanced understanding of the duties and limits of Christian hospitality.

The Didachē, the first-century Church Manual to which reference was made in the introduction to the Second Epistle, shows that early Christian hospitality was sometimes abused. Instructions are given that an 'apostle' may not stay beyond one day or, 'in case of necessity', two. 'If he stays three days, he is a false prophet' (xi. 5). On departing, he may receive enough food to last him his journey. But 'if he asks for money, he is a false prophet' (xi. 6). Again, if a prophet, apparently speaking under the inspiration of the Spirit, says 'give me

money, or something else', he is not to be heeded unless the
money is 'for others in need' (xi. 12). It is recognized that true
prophets have a right to stay and be supported (13), but an
ordinary Christian traveller must not be entertained free for
more than two or three days (xii. 2). If he wants to settle, 'he
must work for his living. . . . If he refuses to do this, he is
trading on Christ' (xii. 3–5).

The Third Epistle contains messages to or concerning Gaius
(1–8), Diotrephes (9, 10), and Demetrius (11, 12), with a
conclusion and greeting (13, 14).

I. THE MESSAGE TO GAIUS (1–8)

1. The writer again announces himself not by his personal
name but by the title which his readers would evidently
recognize, *the elder*. See note on 2 John 1. The recipient of the
letter is called *Gaius*. Several men named Gaius appear in the
pages of the New Testament—Gaius of Corinth, who after his
baptism by Paul became host to the apostle and to 'the whole
church' (1 Cor. i. 14; Rom. xvi. 23), and who, according to
Origen, was traditionally thought to have been the first Bishop
of Thessalonica; Gaius of Macedonia, linked with Aristarchus
of Thessalonica as one of Paul's companions, who suffered in
the riot at Ephesus (Acts xix. 29); and Gaius of Derbe,
who travelled with Paul on his last journey from Greece
through Macedonia at least as far as Troas and was probably
his church's delegate for the transmission of the collection for
the poor in Judaea (Acts xx. 4). According to the fourth-
century so-called 'Apostolical Constitutions' (vii. 46. 9), it
was this last Gaius of Derbe to whom the Third Epistle of John
was sent and whom John appointed the first Bishop of
Pergamum. This latter suggestion has attracted some commentators. Indeed 'there is nothing unlikely about it, but the
document is late and there is no early support for its statement'
(Dodd).

Since 'Gaius' was 'perhaps the most common of all names in
the Roman Empire' (Plummer), it is safer to resist the attempt
to identify the Gaius of this Epistle. We do not know who he

was. It is clear, however, from the terms in which John writes, that he occupied a position of responsibility and leadership in the local church. Visiting evangelists seem to have stayed with him rather than with others, and the Elder would hardly have written so outspokenly of Diotrephes to any but a church leader. Although we can only guess his identity and his position, we do know that he was both highly respected in the Christian community (*the wellbeloved*, 1) and particularly dear to John himself ('Beloved' in verses 2, 5 and 11, rendered in the NEB either 'My dear Gaius' or 'my dear friend'). John's love for him was *in the truth*. As in 2 John 1 there is no definite article in this phrase. C. H. Dodd quotes two letters from an Egyptian farmer in AD 110 in which he sends greetings to 'all who love you (or us) truly'. Nevertheless, the AV and RSV are certainly right to translate the expression here not 'in truth' (RV), or 'sincerely', but *in the truth*, the truth being the sphere in which their mutual love existed and flourished. Perhaps their relationship to each other was more personal even than this and the reference to 'my children' (4) hints that Gaius owed his conversion to John.

2. *Beloved.* Three of the first eleven Greek words with which the Epistle opens refer to love. The Elder's love for Gaius was genuine and now expresses itself in a *wish* (RV, RSV, NEB, 'I pray') for his material well-being. *Above all things* (*peri pantōn*) can hardly mean that this was the dearest of all John's wishes. It is better to take the words as referring not to John's prayer, but to Gaius' prosperity 'in all respects' (Westcott, Smith). RSV and NEB translate 'that all may go well with you'. *Prosper* (*euodousthai*) means literally 'to have a good journey' (Dodd), and metaphorically to 'succeed' or 'prosper' (Rom. i. 10; 1 Cor. xvi. 2). *Be in health* (*hugiainein*) is used by Luke the physician to describe those who are 'fit and well' or 'safe and sound' (Lk. v. 31, vii. 10, xv. 27). Taking the words together, 'the elements of progress and vigour are combined' (Westcott). Both verbs belonged to the conventional language of letter writing, although the concern John thus expressed for Gaius' body and estate was doubtless a sincere one. There was no need to express a similar desire for his spiritual well-being also because he knew, he said, that *thy soul prospereth*. There is biblical warrant here for desiring both the physical as well as the spiritual welfare of our Christian friends.

3. The evidence of Gaius' spiritual well-being, which had caused John greatly to rejoice, had been brought to him by certain *brethren*. They are mentioned in this verse and in verse 5. They had visited the church in which Gaius held a responsible position and had seen certain things about him which enabled them, on their return to the Elder, to bring him a good report. Two characteristics of Gaius' spiritual prosperity are mentioned, *the truth that is in thee* (3), and 'thy charity' (6), or, to translate the Greek literally 'thy truth' (rv) and 'thy love'. Gaius was a balanced Christian. He held the truth in love (cf. Eph. iv. 15). He loved in truth. For the relation between these two qualities see notes on 2 John 1 and 3. Since testimony can be borne only to what has been seen (see note on 1 Jn. i. 2), it is clear that Gaius was a transparent, open Christian who was letting his light shine and not hiding it under a bushel. His truth and love were known to all. Even 'strangers' (5) could see his sterling worth and bear witness to it. For the meaning of *the truth that is in thee*, see note on the next verse.

4. The Elder regarded Gaius as his child, much as all those to whom he addressed his First Epistle were his 'little children'. He had a fatherly affection for them (cf. 1 Cor. iv. 14–16; 1 Thes. ii. 11). Thus his joy as a parent was bound up in the welfare of his children (cf. 1 Thes. iii. 1–10). In particular he rejoiced if his children were continuing to *walk in truth* (cf. the similar statement in 2 Jn. 4). This expression, which has the definite article (*en tē alētheia*), explains the meaning of the two earlier phrases in the previous verse, 'thy truth' (rv; rsv, 'the truth of your life') and 'even as thou walkest in the truth' (which has no definite article). To *walk in* (rsv, 'follow') the *truth* is more than to give assent to it. It means to apply it to one's behaviour. He who 'walks in the truth' is an integrated Christian in whom there is no dichotomy between profession and practice. On the contrary, there is in him an exact correspondence between his creed and his conduct. Such conformity of life to the truth on the part of his children brought John *greater joy* than anything else. To him truth mattered. He did not regard theological issues as unimportant trivialities. It was from truth, believed and obeyed by his children, that he derived his greatest joy. The alternative reading of *charin* 'favour' (meaning 'no greater favour from God') for *charan* (*joy*), followed by the Vulgate and adopted by Westcott and Hort, perhaps because it is found in the Codex Vaticanus, is almost certainly a copyist's error.

5, 6a. The Elder again addresses Gaius as *beloved* and proceeds to write not now of his truth but of his love. He was 'given to hospitality', as all Christians (Rom. xii. 13; Heb. xiii. 2; 1 Pet. iv. 9) and particularly widows (1 Tim. v. 10) and presbyter-bishops (1 Tim. iii. 2; Tit. i. 8) are commanded to be. In each of these verses the Greek word is either the noun *philoxenia* or the adjective *philoxenos*, which indicate literally a love for strangers. In welcoming such, we may not only entertain angels unawares (Heb. xiii. 2), but will be receiving the Lord Jesus Himself (Mt. x. 40–42, xxv. 35, 38; cf. *Didachē* xi. 2, 4, 'welcome him as the Lord'). This love for strangers is just what Gaius possessed, for his ministry had been *to the brethren, and* (RSV, 'especially') *to strangers* (*xenous*). This does not mean that there were two separate groups to whom Gaius showed hospitality. 'The brethren and the strangers are not two classes, but one and the same' (Plummer). His *philadelphia* (love of the brethren) and *philoxenia* (love of strangers) were combined. Cf. Hebrews xiii. 1, 2 where these words occur together. He must have received them into his house and entertained them at his own expense. This service, the Elder comments, was being done *faithfully*. This may signify that John recognized in the hospitable practice of Gaius a token of his loyalty to himself and his principles. He could 'still be counted on' (Dodd); cf. RSV, 'it is a loyal thing you do' and NEB, 'you show a fine loyalty'. Or, as Westcott suggests, the phrase should perhaps be rendered: 'thou makest sure . . .'

i.e. 'such an act . . . will not fail of its due issue and reward.'
But it is noteworthy that what Gaius is said to do *faithfully* is
his 'work' (*ergasē*). His work was the outcome of his faith; it
was 'a faithful work' (RV). The adverb seems to link together
the truth and the love of Gaius. His practical ministry to
strangers was true to his profession. His love was consistent
with the truth which he believed. The verb *have borne witness* is
an aorist (*emarturēsan*) and refers to some definite occasion
when before the assembled congregation, of which John was
leader, the returned travellers spoke appreciatively of the love
Gaius had shown them, and of his truth (3). His truth had not
been kept secret in his mind, nor his love in his heart. Both
were evident. 'The brethren' had seen both, had been
impressed by both, and bore witness to both.

6b. The Elder now turns from the past to the future, from
what 'thou doest' (5) to what *thou shalt do* (6). John is perhaps
anxious lest the vociferous Diotrephes (9, 10) should succeed
in persuading Gaius to change his policy of keeping open
house. So he urges him to continue to entertain travelling
teachers. The implication of extending hospitality to itinerant
missionaries is now clear. They are not just to be received
when they arrive, but to be so refreshed and provided for (no
doubt with supplies of food and money) as to be sent forward
on the next stage of their journey *after a godly sort*, 'as befits
God's service' (RSV), literally 'worthily of God' (RV; *axiōs tou
Theou*; cf. Col. i. 10; I Thes. ii. 12). They are the servants of
God and represent Him. We must treat them as we would
treat Him. 'He that receiveth you receiveth me, and he that
receiveth me receiveth him that sent me' (Mt. x. 40). Such
thoughtful sending forth of missionaries on their journey is not
only 'a loyal thing' (5, RSV), but a 'beautiful' thing (*kalōs
poiēseis, thou shalt do well*). Cf. Mark xiv. 6 for another deed of
love which is recognized as 'a beautiful thing' (RSV).

C. H. Dodd suggests that the verb translated *bring forward
on their journey* (*propempsas*) was 'something like a technical
term of early Christian missions', implying 'the assumption of
financial responsibility for the journey' of departing mis-

sionaries. This is probably the case for, although in Acts xx. 38 and xxi. 5 it seems to mean no more than to 'accompany' or 'escort', in other places, as here, it indicates to receive and entertain someone in preparation for the next stage of his journey (Rom. xv. 24; 1 Cor. xvi. 6, 11; 2 Cor. i. 16) and possibly to supply him with money or provisions as well when he leaves (as in Tit. iii. 13 and possibly Acts xv. 3). Cf. verse 8 here.

7. The reasons for such special hospitality are now given. 'The brethren' and 'strangers' of verse 5 are not ordinary Christians who happen to be travelling from one city to another, but missionaries. John writes of them that *they went forth*. The verb (*exēlthan*) is the same as that used for the false teachers (1 Jn. ii. 19, iv. 1; 2 Jn. 7). It depicts a deliberate setting out on a mission, as when Paul embarked on his second missionary journey (Acts xv. 40). Their motive is described as being *for his name's sake*. The possessive adjective should be omitted and the phrase rendered 'for the sake of the Name' (RV). The Name is the Name of Jesus Christ, that is, the revelation of His divine-human Person and saving work. Jealousy for the Name of Christ is the most compelling of all missionary motives (cf. Rom. i. 5 and, for suffering for the Name, Acts v. 40, 41). *The Gentiles* (*hoi ethnikoi*) refers here not to non-Jews, but to 'the heathen' (RSV) or 'pagans' (NEB), in contrast to Christian believers. The phrase *taking nothing* need not be pressed into meaning that these Christian missionaries would refuse to accept gifts voluntarily offered to them by the unconverted. There is no prohibition here of taking money from non-Christians who may be well disposed to the Christian cause. Jesus Himself asked for and accepted a glass of water from a sinful Samaritan woman. What is here said is that these itinerant evangelists would not (as a matter of policy) seek their support from the heathen and did not (as a matter of fact) receive their support from them. Christian missionaries were not like many wandering non-Christian teachers of those days (or the begging friars of the Middle Ages), who made a living out of their vagrancy. C. H. Dodd writes: 'Devotees of various religions tramped the roads, extolling the virtues of the deity of their choice, and collecting subscriptions from the public. Thus, a "slave" of the Syrian Goddess has put on record (in an inscription cited by Deissmann, *Light from the Ancient East*, pp. 108 et seq.) how he travelled in the service of his "Lady", and "at each journey brought back seventy bags".' Jesus told the Twelve and the Seventy to take with them 'no scrip' (Mk. vi. 8; Lk. x. 4), and Paul condemned those who were 'peddlers of God's word' (2 Cor. ii. 17, RSV; cf. 1 Thes. ii. 5–9). Christian ministers and teachers certainly have the right to be supported by those who benefit from their service, as Paul several times insisted (especially 1 Cor. ix. 1–18; Gal. vi. 6; 1 Tim. v. 17, 18). But a Christian congregation supporting its minister is one thing; missionaries taking money from the heathen is another.

8. This verse is in direct contrast to verse 7. It is because the itinerant evangelists were not supported by the heathen that *we therefore ought to receive such. We* is strongly emphatic in the Greek sentence. There is also a pun in that we ought to receive, or better 'support' (RSV, NEB, reading *hupolambanein* rather than *apolambanein*), those who refuse to receive (*lambanontes*) anything from the heathen. If the first reason for entertaining travelling missionaries is that they are brethren whom we should honour for setting out for the sake of the Name, the second is the much more practical one that they have no other means of support. *We* must do for them what they will not ask the heathen to do. An important principle lies buried here, namely that Christians should finance Christian enterprises which the world will not, or should not be asked to, support. Indeed, Christians have an obligation (*ought*) to do so. There are many good causes which Christians *may* support; but they *must* support their brethren to whom the world should not be asked to contribute. This is a good guiding principle in Christian giving. The third reason for receiving and providing for travelling missionaries is that by so doing we become *fellowhelpers to the truth.* This may mean 'fellow workers in the truth' (RSV), implying that we are co-operating with the

missionaries and 'so play our part in spreading the truth' (NEB).
Or the phrase could be translated 'fellow-workers with the
truth' (RV), 'allies of the Truth' (Moffatt), the truth itself
being personified and regarded as the one with whom we
collaborate. For this construction see James ii. 22. Such a
personification of the truth, the gospel or the word, is not
without precedent in the New Testament (see e.g. verse 12;
2 Cor. xiii. 8; Phil. i. 27; 1 Thes. ii. 13). These itinerant
evangelists are not 'deceivers' (2 Jn. 7), bringing with them
the lie that Jesus is not the Christ, the Son of God. On the
contrary, they bring with them 'the truth'. To receive one of
the former is to be 'partaker of his evil deeds' (2 Jn. 11); to
receive the latter is to be a fellow worker with the truth. The
Christian missionaries co-operate with the truth by proclaiming it; we co-operate with it by entertaining them. The
Christian missionary enterprise is, therefore, not undertaken by
evangelists only, but by those who entertain and support them.

II. THE MESSAGE CONCERNING DIOTREPHES
(9, 10)

9. The Elder now introduces the problem created by
Diotrephes. In character and behaviour he was entirely
different from Gaius. Gaius is portrayed as walking in the
truth, loving the brethren, entertaining strangers. Diotrephes,
on the other hand, is seen as loving himself more than others
and refusing to welcome the travelling evangelists, or to let
others do so. Yet both Gaius and Diotrephes were probably
members of the same congregation, for 'in the visible Church
the evil be ever mingled with the good' (Article 26 of the
Thirty-Nine Articles), although C. H. Dodd thinks they were
members of neighbouring churches. Matters had now come to
a head, John says. *I wrote unto the church: but Diotrephes . . .
receiveth us not.* What this letter was is not clear. It cannot be
the letter he is now writing because, although the verb might
grammatically be an epistolary aorist, the words *Diotrephes . . .
receiveth us not* seem to describe the response which the letter in
question has already (in the past) received. So it must be some

other letter, not a private message to Gaius, but an official directive addressed to *the church*. This can hardly be either the First or Second Epistle of John, since neither recommends the entertainment of travelling missionaries, which evidently was the subject of the letter mentioned in this verse. The letter in question must, therefore, have been lost, possibly because Diotrephes destroyed it.

Whether or not Diotrephes destroyed the letter, or declined to read it to the church, he certainly rejected the Elder's written instruction (*ti*, 'something', RSV) to receive the itinerant evangelists hospitably. He 'does not acknowledge my authority' (RSV). It is noteworthy that the Elder possessed a generally accepted authority. He issued orders and expected them to be obeyed (cf. 2 Thes. iii for apostolic commands requiring obedience). Diotrephes was the exception. He was not going to be dictated to by John. He evidently claimed an authority of his own, even to the point of excommunicating church members who disobeyed him (10).

What were the motives which prompted Diotrephes thus to assert himself against John? Several attempts have been made to reconstruct the situation. There is no evidence that their disagreement was theological. If the truth of the gospel were at stake, the Elder would surely not have hesitated to expose the error in the same uncompromising language which he had used in the First and Second Epistles. Not doctrinal heresy but personal ambition was the cause of the trouble. Findlay points out that the name *Diotrephes* was as rare as *Gaius* was common. Since, literally translated, it means 'Zeus-reared, nursling of Zeus' and was only to be found 'in noble and ancient families', he goes on to make the ingenious conjecture that this Diotrephes 'belonged to the Greek aristocracy of the old royal city' (of Pergamum, to which Findlay believes this Epistle was addressed). In this case it was social prestige which lay behind his disgraceful behaviour. Other writers have tried to trace the rivalry between John and Diotrephes to the changing pattern of church order at the end of the first century AD. The age of the apostles was drawing to a close. Indeed, according to those who deny that the Elder John was the apostle, it had already closed. It is known that by about AD 115, when Bishop Ignatius of Antioch wrote his letters to the Asian churches, 'monarchical episcopacy' (the acceptance of a single bishop with authority over a group of presbyters) was established among them. So this Epistle was written at the end of the apostolic era, or between it and the universal acceptance of episcopacy—a period of transition and tension which C. H. Dodd likens to the handing over of responsibility by foreign missionaries to the indigenous church.

Some commentators believe that the monarchical episcopate was already being introduced, and that Diotrephes, as the lawful bishop of the church, was chafing under the apostolic, or (if C. H. Dodd is right about the Elder; see Introduction) 'subapostolic', authority of John. Others think Diotrephes was rather aspiring to this office, while Gaius was the rival candidate favoured by John. William Barclay suggests that the Epistle reflects the tension between the universal ministry of apostles and prophets and the local ministry of elders. He thinks Diotrephes may have been an elder who was determined to champion the autonomy of the local church and therefore resented both the 'remote control' of John and 'the interference of wandering strangers'. Precisely what his position was depends on whether his excommunication of church members (10) rested on any proper authority or was arrogantly presumptuous. C. H. Dodd is prepared to consider the former a possibility, and that Diotrephes may have been understandably revolting against the old order represented by John. It is clear, however, that John himself held a different view of Diotrephes and, if we recognize his authority as a biblical writer, we must of course accept his standpoint.

To John the motives governing the conduct of Diotrephes were neither theological, nor social, nor ecclesiastical, but moral. The root of the problem was sin. *Diotrephes . . . loveth to have the preeminence* (*philoprōteuōn*; RSV, 'likes to put himself first'). He did not share the Father's purpose that in all things Christ should have the pre-eminence (Col. i. 18, *prōteuōn*). Nor would he kowtow to the Elder. He wanted the pre-eminence himself. He was 'greedy of place and power'

(Findlay). He had not heeded the warnings of Jesus against ambition and the desire to rule (e.g. Mk. x. 42–45; cf. 1 Pet. v. 3). His secret self-love erupted in the antisocial behaviour described in the next verse. David Smith comments that '*proagein* (2 John 9) and *philoprōteuein* denote two tempers which disturbed the Christian life of Asia Minor—intellectual arrogance and personal aggrandisement'.

10. John declares that if he comes in person to the church in question, he *will remember* (or RSV, NEB 'will bring up', that is in public reproof) the *deeds* and *words* of Diotrephes. He knows that evil words, like evil works (2 Jn. 11), emanate from the evil one. He cannot overlook this challenge to his apostolic authority. He will be obliged to take some kind of disciplinary action. The seriousness of Diotrephes' behaviour is now exposed in three phrases. First, he is *prating against us with malicious words*. The word for *prating* (*phluarōn*) means in classical Greek to 'talk nonsense'. 'It conveys the idea that the words were not only wicked, but senseless' (Plummer). The noun *phluaroi* in 1 Timothy v. 13 is translated 'tattlers' in AV and 'gossips' in RSV. The NEB renders the phrase: 'He lays baseless and spiteful charges against us.' Diotrephes evidently regarded John as a dangerous rival to his own assumed authority in the church and sought to undermine his position by slanderous gossip. It was not only against John's person and position, however, that Diotrephes was working, but against his instruction regarding the entertainment of the missionaries. He was *not content* with a campaign of *malicious words* against John, but went further and deliberately defied the Elder by refusing *himself* to *receive the brethren*. Thirdly, he *forbiddeth them that would, and casteth them out of the church*. For some reason Diotrephes resented the intrusion of the itinerant teachers. He did not honour them for setting out 'for the sake of the Name'; he was more concerned for the glory of his own name. Perhaps he had no better reason for refusing to welcome these strangers than that John had commanded it. He would not have them in his home or help them, and those who wanted to obey John and welcome them he first prevented from carrying out their desire and then excommunicated. Self-love vitiates all relation-ships. Diotrephes slandered John, cold-shouldered the mis-sionaries and excommunicated the loyal believers because he loved himself and wanted to have the pre-eminence. Personal vanity still lies at the root of most dissensions in every local church today.

III. THE MESSAGE CONCERNING DEMETRIUS
(11, 12)

11. John turns from his description of the mischief being done by Diotrephes to give a word of personal counsel to Gaius, followed by a commendation of Demetrius. Perhaps he is anxious lest even Gaius should be influenced by Diotrephes. So he writes: *Beloved, follow not that which is evil, but that which is good.* The imperative *follow* is *mimou*, 'imitate' (RV, RSV, NEB). Everybody is an imitator. It is natural for us to look up to other people as our model and to copy them. This is all right, the Elder seems to be saying, but Gaius must choose his model carefully. Diotrephes will not do, for instance. Gaius must 'not imitate evil but imitate good' (RSV), and John adds the reason. It is not just because of the effect which our behaviour has on others, but because of the evidence our behaviour supplies of our spiritual condition. *He that doeth good is of God: but he that doeth evil hath not seen God.* This is the moral test which is often applied in the First Epistle (e.g. ii. 3–6, 28, 29, iii. 4–10, v. 18). Indeed an illustration of each of the three tests is given in this Epistle—truth (verses 3, 4), love (6) and now goodness (11). The true Christian may be described both as being *of God* (cf. 1 Jn. iv. 4, 6) and as having *seen God* (cf. 1 Jn. iii. 6). Birth of God and the vision of God are to some extent equivalent. He who has been born of God has come, with the inner eye of faith, to see God. And this vision of God deeply affects his behaviour. To do good is to give evidence of a divine birth; to do evil is to prove that one has never seen God (cf. 1 Jn. iii. 6). Perhaps in this generalization John has Diotrephes in mind and thus obliquely indicates that he questions whether Diotrephes is a true Christian at all.

12. Just as the thought of Diotrephes led John to write about doing evil, the mention of doing good seems now to remind him of *Demetrius*. A certain Demetrius is mentioned in Acts xix. 23 ff., a silversmith of Ephesus; but there is no evidence that it is he who is here described. Nor can we say that he is the same as Demas in Paul's Epistles (Col. iv. 14; Phm. 24; 2 Tim. iv. 10), although Demas is probably short for Demetrius. According to the *Apostolical Constitutions* John later appointed him Bishop of Philadelphia. We know nothing for certain of this Demetrius beyond what we are told in this one verse. It has been conjectured that John thus commended him because he was the bearer of the Epistle, a 'travelling assistant of the Apostle' (Findlay), or because he was an object of Diotrephes' malice and Gaius needed to be reassured about him. Either is possible; both are speculative. The former is, however, the more probable as John seems to be commending Demetrius to Gaius as if Gaius did not already know him. What is clear is that Demetrius is given an impressive threefold testimony (cf. 1 Jn. v. 8). First, he *hath good report of all men*. The perfect passive *memarturētai* conveys the idea that the testimony of all men to Demetrius in the past remains valid in the present. This testimony is confirmed by *the truth itself*. This can hardly be a reference to the Son or the Spirit, although each is 'the truth' (Jn. xiv. 6; 1 Jn. v. 6). It surely means rather that the Christian genuineness of Demetrius did not need the evidence of men; it was self-evident. The truth he professed was embodied in him, so closely did his life conform to it. But Demetrius had a third witness: *yea, and we also bear record* (*marturoumen*) with a present and continuing testimony. This is the first person plural of authority and by it John is referring to himself (as in verse 9). RSV rightly renders it: 'I testify to him too.' This would be enough for Gaius because, even if he did not know any of the *all men* who had testified to Demetrius and had not yet met Demetrius to see in him the witness of *the truth itself*, he knew and trusted the judgment of John, as John goes on to write: *ye know that our record* (*marturia*) *is true* (cf. Jn. xxi. 24).

IV. THE CONCLUSION AND GREETING (13, 14)

13, 14a. Compare 2 John 12 and notes. There are verbal differences between the two conclusions, such as the tense of the verb and the reference to *ink and pen* (*kalamos*, the reed used by the ancients for a pen) instead of 'paper and ink', but the general sense is identical. He has *many things to write*, much more than he can include on one sheet of papyrus, but these things he prefers to communicate by word of mouth, for he is planning to visit Gaius *shortly*, and then, he says, *we shall speak face to face.*

14b (RSV, 15). *Peace be to thee*, the Hebrew greeting, invested with new meaning by Jesus after the resurrection (Jn. xx. 19, 21, 26), is an appropriate prayer for Gaius if he had to exercise leadership in a church where Diotrephes was stirring up strife. In the Second Epistle, the reference to peace comes at the beginning (verse 3), but a similar greeting of peace at the conclusion of an Epistle occurs in Galatians vi. 16; Ephesians vi. 23; 2 Thessalonians iii. 16, and 1 Peter v. 14. The reciprocal greeting with which the Epistle ends is from and to *the friends*. This designation of Christians is unique in the Epistles. Their relation to each other is normally described in terms of 'brotherhood', not 'friendship'. Nevertheless Jesus called the Twelve His friends (Jn. xv. 13, 14), and Paul's friends in the city of Sidon are mentioned in Acts xxvii. 3. There does not seem to be any hint here that *friends* are less intimately associated with each other than 'brethren' (cf. verses 3, 5, 10), for the instruction Gaius is given is to *greet the friends by name*, which the RSV interprets as meaning 'every one of them', and NEB as 'individually'. Christians should not lose their individual identity and importance in the group. God surely means each local fellowship to be sufficiently small and closely knit for the minister and members to know each other personally and be able to greet each other by name. The Good Shepherd calls His own sheep by name (Jn. x. 3); undershepherds and sheep should know each other by name also.